SELECTED LETTERS

OF

SAMUEL JOHNSON

AMS PRESS
NEW YORK

SELECTED LETTERS

OF

SAMUEL JOHNSON

HUMPHREY MILFORD
OXFORD UNIVERSITY PRESS
London   Edinburgh   Glasgow   Copenhagen
New York   Toronto   Melbourne   Cape Town
Bombay   Calcutta   Madras   Shanghai

Library of Congress Cataloging in Publication Data

Johnson, Samuel, 1709-1784.
  Selected letters of Samuel Johnson.

  Reprint of the 1925 ed. published by Oxford
University Press, London, which was issued as 282
of The World's classics.
  Includes index.
  1. Johnson, Samuel, 1709-1784—Correspondence.
2. Authors, English—18th century—Correspondence.
I. Title.
PR3533.A25   1979   828'.6'09 [B]   76-29446
ISBN 0-404-15312-7

First AMS edition published in 1979.

Reprinted from the edition of 1925, London. [Trim size and text area of the original have been slightly altered in this edition. Original trim size: 9 x 14.8 cm; original text area: 7.3 x 12.7 cm.]

MANUFACTURED
IN THE UNITED STATES OF AMERICA

CONTENTS

	PAGES
INTRODUCTION	vii
LETTERS	1–264
INDEX OF CORRESPONDENTS	265–267

SAMUEL JOHNSON

Born, Lichfield . . . . 18 September, 1709
Died, London . . . . 13 December, 1784

The present selection from his Letters was first published in 'The World's Classics' in 1925.

INTRODUCTION

THE surviving letters of Johnson are like the other records of his life : very full for the last twenty years, and relatively scanty for that earlier period, much longer and much fuller of activity, in which Johnson had as yet no money, no established reputation, and no Boswell. Their editor, Dr. Birkbeck Hill, was acquainted with just over one thousand letters. In that series the letter which Johnson wrote to Lord Bute on 20 July 1762, acknowledging the grant of his pension, is numbered 143. Doubtless when he became a man of leisure, and a literary dictator, he wrote more letters than had formerly been his habit. But the discrepancy is due less to this cause than to the care taken by his later correspondents to preserve the letters of a famous man.

The extant letters are, none the less, remarkable for their range and variety. Johnson's correspondents are of many conditions in life, and the list includes some notable names. The letters arise out of very various occasions, and exhibit many sides of their writer's life and character. Those that concern his books are few and brief, precious fragments. There is a group of very early letters addressed to Edward Cave, otherwise *Sylvanus Urban*, the founder of the *Gentleman's Magazine*. These were written when Johnson was a new-comer to London, just beginning his long struggle to earn a living by literature. They were no doubt preserved in Cave's archives, and fifty years later John Nichols published them in the *Gentleman's Magazine*. Later there are other letters to printers and booksellers—William Strahan, Andrew Millar, Thomas Cadell. From some of these we get brief glimpses of the progress of the great Dictionary, and may picture the drudgery of the lexicographer and his North-British amanuenses in the big room under the roof in Gough Square. A few years later we find him, in great grief for the loss of his mother—' the best of mothers '—throwing off *The Prince of Abissinia* in the evenings of one week, to pay some petty debts she had left.

But many of Johnson's literary letters are addressed to fellow-craftsmen. There are letters to the brothers Warton—Thomas Warton, Fellow of Trinity College, Oxford, and Joseph Warton, Head Master of Winchester; both poets, critics, and romantic enthusiasts. Joseph criticized, not always favourably, the Writings and Genius of Pope; Thomas wrote on *The Faery Queen*, and later compiled a massive

History of English Poetry, a pioneer book which is still valuable. Johnson loved these ingenious and scholarly gentlemen, though he laughed at their enthusiasms. He visited them, and solicited their help in his Dictionary and his edition of Shakespeare. When he was associated with John Hawkesworth in *The Adventurer*, a periodical which followed hard on *The Rambler*, he invited Joseph Warton to be a contributor. Another antiquarian friend was Richard Farmer, Master of Emmanuel, of whose acute and erudite *Essay on the Learning of Shakespeare* Johnson said that it had ' done that which never was done before ; it had finished a controversy beyond all further doubt '. Another was Thomas Percy, an early acquaintance, with whom Johnson stayed when Percy was a humble country clergyman. He saw the *Reliques of Ancient English Poetry* in manuscript, used his influence with the booksellers to secure good terms for the editor, and finally wrote the dedication. ' A mere antiquarian ', he writes, ' is a rugged being.' But Percy's love of poetry had ' given grace and splendour to his studies of antiquity '. Johnson had himself a large share of the curiosity which makes an antiquary. Lack of health and leisure, and, even more, lack of patience, had prevented his exploring antiquity as far as he wished; but he was always eager in promoting the zeal of others. He knew, he said, as well as any man how to write 'an introduction to any literary work, stating what it is to contain, and how it should be executed in the most perfect manner'; and his letters include some admirable persuasions to research. There are two—written at an interval of twenty years—to an Irish antiquary, Charles O'Connor; urging him to compose a history of the Irish in early times—' those times (for such there were) when Ireland was the school of the West, the quiet habitation of sanctity and literature.' He adds advice by which many scholars might have profited: 'do what you can easily do without anxious exactness. Lay the foundations, and leave the superstructure to posterity.'

A number of the letters belong to the kind that may be called letters of ceremony: a class of composition in which, as in the formal dedication, Johnson has no equal in his own tongue. Most of these are in Boswell, and are well known—the letters to Lord Bute, those to Hamilton and to Lord Thurlow, acknowledging the offer of loans; and those to Warren Hastings, in which courtly deference is mingled with a friendly independence; a combination, the effect not of artifice, but of that sincerity which it is a triumph of art to express. Viewed in

INTRODUCTION xi

this light, these letters may be thought superior even to those more famous documents, which though ostensibly private belong in reality to public controversy, and are such as might to-day be addressed to the editor of a newspaper. These are the letters to Chesterfield and to Macpherson, and that addressed to Mr. William Drummond, in which Johnson denounces those who, ' in an assembly convened for the propagation of Christian knowledge ', had from political motives obstructed the translation of the Bible into Gaelic.

One small group of letters is of peculiar interest. Johnson's attitude to the American question has always been notorious. It will surprise many to learn that it had the approval of John Wesley ; but it made most of Johnson's friends uncomfortable, and Boswell himself apologetic. Yet only two years before the publication of *Taxation No Tyranny* Johnson addressed letters to three American gentlemen, of two of which copies were communicated to Boswell by Mr. James Abercrombie of Philadelphia. We have to-day every reason to honour the generosity with which Americans regard Johnson's memory ; it is even more remarkable that about 1795 the originals of these letters, ' being the only relicks of the kind in America, were considered by the possessors of such inestimable value, that no possible consideration would induce them to part with them'. The only sign of hesitancy was shown by one of the recipients, a Mr. B—d, who ' residing in America in a publick character of considerable dignity, desired that his name might not be transcribed at full length '. The others were William White, afterwards Bishop of the Episcopal Church in Pennsylvania, who had sent Johnson a copy of the American edition of *Rasselas*, and Dr. William Samuel Johnson of Connecticut, whom the accident of his name, and the added coincidence that they were both Doctors of the University of Oxford, had brought acquainted with his namesake.

The accidents of time have spared few of Johnson's family letters. We have one to his wife, a few brief notes to his mother on her death-bed, and a fairly long series to his stepdaughter Lucy Porter. Miss Porter seems to have been a rather unattractive spinster. She exacted the attention of regular visits, but it does not appear that she made her visitor very comfortable. His letters to her are affectionate, but not very communicative, and they have sometimes a touch of acerbity which we rarely find in his correspondence.

By far the greater part of the collection consists of letters of pure friendship. Johnson's circle of friends was large and miscellaneous; to give an account of his correspondents would be to retell a great part of his history. He was especially loyal to his early acquaintances, some of them obscure persons whom a smaller man would have found it easy to forget. We owe to this fidelity the letters addressed to Edmund Hector of Birmingham and Mrs. Careless his sister, 'an old love'; to Miss Aston and Mrs. Gastrell, ladies of Lichfield; and to the Rev. Dr. John Taylor, the most oddly incongruous of Johnson's intimates. Taylor was a wealthy pluralist, and it was said that he intended to leave Johnson money. It is certain that Johnson wrote his sermons. But the suggestion that their friendship was kept alive by motives of mutual convenience is incompatible with the tone of the letters. Johnson admitted that though he loved Taylor, his regard for him did not increase; 'his talk was of bullocks'; his habits were 'by no means sufficiently clerical'; Johnson did not conceal his perception of this; and 'no man likes to live under the eye of perpetual disapprobation'. Yet Taylor expected an annual visit, and released his visitor 'in a disposition of mind not very uncommon, at once weary of my stay, and grieved at my departure'. It was not interest, but long habit and blind affection, that kept together two men who 'seemed formed for different elements'.

Many of Johnson's correspondents were more congenial to his tastes and temper, and his letters to them are written with the ease of confidence. Such are the letters to the literary friends already mentioned; to Sir Joshua Reynolds and his sister; to Dr. Burney, the historian of music; to David Garrick. There is one letter, and one only, to Goldsmith, who perhaps did not keep letters. It is more surprising that there are hardly any to the accomplished ladies whom Johnson helped in their literary ventures—notably Charlotte Lennox and Elizabeth Carter. But there are several letters of ceremony to that very great lady, Mrs. Elizabeth Montagu; and there are some to Miss Hill Boothby, who was almost his contemporary, and to whom he was deeply attached.

It is evidence of the subtlety and delicacy of Johnson's mind—qualities which he is often held to have lacked—that though all his letters are markedly and unmistakably his own, they are also strongly coloured by the individuality of his correspondents. Thus the letters to Boswell are strikingly different from those, equally unreserved and affectionate, which he wrote to other men much younger than himself—to Bennet Langton or to Joseph Baretti. All Johnson's letters abound in reflexion and in maxims of prudence; but the letters to Boswell are distinguished by their wealth of argument and their fervour of admonition. This is due not only to Boswell's palpable want of good advice, but also to his unequalled power of stimulation. Johnson's letters to him, like the *Life* of which they form part, are the work of Boswell's genius as well as of Johnson's.

Johnson's letters to Hester Thrale make a distinct chapter of his history. For nearly twenty years he had his rooms in the Thrales' house at Streatham. He retained his own establishment in London; but his habit was to leave Streatham on Saturday and to return there on Monday. This routine was not often interrupted save by the Thrales' visit to Brighthelmstone or Bath—whither he sometimes accompanied them—and by his own annual ' ramble ' to Oxford, Lichfield, and Ashbourne.

Johnson was deeply and gratefully devoted to Henry Thrale. ' I have lost a friend ', he wrote at his death, ' of boundless kindness.' But his attachment to Mrs. Thrale was the romance of his old age. To write to her, in the short intervals of absence, was the chief solace of his loneliness, and his most settled habit. The lady's character is, perhaps, sufficiently suggested by the correspondence itself. However we regard her, there is no doubt that she possessed in an eminent degree the faculty which Fanny Burney shared, and which Boswell conspicuously lacked, of drawing out Johnson's playful and whimsical humour. His letters to her are very like the conversations which she and Miss Burney have recorded, and rather unlike those which Boswell transcribed. They are never argumentative, or excessively dogmatic; they are gentle, sometimes trivial; allusive, and even inconsequent. These graces add a moral charm to the sterner qualities which Johnson's writing never lacks. The letters to Mrs. Thrale are the fullest and best of all supplements to Boswell's *Life*.

Johnson has never been in high estimation as a letter-writer. Many of his best letters, it is true, are in the *Life*, and are familiar in that setting. But they are not there printed, or read, continuously; and, like the other components of that great whole, they obey a law of subordination, and seem to shine not by their own light, but as fragments of a vaster constellation. The other letters have been neglected. Only two substantial collections of them have ever been printed as such—Mrs. Piozzi's *Letters to and from the late Samuel Johnson, LL.D.*, which was published in 1788

INTRODUCTION

and has not been reprinted ; and Dr. Birkbeck Hill's elaborate edition, published more than thirty years ago, of all the letters *not* printed by Boswell. No popular edition or selection of the letters has been produced.

This neglect is not unintelligible. Of the extant letters not printed by Boswell a very large proportion are the letters of a tired and lonely old man. Their burden is disease and despondency. Again, Johnson's letters do not, in any important degree, show a side of him that is unfamiliar. They do not, like the letters of Walpole and Cowper, unfold a personality of which we otherwise know little ; nor do they, like those of Lamb, furnish an ample commentary to a brief and precious text. Johnson is always Johnson, and is above all things the Johnson we have always known.

Yet even in this massive identity we may trace minor differences. His letters are very like his talk ; that they are less ' good ' than the sayings preserved by Boswell is mainly because Boswell recorded what he wrote down from memory, and his memory retained the best things. Even Boswell, it should not be forgotten, regretted his inability to ' take down the full strain of Johnson's eloquence '. What he gives us is not typical specimens, but a collection of gems. The result is a certain distortion, which led Macaulay to state a plausible, but grossly erroneous antithesis between Johnson's talk and written Johnsonese. The truth is rather the contrary. It was again and again remarked by Johnson's contemporaries that he talked like a book, and like his own books; that his oral discourses might have been printed without correction. This, too, was of course an exaggeration; but an exaggeration far less misleading than the other.

In his letters, if anywhere, we should find the real Johnson: the Johnson whom Boswell loved and revered, though he does not quote him so often as he quotes the Autocrat of the Mitre. The letters have, indeed, all the qualities which should commend the letters of a great man to the esteem and affection of his readers. They are spontaneous, and they are sincere; they abound in wit and wisdom, in humour and fancy. In one of his letters to Mrs. Thrale,[1] Johnson dwells on ' the pleasure of corresponding with a friend, where doubt and mistrust have no place, and everything is said as it is thought'. The passage begins in playfulness; but the end is serious: ' I have indeed concealed nothing from you, nor do I expect ever to repent of having thus opened my heart.'

But when this has been said, there is yet

[1] No. 559.

more to say. There are, in the best of these letters, not a few passages which it would be hard to overpraise; which are as memorable as the most famous sentences in Johnson's published writings; and which it would not be easy to match from any other writer. Such is the conclusion of his valediction to Mrs. Thrale:

> When Queen Mary took the resolution of sheltering herself in England, the Archbishop of St. Andrew's, attempting to dissuade her, attended on her journey; and when they came to the irremeable stream that separated the two kingdoms, walked by her side into the water, in the middle of which he seized her bridle, and with earnestness proportioned to her danger and his own affection pressed her to return. The Queen went forward.——If the parallel reaches thus far, may it go no further.—The tears stand in my eyes.

Such is the letter written to Garrick's widow on her bereavement:

> Dr. Johnson sends most respectful condolence to Mrs. Garrick, and wishes that any endeavour of his could enable her to support a loss which the world cannot repair.

Johnson's prose, when he is deeply moved, achieves sometimes a harmony of thought and language, which the noblest prose rarely attains; which is not altogether unworthy of comparison with the splendours of great poetry.

R. W. C.

The numbers prefixed to the letters are those of Birkbeck Hill's edition. A few have been included which were not in that edition; to these no number is given.

SELECTED LETTERS

OF

SAMUEL JOHNSON

1. To Gregory Hickman

Sir   Lichfield, Oct. 30, 1731.

    I have so long neglected to return you thanks for the favour and assistance received from you at Stourbridge, that I am afraid you have now done expecting it. I can, indeed, make no apology, but by assuring you, that this delay, whatever was the cause of it, proceeded neither from forgetfulness, disrespect, nor ingratitude. Time has not made the sense of obligation less warm, nor the thanks I return less sincere. But while I am acknowledging one favour, I must beg another—that you would excuse the composition of the verses you desired. Be pleased to consider, that versifying against one's inclination is the most disagreeable thing in the world ; and that one's own disappointment is no inviting subject ; and that though the desire of gratifying you might have prevailed over my dislike of it, yet it proves, upon reflection, so barren, that to attempt to write upon it, is to undertake to build without materials. As I am yet unemployed, I hope you will, if any thing should offer, remember and recommend,

                Sir,
                    Your humble servant,
                        Sam : Johnson.

4. To Edward Cave[1]

Greenwich, next door to the Golden Heart,
Church-street, July 12, 1737.

Sir

Having observed in your papers very uncommon offers of encouragement to men of letters, I have chosen, being a stranger in London, to communicate to you the following design, which, I hope, if you join in it, will be of advantage to both of us.

The History of the Council of Trent having been lately translated into French, and published with large Notes by Dr. Le Courayer, the reputation of that book is so much revived in England, that, it is presumed, a new translation of it from the Italian, together with Le Courayer's Notes from the French, could not fail of a favourable reception.

If it be answered, that the History is already in English, it must be remembered, that there was the same objection against Le Courayer's undertaking, with this disadvantage, that the French had a version by one of their best translators, whereas you cannot read three pages of the English History without discovering that the style is capable of great improvements ; but whether those improvements are to be expected from the attempt, you must judge from the specimen, which, if you approve the proposal, I shall submit to your examination.

Suppose the merit of the versions equal, we may hope that the addition of the Notes will turn the balance in our favour, considering the reputation of the Annotator.

Be pleased to favour me with a speedy answer, if you are not willing to engage in this scheme ; and appoint me a day to wait upon you, if you are.

I am, Sir, your humble servant,
Sam : Johnson.

[Editor of *The Gentleman's Magazine*.]

5. To Edward Cave

Castle-street, Wednesday Morning.
[*No date.* 1738.]

Sir

When I took the liberty of writing to you a few days ago, I did not expect a repetition of the same pleasure so soon ; for a pleasure I shall always think it, to converse in any manner with an ingenious and candid man ; but having the inclosed poem [1] in my hands to dispose of for the benefit of the authour, (of whose abilities I shall say nothing, since I send you his performance,) I believed I could not procure more advantageous terms from any person than from you, who have so much distinguished yourself by your generous encouragement of poetry ; and whose judgment of that art nothing but your commendation of my trifle [2] can give me any occasion to call in question. I do not doubt but you will look over this poem with another eye, and reward it in a different manner, from a mercenary bookseller, who counts the lines he is to purchase, and considers nothing but the bulk. I cannot help taking notice, that, besides what the authour may hope for on account of his abilities, he has likewise another claim to your regard, as he lies at present under very disadvantageous circumstances of fortune. I beg, therefore, that you will favour me with a letter to-morrow, that I may know what you can afford to allow him, that he may either part with it to you, or find out, (which I do not expect,) some other way more to his satisfaction.

I have only to add, that as I am sensible I have transcribed it very coarsely, which, after having altered it, I was obliged to do, I will, if you please to transmit the sheets from the press, correct it for you ; and will take the trouble of altering any stroke of satire which you may dislike.

By exerting on this occasion your usual generosity,

[1] [*London.*]
[2] His Ode *Ad Urbanum* probably. Nichols.

you will not only encourage learning, and relieve distress, but (though it be in comparison of the other motives of very small account) oblige in a very sensible manner,

> Sir, your very humble servant,
> SAM: JOHNSON.

10. To EDWARD CAVE

Sir [*No date.*]

I am pretty much of your opinion, that the Commentary cannot be prosecuted with any appearance of success; for as the names of the authours concerned are of more weight in the performance than its own intrinsick merit, the publick will be soon satisfied with it. And I think the Examen should be pushed forward with the utmost expedition. Thus, 'This day, &c., An Examen of Mr. Pope's Essay, &c., containing a succinct Account of the Philosophy of Mr. Leibnitz or the System of the Fatalists, with a Confutation of their Opinions, and an Illustration of the Doctrine of Free-will;' with what else you think proper.

It will, above all, be necessary to take notice, that it is a thing distinct from the Commentary.

I was so far from imagining they stood still,[1] that I conceived them to have a good deal before-hand, and therefore was less anxious in providing them more. But if ever they stand still on my account, it must doubtless be charged to me; and whatever else shall be reasonable, I shall not oppose; but beg a suspense of judgment till morning, when I must entreat you to send me a dozen proposals, and you shall then have copy to spare.

> I am, Sir, your's, *impransus*,
> SAM: JOHNSON.

Pray muster up the Proposals if you can, or let the boy recall them from booksellers.

[1] The Compositors in Mr. Cave's printing-office, who appear by this letter to have then waited for copy. NICHOLS

12. To Mrs. Johnson

Dearest Tetty

After hearing that you are in so much danger, as I apprehend from a hurt on a tendon, I shall be very uneasy till I know that you are recovered, and beg that you will omit nothing that can contribute to it, nor deny yourself any thing that may make confinement less melancholy. You have already suffered more than I can bear to reflect upon, and I hope more than either of us shall suffer again. One part at least I have often flattered myself we shall avoid for the future, our troubles will surely never separate us more. If [   ] does not easily succeed in his endeavours, let him not [scruple] to call in another Surgeon to consult with him, Y[ou may] have two or three visits from Ranby or Shipton, who is [thought] to be the best, for a guinea, which you need not fear to part with on so pressing an occasion, for I can send you twenty pouns more on Monday, which I have received this night ; I beg therefore that you will more regard my happiness, than to expose yourself to any hazards. I still promise myself many happy years from your tenderness and affection, which I sometimes hope our misfortunes have not yet deprived me of. David wrote to me this day on the affair of Irene, who is at last become a kind of Favourite among the Players, Mr. Fletewood promises to give a promise in writing that it shall be the first next season, if it cannot be introduced now, and Chetwood the Prompter is desirous of bargaining for the copy, and offers fifty Guineas for the right of printing after it shall be played. I hope it will at length reward me for my perplexities.

Of the time which I have spent from thee, and of my dear Lucy and other affairs, my heart will be at ease on Monday to give Thee a particular account, especially if a Letter should inform me that thy leg is better, for I hope you do not think so unkindly of me as to imagine that I can be at rest while I believe my dear Tetty in pain.

Be assured, my dear Girl, that I have seen nobody in these rambles upon which I have been forced, that has not contributed to confirm my esteem and affection for thee, though that esteem and affection only contributed to encrease my unhappiness when I reflected that the most amiable woman in the world was exposed by my means to miseries which I could not relieve.

     I am
      My charming Love
       Yours
        Sam: Johnson.

      Jan. 31st, 1739–40.

Lucy always sends her Duty and my Mother her Service.

25. To Miss Porter

     Goff Square, July 12, 1749.
Dear Miss

I am extremely obliged to you for your letter, which I would have answered last post, but that illness prevented me. I have been often out of order of late, and have very much neglected my affairs. You have acted very prudently with regard to Levett's affair, which will, I think, not at all embarrass me, for you may promise him, that the mortgage shall be taken up at Michaelmas, or, at least, some time between that and Christmas; and if he requires to have it done sooner, I will endeavour it. I make no doubt, by that time, of either doing it myself, or persuading some of my friends to do it for me.

Please to acquaint him with it, and let me know if he be satisfied. When he once called on me, his name was mistaken, and therefore I did not see him; but, finding the mistake, wrote to him the same day, but never heard more of him, though I entreated him to let me know where to wait on him. You frighted me, you little gipsy, with your black wafer, for I had forgot you were in mourning, and was afraid your letter had brought me ill news of my mother, whose death is one of the few calamities on which I think with terror. I long to know how she does, and how you all do. Your poor mamma is come home, but very weak; yet I hope she will grow better, else she shall go into the country. She is now up-stairs, and knows not of my writing.

I am, dear Miss,
Your most humble servant,
SAM: JOHNSON.

30. TO JAMES ELPHINSTON

Dear Sir   September 25, 1750.

You have, as I find by every kind of evidence, lost an excellent mother; and I hope you will not think me incapable of partaking of your grief. I have a mother, now eighty-two years of age, whom, therefore, I must soon lose, unless it please GOD that she rather should mourn for me. I read the letters in which you relate your mother's death to Mrs. Strahan, and think I do myself honour, when I tell you that I read them with tears; but tears are neither to *you* nor to *me* of any further use, when once the tribute of nature has been paid. The business of life summons us away from useless grief, and calls us to the exercise of those virtues of which we are lamenting our deprivation. The greatest benefit which one friend can confer upon another, is to guard, and excite, and elevate his virtues. This your mother will still perform, if you diligently preserve the memory of her life, and of her death: a life, so far as I can learn, useful, wise, and innocent; and a death resigned, peaceful, and holy. I cannot forbear to mention, that neither reason nor revelation denies you to hope, that you may increase her happiness by obeying her precepts; and that she may, in her present state, look with pleasure upon every act of virtue to which her instructions or example have contributed. Whether this be more than a pleasing dream, or a just opinion of separate spirits, is, indeed, of no great importance to us, when we consider ourselves as acting under the eye of GOD : yet, surely, there is something pleasing in the belief, that our separation from those whom we love is merely corporeal ; and it may be a great incitement to virtuous friendship, if it can be made probable, that that union that has received the divine approbation shall continue to eternity.

There is one expedient by which you may, in some degree, continue her presence. If you write down minutely what you remember of her from your earliest years, you will read it with great pleasure, and receive from it many hints of soothing recollection, when time shall remove her yet farther from you, and your grief shall be matured to veneration. To this, however painful for the present, I cannot but advise you, as to a source of comfort and satisfaction in the time to come ; for all comfort and all satisfaction is sincerely wished you by,

dear Sir, your most obliged,
most obedient, and most humble servant,
SAM: JOHNSON.

31. To SAMUEL RICHARDSON

Dear Sir March 9, 1750–1.

Though Clarissa wants no help from external splendour, I was glad to see her improved in her appearance, but more glad to find that she was now got above all fears of prolixity, and confident enough of success to supply whatever had been hitherto suppressed. I never indeed found a hint of any such defalcation, but I fretted ; for though the story is long, every letter is short.

I wish you would add an *index rerum*, that when the reader recollects any incident, he may easily find it, which at present he cannot do, unless he knows in which volume it is told; for Clarissa is not a performance to be read with eagerness, and laid aside for ever; but will be occasionally consulted by the busy, the aged, and the studious; and therefore I beg that this edition, by which I suppose posterity is to abide, may want nothing that can facilitate its use.

I am, Sir,
Your obliged humble servant,
SAM: JOHNSON.

35. TO WILLIAM STRAHAN

Dearest Sir   Nov. 1, 1751.

The message which you sent me by Mr. Stuart I do not consider as at all your own, but if you were contented to be the deliverer of it to me, you must favour me so far as to return my answer, which I have written down to spare you the unpleasing office of doing it in your own words. You advise me to write, I know with very kind intentions, nor do I intend to treat your counsel with any disregard when I declare that in the present state of the matter ' I shall *not* write ' otherwise than the words following :—

' That my resolution has long been, and is *not* now altered, and is now *less* likely to be altered, that I shall *not* see the Gentlemen Partners [1] till the first volume is in the press, which they may forward or retard by dispensing or not dispensing with the last message.'

Be pleased to lay this my determination before them this morning, for I shall think of taking my measures accordingly to-morrow evening, only this that I mean no harm, but that my citadel shall not be taken by storm while I can defend it, and that if a blockade is intended, the country is under the command of my

---

[1] [The Partners were the publishers of the Dictionary. It appears that they threatened to stop supplies, and that Johnson in return threatens to stop composition. They could not proceed without him.]

batteries, I shall think of laying it under contribution to-morrow Evening.

   I am, Sir,
    Your most obliged, most obedient,
     and most humble servant,
      SAM: JOHNSON.

38. To WILLIAM STRAHAN

Dear Sir

I must desire you to add to your other civilities this one, to go to Mr. Millar and represent to him our manner of going on, and inform him that I know not how to manage. I pay three and twenty shillings a week to my assistants, in truth without having much assistance from them, but they tell me they shall be able to fall better in method, as indeed I intend they shall. The point is to get two Guineas for

    Your humble servant,
     SAM: JOHNSON.

39. To WILLIAM STRAHAN

Sir

I have often suspected that it is as you say, and have told Mr. Dodsley of it. It proceeds from the haste of the amanuensis to get to the end of his day's work. I have desired the passages to be clipped close, and then perhaps for two or three leaves it is done. But since poor Stuart's time I could never get that part of the work into regularity, and perhaps never shall. I will try to take some more care, but can promise nothing; when I am told there is a sheet or two I order it away. You will find it sometimes close; when I make up any myself, which never happens but when I have nobody with me, I generally clip it close, but one cannot always be on the watch.

   I am, Sir,
    Your most, &c.,
     SAM: JOHNSON.

46. To Joseph Warton

Dear Sir

I ought to have written to you before now, but I ought to do many things which I do not; nor can I, indeed, claim any merit from this letter; for being desired by the authours and proprietor of *The Adventurer* to look out for another hand, my thoughts necessarily fixed upon you, whose fund of literature will enable you to assist them, with very little interruption of your studies.

They desire you to engage to furnish one paper a month, at two guineas a paper, which you may very readily perform. We have considered that a paper should consist of pieces of imagination, pictures of life, and disquisitions of literature. The part which depends on the imagination is very well supplied, as you will find when you read the paper; for descriptions of life, there is now a treaty almost made with an authour and an authouress; and the province of criticism and literature they are very desirous to assign to the commentator on Virgil.

I hope this proposal will not be rejected, and that the next post will bring us your compliance. I speak as one of the fraternity, though I have no part in the paper, beyond now and then a motto; but two of the writers are my particular friends, and I hope the pleasure of seeing a third united to them, will not be denied to,

              dear Sir, your most obedient,
              and most humble servant,
March 8, 1753.   Sam: Johnson.

49. To Samuel Richardson

Dear Sir   September 26, 1753.

I return you my sincerest thanks for the volumes of your new work[1]; but it is a kind of tyrannical kindness to give only so much at a time, as makes

[1] [*Sir Charles Grandison.*]

more longed for; but that will probably be thought, even of the whole, when you have given it.

I have no objection but to the preface, in which you first mention the letters as fallen by some chance into your hands, and afterwards mention your health as such, that you almost despaired of going through your plan. If you were to require my opinion which part should be changed, I should be inclined to the suppression of that part which seems to disclaim the composition. What is modesty, if it deserts from truth? Of what use is the disguise by which nothing is concealed?

You must forgive this, because it is meant well.

I thank you once more, dear Sir, for your books; but cannot I prevail this time for an index?—such I wished, and shall wish, to Clarissa. Suppose that in one volume an accurate index was made to the three works—but while I am writing an objection arises—such an index to the three would look like the preclusion of a fourth, to which I will never contribute; for if I cannot benefit mankind, I hope never to injure them.

I am, Sir,
Your most obliged and most humble servant,
SAM: JOHNSON.

51. TO JOSEPH WARTON

Dear Sir
March 8th, 1754.

I cannot but congratulate you upon the conclusion of a work[1], in which you have borne so great a part with so much reputation. I immediately determined that your name should be mentioned, but the paper having been some time written, Mr. Hawkesworth, I suppose, did not care to disorder its text, and therefore put your eulogy in a note. He and every other man mention your papers of Criticism with great commendation, though not with greater than they deserve.

But how little can we venture to exult in any

[1] [*The Adventurer.*]

intellectual powers or literary attainments, when we consider the condition of poor Collins. I knew him a few years ago full of hopes and full of projects, versed in many languages, high in fancy, and strong in retention. This busy and forcible mind is now under the government of those who lately would not have been able to comprehend the least and most narrow of its designs. What do you hear of him? are there hopes of his recovery? or is he to pass the remainder of his life in misery and degradation? perhaps with complete consciousness of his calamity.

You have flattered us, dear Sir, for some time, with hopes of seeing you; when you come you will find your reputation increased, and with it the kindness of those friends who do not envy you; for success always produces either love or hatred. I enter my name among those that love, and that love you more and more in proportion as by writing more you are more known; and believe, that as you continue to diffuse among us your integrity and learning, I shall be still with greater esteem and affection,

Dear Sir,
Your most obedient and most humble servant,
SAM: JOHNSON.

53. TO THOMAS WARTON

Sir

It is but an ill return for the book with which you were pleased to favour me, to have delayed my thanks for it till now. I am too apt to be negligent; but I can never deliberately shew any disrespect to a man of your character: and I now pay you a very honest acknowledgement for the advancement of the literature of our native country. You have shewn to all, who shall hereafter attempt the study of our ancient authours, the way to success, by directing them to the perusal of the books which those authours had read. Of this method, Hughes and men much greater than Hughes seem never to have thought. The reason why the authours which are yet read of the sixteenth century, are so little understood, is, that they are read alone ; and no help is borrowed from those who lived with them, or before them. Some part of this ignorance I hope to remove by my book, which now draws towards its end, but which I cannot finish to my mind, without visiting the libraries at Oxford, which I, therefore, hope to see in about a fortnight. I know not how long I shall stay, or where I shall lodge, but shall be sure to look for you at my arrival, and we shall easily settle the rest.

    I am, dear Sir, your most obedient,
                and most humble servant
[London,] July 16, 1754.   SAM : JOHNSON.

56. To THOMAS WARTON

Dear Sir

I am extremely sensible of the favour done me, both by Mr. Wise and yourself. The book [1] cannot, I think, be printed in less than six weeks, nor probably so soon ; and I will keep back the title-page, for such an insertion as you seem to promise me. Be pleased to let me know what money I should send you, for bearing the expence of the affair, and I will take care that you may have it ready in your hand.

I had lately the favour of a letter from your brother, with some account of poor Collins, for whom I am much concerned. I have a notion, that by very great temperance, or more properly abstinence, he might yet recover.

There is an old English and Latin book of poems by Barclay, called ' The Ship of Fools ; ' at the end of which are a number of *Eglogues* (so he writes it, from *Ægloga*) which are probably the first in our language. If you cannot find the book I will get Mr. Dodsley to send it you.

I shall be extremely glad to hear from you soon again,

---

[1] His Dictionary. WARTON.

to know if the affair proceeds.[1] I have mentioned it to none of my friends for fear of being laughed at for my disappointment.

You know poor Mr. Dodsley has lost his wife; I believe he is much affected. I hope he will not suffer so much as I yet suffer for the loss of mine.

Οἴμοι. τί δ᾽ οἴμοι; θνῆια γὰρ πεπόνθαμεν.[2]

I have ever since seemed to myself broken off from mankind; a kind of solitary wanderer in the wild of life, without any certain direction, or fixed point of view: a gloomy gazer on a world to which I have little relation. Yet I would endeavour, by the help of you and your brother, to supply the want of closer union, by friendship: and hope to have long the pleasure of being,

dear Sir, most affectionately your's,
[London,] Dec. 21, 1754.   SAM: JOHNSON.

58. To THOMAS WARTON

Dear Sir

I wrote to you some weeks ago, but I believe did not direct accurately, and therefore know not whether you had my letter. I would likewise write to your brother, but know not where to find him. I now begin to see land, after having wandered, according to Mr. Warburton's phrase, in this vast sea of words. What reception I shall meet with upon the shore, I know not; whether the sound of bells, and acclamations of the people, which Ariosto talks of in his last Canto, or a general murmur of dislike, I know not: whether I shall find upon the coast a Calypso that will court, or a Polypheme that will eat me. But if Polypheme comes to me, have at his eye. I hope, however, the criticks will let me be at peace; for though I do not much fear their skill or strength, I am a little afraid

[1] Of the degree at Oxford. WARTON.

[2] ['Alas! Yet why should I cry, Alas? What I have suffered is the common lot of man.' EURIPIDES.]

of myself, and would not willingly feel so much ill-will in my bosom as literary quarrels are apt to excite.

Mr. Baretti is about a work for which he is in great want of *Crescembeni*, which you may have again when you please.

There is nothing considerable done or doing among us here. We are not, perhaps, as innocent as villagers, but most of us seem to be as idle. I hope, however, you are busy; and should be glad to know what you are doing.

   I am, dearest Sir, your humble servant,
[London,] Feb. 4, 1755.   SAM: JOHNSON.

59. To THOMAS WARTON

Dear Sir

I received your letter this day, with great sense of the favour that has been done me;[1] for which I return you my most sincere thanks: and entreat you to pay to Mr. Wise such returns as I ought to make for so much kindness so little deserved.

I sent Mr. Wise the *Lexicon*, and afterwards wrote to him; but know not whether he had either the book or letter. Be so good as to contrive to enquire.

But why does my dear Mr. Warton tell me nothing of himself? Where hangs the new volume?[2] Can I help? Let not the past labour be lost, for want of a little more: but snatch what time you can from the hall, and the pupils, and the coffee-house, and the parks, and complete your design.

     I am, dear Sir, &c.
[London,] Feb. 4, 1755.   SAM: JOHNSON.

---

[1] His degree had now past, according to the usual form, the suffrages of the heads of Colleges; but was not yet finally granted by the University. It was carried without a single dissentient voice. WARTON.

[2] On Spenser. WARTON.

61. To the Right Honourable the Earl of Chesterfield [1]

My Lord   February 7, 1755.

I have been lately informed, by the proprietor of *The World*, that two papers, in which my Dictionary is recommended to the publick, were written by your Lordship. To be so distinguished, is an honour, which, being very little accustomed to favours from the great, I know not well how to receive, or in what terms to acknowledge.

When, upon some slight encouragement, I first visited your Lordship, I was overpowered, like the rest of mankind, by the enchantment of your address ; and could not forbear to wish that I might boast myself *Le vainqueur du vainqueur de la terre* ;—that I might obtain that regard for which I saw the world contending ; but I found my attendance so little encouraged, that neither pride nor modesty would suffer me to continue it. When I had once addressed your Lordship in publick, I had exhausted all the art of pleasing which a retired and uncourtly scholar can possess. I had done all that I could ; and no man is well pleased to have his all neglected, be it ever so little.

Seven years, my Lord, have now past, since I waited in your outward rooms, or was repulsed from your door ; during which time I have been pushing on my

---

[1] Dr. Johnson appeared to have had a remarkable delicacy with respect to the circulation of this letter ; for Dr. Douglas, Bishop of Salisbury, informs me that, having many years ago pressed him to be allowed to read it to the second Lord Hardwicke, who was very desirous to hear it (promising at the same time, that no copy of it should be taken), Johnson seemed much pleased that it had attracted the attention of a nobleman of such a respectable character ; but after pausing some time, declined to comply with the request, saying, with a smile, ' No, Sir ; I have hurt the dog too much already; ' or words to that purpose. BOSWELL.

work through difficulties, of which it is useless to complain, and have brought it, at last, to the verge of publication, without one act of assistance,[1] one word of encouragement, or one smile of favour. Such treatment I did not expect, for I never had a Patron before.

The shepherd in Virgil grew at last acquainted with Love, and found him a native of the rocks.

Is not a Patron, my Lord, one who looks with unconcern on a man struggling for life in the water, and, when he has reached ground, encumbers him with help ? The notice which you have been pleased to take of my labours, had it been early, had been kind ; but it has been delayed till I am indifferent, and cannot enjoy it ; till I am solitary, and cannot impart it ;[2] till I am known, and do not want it. I hope it is no very cynical asperity not to confess obligations where no benefit has been received, or to be unwilling that the Publick should consider me as owing that to a Patron, which Providence has enabled me to do for myself.

Having carried on my work thus far with so little

---

[1] The following note is subjoined by Mr. Langton :—
'Dr. Johnson, when he gave me this copy of his letter, desired that I would annex to it his information to me, that whereas it is said in the letter that " no assistance has been received ", he did once receive from Lord Chesterfield the sum of ten pounds ; but as that was so inconsiderable a sum, he thought the mention of it could not properly find place in a letter of the kind that this was.' BOSWELL.

[2] In this passage Dr. Johnson evidently alludes to the loss of his wife. We find the same tender recollection recurring to his mind upon innumerable occasions : and, perhaps no man ever more forcibly felt the truth of the sentiment so elegantly expressed by my friend Mr. Malone, in his Prologue to Mr. Jephson's tragedy of JULIA :—

'Vain—wealth, and fame, and fortune's fostering care,
If no fond breast the splendid blessings share ;
And, each day's bustling pageantry once past,
There, only there, our bliss is found at last.' BOSWELL.

obligation to any favourer of learning, I shall not be disappointed though I should conclude it, if less be possible, with less; for I have been long wakened from that dream of hope, in which I once boasted myself with so much exultation, my Lord,
  your Lordship's most humble,
    most obedient servant,
      SAM: JOHNSON.[1]

64. TO THOMAS WARTON

Dear Sir

After I received my diploma, I wrote you a letter of thanks, with a letter to the Vice-Chancellor, and sent another to Mr. Wise; but have heard from nobody since, and begin to think myself forgotten. It is true, I sent you a double letter, and you may fear an expensive correspondent; but I would have taken it kindly, if you had returned it treble: and what is a double letter to a *petty king*, that having *fellowship and fines*, can sleep without a *modus in his head* ? [2]

Dear Mr. Warton, let me hear from you, and tell me something, I care not what, so I hear it but from you. Something I will tell you:—I hope to see my *Dictionary* bound and lettered, next week;—*vastâ mole superbus*. And I have a great mind to come to Oxford at Easter; but you will not invite me. Shall I come uninvited, or stay here where nobody perhaps would miss me if I went ? A hard choice ! But such is the world to,

  dear Sir, your most humble servant
[London,] March 20, 1755.   SAM: JOHNSON.

[1] Upon comparing this copy with that which Dr. Johnson dictated to me from recollection, the variations are found to be so slight, that this must be added to the many other proofs which he gave of the wonderful extent and accuracy of his memory. To gratify the curious in composition, I have deposited both the copies in the British Museum. BOSWELL.

[2] The words in Italicks are allusions to passages in Mr. Warton's poem, called *The Progress of Discontent*, now lately published. WARTON.

67. To CHARLES BURNEY

Sir

If you imagine that by delaying my answer I intended to shew any neglect of the notice with which you have favoured me, you will neither think justly of yourself nor of me. Your civilities were offered with too much elegance not to engage attention ; and I have too much pleasure in pleasing men like you, not to feel very sensibly the distinction which you have bestowed upon me.

Few consequences of my endeavours to please or to benefit mankind have delighted me more than your friendship thus voluntarily offered, which now I have it I hope to keep, because I hope to continue to deserve it.

I have no *Dictionaries* to dispose of for myself, but shall be glad to have you direct your friends to Mr. Dodsley, because it was by his recommendation that I was employed in the work.

When you have leisure to think again upon me, let me be favoured with another letter ; and another yet, when you have looked into my *Dictionary*. If you find faults, I shall endeavour to mend them ; if you find none, I shall think you blinded by kind partiality : but to have made you partial in his favour, will very much gratify the ambition of,

Sir,
your most obliged and most humble servant,
SAM : JOHNSON.

Gough-square, Fleet-street, April 8, 1755.

70. To BENNET LANGTON, ESQ., AT LANGTON NEAR SPILSBY, LINCOLNSHIRE

Sir

It has been long observed, that men do not suspect faults which they do not commit ; your own elegance of manners, and punctuality of complaisance, did not suffer you to impute to me that negligence of which I was guilty, and which I have not since atoned. I received both your letters, and received them with pleasure proportionate to the esteem which so short an acquaintance strongly impressed, and which I hope to confirm by nearer knowledge, though I am afraid that gratification will be for a time withheld.

I have, indeed, published my Book,[1] of which I beg to know your father's judgement, and yours; and I have now staid long enough to watch its progress into the world. It has, you see, no patrons, and, I think, has yet had no opponents, except the criticks of the coffee-house, whose outcries are soon dispersed into the air, and are thought on no more: from this, therefore, I am at liberty, and think of taking the opportunity of this interval to make an excursion; and why not then into Lincolnshire? or, to mention a stronger attraction, why not to dear Mr. Langton? I will give the true reason, which I know you will approve:—I have a mother more than eighty years old, who has counted the days to the publication of my book, in hopes of seeing me; and to her, if I can disengage myself here, I resolve to go.

As I know, dear Sir, that to delay my visit for a reason like this, will not deprive me of your esteem, I beg it may not lessen your kindness. I have very seldom received an offer of friendship which I so earnestly desire to cultivate and mature. I shall rejoice to hear from you till I can see you, and will see you as soon as I can , for when the duty that calls me to Lichfield is discharged, my inclination will carry me to Langton. I shall delight to hear the ocean roar, or see the stars twinkle, in the company of men to whom Nature does not spread her volumes or utter her voice in vain.

Do not, dear Sir, make the slowness of this letter a precedent for delay, or imagine that I approved the incivility that I have committed; for I have known you enough to love you, and sincerely to wish a further

---

[1] His *Dictionary*. BOSWELL.

knowledge; and I assure you, once more, that to live in a house that contains such a father and such a son, will be accounted a very uncommon degree of pleasure, by,

dear Sir, your most obliged,
and most humble servant,

May 6, 1755.   SAM: JOHNSON.

74. TO MISS COTTERELL

Madam   July 19, 1755.

I know not how liberally your generosity would reward those who should do you any service, when you can so kindly acknowledge a favour which I intended only to myself. That accidentally hearing that you were in town, I made haste to enjoy an interval of pleasure which I found would be short, was the natural consequence of that self-love which is always busy in quest of happiness; of that happiness which we often miss when we think it near, and sometimes find when we imagine it lost. When I had missed you, I went away disappointed; and did not know that my vexation would be so amply repaid by so kind a letter. A letter indeed can but imperfectly supply the place of its writer, at least of such a writer as you; and a letter which makes me still more desire your presence, is but a weak consolation under the necessity of living longer without you: with this however I must be for a time content, as much content at least as discontent will suffer me; for Mr. Baretti being a single being in this part of the world, and entirely clear from all engagements, takes the advantage of his independence, and will come before me; for which if I could blame him, I should punish him; but my own heart tells me, that he only does to me, what, if I could, I should do to him.

I hope Mrs. Porter, when she came to her favourite place, found her house dry, and her woods growing, and the breeze whistling, and the birds singing, and her

own heart dancing. And for you, Madam, whose heart cannot yet dance to such musick, I know not what to hope ; indeed I could hope every thing that would please you, except that perhaps the absence of higher pleasures is necessary to keep some little place vacant in your remembrance for,
> Madam,
> Your, &c.,
> SAM : JOHNSON.

78. To MISS BOOTHBY

Dear Madam Dec. 30, 1755.

It is again midnight, and I am again alone. With what meditation shall I amuse this waste hour of darkness and vacuity ? If I turn my thoughts upon myself, what do I perceive but a poor helpless being, reduced by a blast of wind to weakness and misery ? How my present distemper was brought upon me I can give no account, but impute it to some sudden succession of cold to heat ; such as in the common road of life cannot be avoided, and against which no precaution can be taken.

Of the fallaciousness of hope, and the uncertainty of schemes, every day gives some new proof ; but it is seldom heeded, till something rather felt than seen awakens attention. This illness, in which I have suffered something and feared much more, has depressed my confidence and elation, and made me consider all that I have promised myself, as less certain to be attained or enjoyed. I have endeavoured to form resolutions of a better life ; but I form them weakly, under the consciousness of an external motive. Not that I conceive a time of sickness a time improper for recollection and good purposes, which I believe diseases and calamities often sent to produce ; but because no man can know how little his performance will answer to his promises ; and designs are nothing in human eyes till they are realised by execution.

Continue, my Dearest, your prayers for me, that no good resolution may be vain. You think, I believe, better of me than I deserve. I hope to be in time what I wish to be, and what I have hitherto satisfied myself too readily with only wishing.

Your billet brought me what I much wished to have, a proof that I am still remembered by you at the hour in which I most desire it!

The Doctor is anxious about you. He thinks you too negligent of yourself; if you will promise to be cautious, I will exchange promises, as we have already exchanged injunctions. However, do not write to me more than you can easily bear; do not interrupt your ease to write at all.

Mr. Fitzherbert sent to-day to offer me some wine; the people about me say I ought to accept it, I shall therefore be obliged to him if he will send me a bottle.

There has gone about a report that I died to-day, which I mention, lest you should hear it and be alarmed. You see that I think my death may alarm you, which for me is to think very highly of earthly friendship. I believe it arose from the death of one of my neighbours. You know Des Cartes's argument, ' I think, therefore I am.' It is as good a consequence, ' I write, therefore I am alive.' I might give another, ' I am alive, therefore I love Miss Boothby'; but that I hope our friendship may be of far longer duration than life.

> I am, dearest Madam,
> with sincere affection,
> Your most obliged and most humble servant,
> Sam: Johnson.

81. To Miss Boothby

Dearest Madam   Jan. 3, 1755 [1756].

Nobody but you can recompense me for the distress which I suffered on Monday night. Having engaged Dr. Lawrence to let me know, at whatever hour, the state in which he left you; I concluded when he staid so long, that he staid to see my dearest expire. I was composing myself as I could to hear what yet I hoped not to hear, when his servant brought me word that you were better. Do you continue to grow better? Let my dear little Miss inform me on a card. I would not have you write lest it should hurt you, and consequently hurt likewise,

     Dearest Madam,
      Your, &c.,
       SAM: JOHNSON.

87. TO MISS CARTER

Madam

From the liberty of writing to you if I have hitherto been deterred by the fear of your understanding, I am now encouraged to it by the confidence of your goodness.

I am soliciting a benefit for Miss Williams, and beg that if you can by letters influence any in her favour, and who is there whom you cannot influence? you will be pleased to patronise her on this occasion. You see the time is short, and as you were not in town, I did not till this day remember that you might help us, or recollect how widely and how rapidly light is diffused.

To every joy is appended a sorrow. The name of Miss Carter introduces the memory of Cave. Poor dear Cave! I owed him much; for to him I owe that I have known you. He died, I am afraid, unexpectedly to himself, yet surely unburthened with any great crime; and for the positive duties of religion, I have yet no right to condemn him for neglect.

I am, with respect which I neither owe nor pay to any other,

    Madam,
     Your most obedient
      and most humble servant,
       SAM: JOHNSON.

Gough Square,
 Jan. 14, 1756.

94. To Samuel Richardson

Sir

I am obliged to entreat your assistance. I am now under an arrest for five pounds eighteen shillings. Mr. Strahan, from whom I should have received the necessary help in this case, is not at home; and I am afraid of not finding Mr. Millar. If you will be so good as to send me this sum, I will very gratefully repay you, and add it to all former obligations.

I am, Sir,
Your most obedient
and most humble servant,
SAM: JOHNSON.

Gough Square, March 16, [1756].

96. To Joseph Warton

April 15th, 1756.

Dear Sir

Though when you and your brother were in town you did not think my humble habitation worth a visit, yet I will not so far give way to sullenness as not to tell you that I have lately seen an octavo book [1] which I suspect to be yours, though I have not yet read above ten pages. That way of publishing, without acquainting your friends, is a wicked trick. However, I will not so far depend upon a mere conjecture as to charge you with a fraud which I cannot prove you to have committed.

I should be glad to hear that you are pleased with your new situation.[2] You have now a kind of royalty, and are to be answerable for your conduct to posterity. I suppose you care not now to answer a letter except there be a lucky concurrence of a post-day with a holiday. These restraints are troublesome for a time, but custom makes them easy, with the help of some honour, and a great deal of profit, and I doubt not but your abilities will obtain both.

For my part, I have not lately done much. I have

---

[1] [His Essay on Pope.]
[2] [Second Master of Winchester.]

been ill in the winter, and my eye has been inflamed; but I please myself with the hopes of doing many things, with which I have long pleased and deceived myself.

What becomes of poor dear Collins? I wrote him a letter which he never answered. I suppose writing is very troublesome to him. That man is no common loss. The moralists all talk of the uncertainty of fortune, and the transitoriness of beauty; but it is yet more dreadful to consider that the powers of the mind are equally liable to change; that understanding may make its appearance and depart, that it may blaze and expire.

Let me not be long without a letter, and I will forgive you the omission of the visit; and if you can tell me that you are now more happy than before, you will give great pleasure to,
Dear Sir,
Your most affectionate
and most humble servant,
SAM: JOHNSON.

106. To Dr. Taylor

Dear Sir

You have no great title to a very speedy answer, yet I did not intend to have delayed so long. I am now in doubt whether you are not come to town, if you are double postage is a proper fine.

There is one honest reason why those things are most subject to delays which we most desire to do. What we think of importance we wish to do well, to do anything well requires time, and what requires time commonly finds us too idle or too busy to undertake it. To be idle is not the best excuse, though if a man studies his own reformation it is the best reason he can allege to himself, both because it is commonly true, and because it contains no fallacy, for every man that thinks he is idle condemns himself and has therefore a chance to endeavour amendment, but the busy mortal has often his own commendation, even when his very business is the consequence of Idleness, when he engages himself in trifles only to put the thoughts of more important duties out of his mind, or to gain an excuse to his own heart for omitting them.

I am glad however that while you forgot me you were gaining upon the affections of other people.

It is in your power to be very useful as a neighbour, a magistrate, and a Clergyman, and he that is useful, must conduct his life very imprudently not to be beloved. If Mousley makes advances, I would wish you not to reject them. You once esteemed him, and the quarrel between you arose from misinformation and ought to be forgotten.

When you come to town let us contrive to see one another more frequently, at least once a week. We have both lived long enough to bury many friends, and have therefore learned to set a value on those who are left. Neither of us now can find many whom he has known so long as we have known each other. Do not let us lose our intimacy at a time when we ought rather to think of encreasing it. We both stand almost single in the world, I have no brother, and with your sister you have little correspondence. But if you will take my advice, you will make some overtures of reconciliation to her. If you have been to blame, you know it is your duty first to seek a renewal of kindness. If she has been faulty, you have an opportunity to exercise the virtue of forgiveness. You must consider that of her faults and follies no very great part is her own. Much has been the consequence of her education, and part may be imputed to the neglect with which you have sometime treated her. Had you endeavoured to gain her kindness and her confidence, you would have had more influence over her. I hope that before I shall see you, she will have had a visit or a letter from you. The longer you delay the more you will sometime repent. When I am musing alone, I feel a pang for every moment that any human being has by my peevishness or obstinacy spent in uneasiness. I know not how I have fallen upon this, I had no thought of it, when I began the letter, yet am glad that I have written it.

     I am, dearest Sir,
       Your most affectionate
Nov. 18, 1756.   SAM: JOHNSON.

107. TO CHARLES O'CONNOR

Sir

I have lately, by the favour of Mr. Faulkner, seen your account of Ireland, and cannot forbear to solicit a prosecution of your design. Sir William Temple complains that Ireland is less known than any other country, as to its ancient state. The natives have had little leisure, and little encouragement for enquiry; and strangers, not knowing the language, have had no ability.

I have long wished that the Irish literature were cultivated. Ireland is known by tradition to have been once the seat of piety and learning; and surely it would be very acceptable to all those who are curious either in the original of nations, or the affinities of languages, to be further informed of the revolutions of a people so ancient, and once so illustrious.

What relation there is between the Welsh and Irish languages, or between the language of Ireland and that of Biscay, deserves enquiry. Of these provincial and unextended tongues, it seldom happens that more than one are understood by any one man; and, therefore, it seldom happens that a fair comparison can be made. I hope you will continue to cultivate this kind of learning, which has lain too long neglected, and which, if it be suffered to remain in oblivion for another century, may, perhaps, never be retrieved. As I wish well to all useful undertakings, I would not forbear to let you know how much you deserve, in my opinion, from all lovers of study, and how much pleasure your work has given to,

  Sir, your most obliged, and most humble servant,
London, April 9, 1757.   SAM: JOHNSON.

110. To BENNET LANGTON

Dear Sir

Though I might have expected to hear from you, upon your entrance into a new state of life at a new place, yet recollecting, (not without some degree of shame,) that I owe you a letter upon an old account, I think it my part to write first. This, indeed, I do not only from complaisance but from interest; for living on in the old way, I am very glad of a correspondent so capable as yourself, to diversify the hours. You have, at present, too many novelties about you to need any help from me to drive along your time.

I know not any thing more pleasant, or more instructive, than to compare experience with expectation, or to register from time to time the difference between idea and reality. It is by this kind of observation that we grow daily less liable to be disappointed. You, who are very capable of anticipating futurity, and raising phantoms before your own eyes, must often have imagined to yourself an academical life, and have conceived what would be the manners, the views, and the conversation, of men devoted to letters; how they would choose their companions, how they would direct their studies, and how they would regulate their lives. Let me know what you expected, and what you have found. At least record it to yourself before custom has reconciled you to the scenes before you, and the disparity of your discoveries to your hopes has vanished from your mind. It is a rule never to be forgotten, that whatever strikes strongly, should be described while the first impression remains fresh upon the mind.

I love, dear Sir, to think on you, and therefore, should willingly write more to you, but that the post will not now give me leave to do more than send my compliments to Mr. Warton, and tell you that

I am, dear Sir, most affectionately,
your very humble servant,

June 28, 1757.   SAM: JOHNSON.

112. To Charles Burney

Sir

That I may shew myself sensible of your favours, and not commit the same fault a second time, I make haste to answer the letter which I received this morning. The truth is, the other likewise was received, and I wrote an answer; but being desirous to transmit you some proposals and receipts, I waited till I could find a convenient conveyance, and day was passed after day, till other things drove it from my thoughts; yet not so, but that I remember with great pleasure your commendation of my *Dictionary*. Your praise was welcome, not only because I believe it was sincere, but because praise has been very scarce. A man of your candour will be surprised when I tell you, that among all my acquaintance there were only two, who upon the publication of my book did not endeavour to depress me with threats of censure from the publick, or with objections learned from those who had learned them from my own Preface. Your's is the only letter of goodwill that I have received; though, indeed, I am promised something of that sort from Sweden.

How my new edition will be received I know not; the subscription has not been very successful. I shall publish about March.[1]

If you can direct me how to send proposals, I should wish that they were in such hands.

I remember, Sir, in some of the first letters with which you favoured me, you mentioned your lady. May I enquire after her? In return for the favours which you have shewn me, it is not much to tell you, that I wish you and her all that can conduce to your happiness.

I am, Sir, your most obliged,
and most humble servant,
Gough-square, Dec. 24, 1757.   Sam: Johnson.

[1] [His edition of Shakespeare was published in 1765.]

113. To CHARLES BURNEY, AT LYNNE, NORFOLK

Sir

Your kindness is so great, and my claim to any particular regard from you so little, that I am at a loss how to express my sense of your favours;[1] but I am, indeed, much pleased to be thus distinguished by you.

I am ashamed to tell you that my *Shakspeare* will not be out so soon as I promised my subscribers; but I did not promise them more than I promised myself. It will, however, be published before summer.

I have sent you a bundle of proposals, which, I think, do not profess more than I have hitherto performed. I have printed many of the plays, and have hitherto left very few passages unexplained; where I am quite at a loss, I confess my ignorance, which is seldom done by commentators.

I have, likewise, enclosed twelve receipts; not that I mean to impose upon you the trouble of pushing them, with more importunity than may seem proper, but that you may rather have more than fewer than you shall want. The proposals you will disseminate as there shall be an opportunity. I once printed them at length in the *Chronicle*, and some of my friends (I believe Mr. Murphy, who formerly wrote the *Gray's-Inn Journal*) introduced them with a splendid encomium.

Since the *Life of Browne*, I have been a little engaged, from time to time, in the *Literary Magazine*, but not very lately. I have not the collection by me, and therefore cannot draw out a catalogue of my own parts, but will do it, and send it. Do not buy them, for I will gather all those that have anything of mine in them, and send them to Mrs. Burney, as a small token of gratitude for the regard which she is pleased to bestow upon me.

I am, Sir,
your most obliged and most humble servant,
London, March 8, 1758. SAM: JOHNSON.

[1] This letter was an answer to one in which was enclosed a draft for the payment of some subscriptions to his *Shakspeare*. BOSWELL.

114. To Thomas Warton

Dear Sir

Your notes upon my poet were very acceptable to me, I beg that you will be so kind as to continue your searches. It will be reputable to my work, and suitable to your professorship, to have something of yours in the notes. You have given no directions about your name, I shall therefore put it. I wish your brother would take the same trouble. A commentary must arise from the fortuitous discoveries of many men in devious walks of literature. Some of your remarks are on plays already printed: but I purpose to add an Appendix of Notes, so that nothing comes too late.

You give yourself too much uneasiness, dear Sir, about the loss of the papers.[1] The loss is nothing, if nobody has found them; nor even then, perhaps, if the numbers be known. You are not the only friend that has had the same mischance. You may repair your want out of a stock, which is deposited with Mr. Allen, of Magdalen-Hall; or out of a parcel which I have just sent to Mr. Chambers[2] for the use of any body that will be so kind as to want them. Mr. Langtons are well; and Miss Roberts, whom I have at last brought to speak, upon the information which you gave me, that she had something to say.

I am, &c.

[London,] April 14, 1758. SAM: JOHNSON.

116. To Bennet Langton, Esq., at Langton, near Spilsby, Lincolnshire

Dear Sir

I should be sorry to think that what engrosses

---

[1] Receipts for *Shakespeare*. WARTON.
[2] Then of Lincoln College. Now Sir Robert Chambers, one of the Judges in India. WARTON.

the attention of my friend, should have no part of
mine. Your mind is now full of the fate of Dury;[1]
but his fate is past, and nothing remains but to try
what reflection will suggest to mitigate the terrours
of a violent death, which is more formidable at the
first glance, than on a nearer and more steady view.
A violent death is never very painful; the only danger
is lest it should be unprovided. But if a man can be
supposed to make no provision for death in war, what
can be the state that would have awakened him to the
care of futurity? When would that man have prepared
himself to die, who went to seek death without preparation?
What then can be the reason why we lament
more him that dies of a wound, than him that dies
of a fever? A man that languishes with disease, ends
his life with more pain, but with less virtue; he leaves
no example to his friends, nor bequeaths any honour
to his descendants. The only reason why we lament
a soldier's death, is, that we think he might have
lived longer; yet this cause of grief is common to
many other kinds of death which are not so passionately
bewailed. The truth is, that every death is violent
which is the effect of accident; every death, which
is not gradually brought on by the miseries of age, or
when life is extinguished for any other reason than
that it is burnt out. He that dies before sixty, of a cold
or consumption, dies, in reality, by a violent death;
yet his death is borne with patience only because the
cause of his untimely end is silent and invisible. Let
us endeavour to see things as they are, and then
enquire whether we ought to complain. Whether to
see life as it is, will give us much consolation, I know
not; but the consolation which is drawn from truth,
if any there be, is solid and durable; that which may

[1] Major-General Alexander Dury, of the first regiment
of foot-guards, who fell in the gallant discharge of his
duty, near St. Cas, in the well-known unfortunate
expedition against France, in 1758. His lady and
Mr. Langton's mother were sisters. BOSWELL.

be derived from errour must be, like its original, fallacious and fugitive.

     I am, dear, dear Sir,
       your most humble servant,
Sept. 21, 1758.   Sam: Johnson.

117. To Bennet Langton

Dearest Sir

I must indeed have slept very fast, not to have been awakened by your letter. None of your suspicions are true; I am not much richer than when you left me; and, what is worse, my omission of an answer to your first letter, will prove that I am not much wiser. But I go on as I formerly did, designing to be some time or other both rich and wise; and yet cultivate neither mind nor fortune. Do you take notice of my example, and learn the danger of delay. When I was as you are now, towering in the confidence of twenty-one, little did I suspect that I should be at forty-nine, what I now am.

But you do not seem to need my admonition. You are busy in acquiring and in communicating knowledge, and while you are studying, enjoy the end of study, by making others wiser and happier. I was much pleased with the tale that you told me of being tutour to your sisters. I, who have no sisters nor brothers, look with some degree of innocent envy on those who may be said to be born to friends; and cannot see, without wonder, how rarely that native union is afterwards regarded. It sometimes, indeed, happens, that some supervenient cause of discord may overpower this original amity; but it seems to me more frequently thrown away with levity, or lost by negligence, than destroyed by injury or violence. We tell the ladies that good wives make good husbands; I believe it is a more certain position that good brothers make good sisters.

I am satisfied with your stay at home, as Juvenal

with his friend's retirement to Cumæ: I know that
your absence is best, though it be not best for me.

> *Quamvis digressu veteris confusus amici,*
> *Laudo tamen vacuis quod sedem figere Cumis*
> *Destinet, atque unum civem donare Sibyllæ.*¹

Langton is a good Cumæ, but who must be Sibylla?
Mrs. Langton is as wise as Sibyl, and as good; and
will live, if my wishes can prolong life, till she shall
in time be as old. But she differs in this, that she has
not scattered her precepts in the wind, at least not
those which she bestowed upon you.

The two Wartons just looked into the town, and were
taken to see *Cleone*, where, David ² says, they were
starved for want of company to keep them warm.
David and Doddy ³ have had a new quarrel, and,
I think, cannot conveniently quarrel any more. *Cleone*
was well acted by all the characters, but Bellamy left
nothing to be desired. I went the first night, and
supported it, as well as I might; for Doddy, you
know, is my patron, and I would not desert him. The
play was very well received. Doddy, after the danger
was over, went every night to the stage-side, and cried
at the distress of poor Cleone.

I have left off housekeeping, and therefore made
presents of the game which you were pleased to send
me. The pheasant I gave to Mr. Richardson,⁴ the
bustard to Dr. Lawrence, and the pot I placed with
Miss Williams, to be eaten by myself. She desires
that her compliments and good wishes may be accepted
by the family; and I make the same request for
myself.

Mr. Reynolds has within these few days raised his
price to twenty guineas a head, and Miss is much

---

¹ [Juvenal's Third Satire; see the opening lines of
Johnson's *London*.]

² Mr. Garrick. BOSWELL.

³ Mr. Dodsley, the Authour of *Cleone*. BOSWELL.

⁴ Mr. Samuel Richardson, authour of *Clarissa*.
BOSWELL.

employed in miniatures. I know not any body else whose prosperity has encreased since you left them.

Murphy is to have his *Orphan of China* acted next month; and is therefore, I suppose, happy. I wish I could tell you of any great good to which I was approaching, but at present my prospects do not much delight me; however, I am always pleased when I find that you, dear Sir, remember

your affectionate, humble servant,

Jan. 9, 1759.   SAM: JOHNSON.

118. To MRS. JOHNSON

Honoured Madam

The account which Miss gives me of your health pierces my heart. God comfort and preserve you and save you, for the sake of Jesus Christ.

I would have Miss read to you from time to time the Passion of our Saviour, and sometimes the sentences in the Communion Service, beginning ' *Come unto me all ye that travail and are heavy laden, and I will give you rest* '.

I have just now read a physical book, which inclines me to think that a strong infusion of the bark would do you good. Do, dear mother, try it.

Pray, send me your blessing, and forgive all that I have done amiss to you. And whatever you would have done, and what debts you would have paid first, or anything else that you would direct, let Miss put it down; I shall endeavour to obey you.

I have got twelve guineas to send you, but unhappily am at a loss how to send it to-night. If I cannot send it to-night, it will come by the next post.

Pray, do not omit any thing mentioned in this letter : God bless you for ever and ever.

I am your dutiful son,

Jan. 13, 1759.   SAM: JOHNSON.

To Mrs. Johnson in Lichfield.

120. To Mrs. Johnson

Dear honoured Mother

Your weakness afflicts me beyond what I am willing to communicate to you. I do not think you unfit to face death, but I know not how to bear the thought of losing you. Endeavour to do all you can for yourself. Eat as much as you can.

I pray often for you; do you pray for me. I have nothing to add to my last letter.

                I am, dear, dear mother,
                  Your dutiful son,

Jan. 16, 1759.   Sam: Johnson.

121. To Mrs. Johnson

Dear honoured Mother

I fear you are too ill for long letters; therefore I will only tell you, you have from me all the regard that can possibly subsist in the heart. I pray God to bless you for evermore, for Jesus Christ's sake. Amen.

Let Miss write to me every post, however short.

                I am, dear mother,
                  Your dutiful son,

Jan. 18, 1759.   Sam: Johnson.

122. To Miss Porter

Dear Miss

I will, if it be possible, come down to you. God grant I may yet find my dear mother breathing and sensible. Do not tell her lest I disappoint her. If I miss to write next post, I am on the road.

                I am, my dearest Miss,
                  Your most humble servant,

Jan. 20, 1759.   Sam: Johnson.

123. To Mrs. Johnson

Dear honoured Mother

Neither your condition nor your character make

it fit for me to say much. You have been the best mother, and I believe the best woman in the world. I thank you for your indulgence to me, and beg forgiveness of all that I have done ill, and all that I have omitted to do well. God grant you his Holy Spirit, and receive you to everlasting happiness, for Jesus Christ's sake. Amen. Lord Jesus receive your spirit. Amen.

I am, dear, dear mother,
Your dutiful son,
Jan. 20, 1759. SAM: JOHNSON.

124. TO WILLIAM STRAHAN
Sir

When I was with you last night I told you of a thing which I was preparing for the press. The title will be

'The Choice of Life

or

The History of . . . Prince of Abissinia.'

It will make about two volumes like little Pompadour, that is about one middling volume. The bargain which I made with Mr. Johnston was seventy five pounds (or guineas) a volume, and twenty-five pounds for the second edition. I will sell this either at that price or for sixty pounds the first edition of which he shall himself fix the number, and the property then to revert to me, or for forty pounds, and share the profit, that is retain half the copy. I shall have occasion for thirty pounds on Monday night when I shall deliver the book which I must entreat you upon such delivery to procure me. I would have it offered to Mr. Johnston, but have no doubt of selling it, on some of the terms mentioned.

I will not print my name, but expect it to be known.
I am, dear Sir,
Your most humble servant,
Jan. 20, 1759. SAM: JOHNSON.

Get me the money if you can.

125. To Miss Porter

You will conceive my sorrow for the loss of my mother, of the best mother. If she were to live again, surely I should behave better to her. But she is happy, and what is past is nothing to her; and for me, since I cannot repair my faults to her, I hope repentance will efface them. I return you and all those that have been good to her my sincerest thanks, and pray God to repay you all with infinite advantage. Write to me, and comfort me, dear child. I shall be glad likewise, if Kitty will write to me. I shall send a bill of twenty pounds in a few days, which I thought to have brought to my mother; but God suffered it not. I have not power or composure to say much more. God bless you and bless us all.

> I am, dear Miss,
> Your affectionate humble servant,

Jan. 23, 1759.   SAM: JOHNSON.

To Miss Porter

Dear Madam

I have sent you a note of twenty pounds with which I would have done what you suppose my dear mother should have directed. I repose wholly on your prudence and can send ten pounds more when you please.

I am not able to determine my stay. My grief makes me afraid to be alone. Write to me dear child.

I should think it best that you staid in the house and that Kitty carried on the trade. She has been very good and is my old friend. Tell me what you would have done. God bless you.

> I am, my dearest,
> Your affectionate servant,

Jan. 27, 1759.   SAM: JOHNSON.

127. To Miss Porter

Dear Miss

I have no reason to forbear writing, but that it

makes my heart heavy, and I had nothing particular to say which might not be delayed to the next post; but had no thoughts of ceasing to correspond with my dear Lucy, the only person now left in the world with whom I think myself connected. There needed not my dear mother's desire, for every heart must lean to somebody, and I have nobody but you; in whom I put all my little affairs with too much confidence to desire you to keep receipts, as you prudently proposed.

If you and Kitty will keep the house, I think I shall like it best. Kitty may carry on the trade for herself, keeping her own stock apart, and laying aside any money that she receives for any of the goods which her good mistress has left behind her. I do not see, if this scheme be followed, any need of appraising the books. My mother's debts, dear mother, I suppose I may pay with little difficulty; and the little trade may go silently forward. I fancy Kitty can do nothing better; and I shall not want to put her out of a house, where she has lived so long, and with so much virtue. I am very sorry that she is ill, and earnestly hope that she will soon recover; let her know that I have the highest value for her, and would do any thing for her advantage. Let her think of this proposal. I do not see any likelier method by which she may pass the remaining part of her life in quietness and competence.

You must have what part of the house you please, while you are inclined to stay in it; but I flatter myself with the hope that you and I shall some time pass our days together. I am very solitary and comfortless, but will not invite you to come hither till I can have hope of making you live here so as not to dislike your situation. Pray, my dearest, write to me as often as you can.

    I am, dear Madam,
     Your affectionate humble servant,
Feb. 6, 1759.   SAM: JOHNSON.

131. To Miss Porter

Dear Madam May 10, 1759.

I am almost ashamed to tell you that all your letters came safe, and that I have been always very well, but hindered, I hardly know how, from writing. I sent, last week, some of my works,[1] one for you, one for your aunt Hunter, who was with my poor dear mother when she died, one for Mr. Howard, and one for Kitty.

I beg you, my dear, to write often to me, and tell me how you like my little book.

I am, dear love,
Your affectionate humble servant,
SAM: JOHNSON.

133. To Mrs. Montagu

Madam Gray's Inn, Dec. 17, 1759.

Goodness so conspicuous as yours will be often solicited, and perhaps sometimes solicited by those who have little pretension to your favour. It is now my turn to introduce a petitioner, but such as I have reason to believe you will think worthy of your notice. Mrs. Ogle, who kept the music-room in Soho Square, a woman who struggles with great industry for the support of eight children, hopes by a benefit concert to set herself free from a few debts, which she cannot otherwise discharge. She has, I know not why, so high an opinion of me as to believe that you will pay less regard to her application than to mine. You know, Madam, I am sure you know, how hard it is to deny, and therefore would not wonder at my compliance, though I were to suppress a motive which you know not, the vanity of being supposed to be of any importance to Mrs. Montagu. But though I may be willing to see the world deceived for my advantage, I am not deceived myself, for I know that Mrs. Ogle will owe whatever favours she shall receive from the

---

[1] [Copies of *Rasselas*.]

patronage which we humbly entreat on this occasion, much more to your compassion for honesty in distress, than to the request of,

             Madam,

    Your most obedient and most humble servant,

                          SAM: JOHNSON.

135. TO BENNET LANGTON

Dear Sir

You that travel about the world, have more materials for letters, than I who stay at home; and should, therefore, write with frequency equal to your opportunities. I should be glad to have all England surveyed by you, if you would impart your observations in narratives as agreeable as your last. Knowledge is always to be wished to those who can communicate it well. While you have been riding and running, and seeing the tombs of the learned, and the camps of the valiant, I have only staid at home, and intended to do great things, which I have not done. Beau[1] went away to Cheshire, and has not yet found his way back. Chambers passed the vacation at Oxford.

I am very sincerely solicitous for the preservation or curing of Mr. Langton's sight, and am glad that the chirurgeon at Coventry gives him so much hope. Mr. Sharpe is of opinion that the tedious maturation of the cataract is a vulgar errour, and that it may be removed as soon as it is formed. This notion deserves to be considered; I doubt whether it be universally true; but if it be true in some cases, and those cases can be distinguished, it may save a long and uncomfortable delay.

Of dear Mrs. Langton you give me no account; which is the less friendly, as you know how highly I think of her, and how much I interest myself in her health. I suppose you told her of my opinion, and likewise suppose it was not followed; however, I still believe it to be right.

[1] Topham Beauclerk, Esq. BOSWELL.

Let me hear from you again, wherever you are, or whatever you are doing; whether you wander or sit still, plant trees or make *Rusticks*,[1] play with your sisters or muse alone; and in return I will tell you the success of Sheridan, who at this instant is playing Cato, and has already played Richard twice. He had more company the second than the first night, and will make, I believe, a good figure in the whole, though his faults seem to be very many; some of natural deficience, and some of laborious affectation. He has, I think, no power of assuming either that dignity or elegance which some men, who have little of either in common life, can exhibit on the stage. His voice when strained is unpleasing, and when low is not always heard. He seems to think too much on the audience, and turns his face too often to the galleries.

However, I wish him well; and among other reasons, because I like his wife.[2] Make haste to write to,

  dear Sir, your most affectionate servant,
Oct. 18, 1760.   SAM: JOHNSON

136. To THOMAS PERCY

Dear Sir

I went this morning to Mr. Millar, and found him very well disposed to your project.[3] I told him the price of 3 vols. was an hundred guineas, to which he made no objection. I said nothing of advancing any money, for he was in great haste, and I did not at once recollect it. There is only one thing which I dislike. He wants the Sheets that are in my hands to shew to I know not whom. In that there is yet some danger.

---

[1] Essays with that title, written about this time by Mr. Langton, but not published. BOSWELL.

[2] Mrs. Sheridan was authour of *Memoirs of Miss Sydney Biddulph*, a novel of great merit, and of some other pieces. BOSWELL.

[3] [The reference is to Percy's *Reliques of Ancient English Poetry*. It appeared in three volumes in 1765. The dedication was written by Johnson.]

If we had not had this Specimen I think we should have immediately bargained. Perhaps after all the bargain is made. You will know from his own Letter, which he promised me to write to-night, and which, if he writes it, will make this superfluous. But, this business being of moment, I would not appear to neglect it. Make all compliments to Mrs. Percy, for

Sir,

Your most humble servant,

Nov. 29, 1760.   SAM: JOHNSON.

138. To JOSEPH BARETTI

You reproach me very often with parsimony of writing: but you may discover by the extent of my paper, that I design to recompence rarity by length. A short letter to a distant friend is, in my opinion, an insult like that of a slight bow or cursory salutation;— a proof of unwillingness to do much, even where there is a necessity of doing something. Yet it must be remembered, that he who continues the same course of life in the same place, will have little to tell. One week and one year are very like one another. The silent changes made by time are not always perceived; and if they are not perceived, cannot be recounted. I have risen and lain down, talked and mused, while you have roved over a considerable part of Europe; yet I have not envied my Baretti any of his pleasures, though, perhaps, I have envied others his company: and I am glad to have other nations made acquainted with the character of the English, by a traveller who has so nicely inspected our manners, and so successfully studied our literature. I received your kind letter from Falmouth, in which you gave me notice of your departure for Lisbon, and another from Lisbon, in which you told me, that you were to leave Portugal in a few days. To either of these how could any answer be returned? I have had a third from Turin, complaining that I have not answered the former. Your English style still continues in its purity and vigour.

With vigour your genius will supply it; but its purity must be continued by close attention. To use two languages familiarly, and without contaminating one by the other, is very difficult: and to use more than two is hardly to be hoped. The praises which some have received for their multiplicity of languages, may be sufficient to excite industry, but can hardly generate confidence.

I know not whether I can heartily rejoice at the kind reception which you have found, or at the popularity to which you are exalted. I am willing that your merit should be distinguished; but cannot wish that your affections may be gained. I would have you happy wherever you are: yet I would have you wish to return to England. If ever you visit us again, you will find the kindness of your friends undiminished. To tell you how many enquiries are made after you, would be tedious, or if not tedious, would be vain; because you may be told in a very few words, that all who knew you wish you well; and that all that you embraced at your departure, will caress you at your return: therefore do not let Italian academicians nor Italian ladies drive us from your thoughts. You may find among us what you will leave behind, soft smiles and easy sonnets. Yet I shall not wonder if all our invitations should be rejected: for there is a pleasure in being considerable at home, which is not easily resisted.

By conducting Mr. Southwell to Venice, you fulfilled, I know, the original contract: yet I would wish you not wholly to lose him from your notice, but to recommend him to such acquaintance as may best secure him from suffering by his own follies, and to take such general care both of his safety and his interest as may come within your power. His relations will thank you for any such gratuitous attention: at least they will not blame you for any evil that may happen, whether they thank you or not for any good.

You know that we have a new King and a new Parliament. Of the new Parliament Fitzherbert is a member.

We were so weary of our old King, that we are much pleased with his successor; of whom we are so much inclined to hope great things, that most of us begin already to believe them. The young man is hitherto blameless; but it would be unreasonable to expect much from the immaturity of juvenile years, and the ignorance of princely education. He has been long in the hands of the Scots, and has already favoured them more than the English will contentedly endure. But, perhaps, he scarcely knows whom he has distinguished, or whom he has disgusted.

The Artists have instituted a yearly Exhibition of pictures and statues, in imitation, as I am told, of foreign academies. This year was the second Exhibition. They please themselves much with the multitude of spectators, and imagine that the English School will rise in reputation. Reynolds is without a rival, and continues to add thousands to thousands, which he deserves, among other excellencies, by retaining his kindness for Baretti. This Exhibition has filled the heads of the Artists and lovers of art. Surely life, if it be not long, is tedious, since we are forced to call in the assistance of so many trifles to rid us of our time, of that time which never can return.

I know my Baretti will not be satisfied with a letter in which I give him no account of myself: yet what account shall I give him ? I have not, since the day of our separation, suffered or done any thing considerable. The only change in my way of life is, that I have frequented the theatre more than in former seasons. But I have gone thither only to escape from myself. We have had many new farces, and the comedy called *The Jealous Wife*, which, though not written with much genius, was yet so well adapted to the stage, and so well exhibited by the actors, that it was crowded for near twenty nights. I am digressing from myself to the playhouse : but a barren plan must be filled with episodes. Of myself I have nothing to say, but that I have hitherto lived without the concurrence of my own judgment; yet I continue to flatter myself, that, when you return, you will find me mended. I do not wonder that, where the monastick life is permitted, every order finds votaries, and every monastery inhabitants. Men will submit to any rule, by which they may be exempted from the tyranny of caprice and of chance. They are glad to supply by external authority their own want of constancy and resolution, and court the government of others, when long experience has convinced them of their own inability to govern themselves. If I were to visit Italy, my curiosity would be more attracted by convents than by palaces : though I am afraid that I should find expectation in both places equally disappointed, and life in both places supported with impatience and quitted with reluctance. That it must be so soon quitted, is a powerful remedy against impatience ; but what shall free us from reluctance ? Those who have endeavoured to teach us to die well, have taught few to die willingly : yet I cannot but hope that a good life might end at last in a contented death.

You see to what a train of thought I am drawn by the mention of myself. Let me now turn my attention upon you. I hope you take care to keep an exact journal, and to register all occurrences and observations ; for your friends here expect such a book of travels as has not been often seen. You have given us good specimens in your letters from Lisbon. I wish you had staid longer in Spain, for no country is less known to the rest of Europe ; but the quickness of your discernment must make amends for the celerity of your motions. He that knows which way to direct his view, sees much in a little time.

Write to me very often, and I will not neglect to write to you ; and I may, perhaps, in time, get something to write : at least, you will know by my letters, whatever else they may have or want, that I continue to be your most affectionate friend,

London, June 10, 1761.   Sam : Johnson.

139. To Thomas Percy

Dear Sir

The kindness of your invitation would tempt me to leave pomp and tumult behind, and hasten to your retreat; however, as I cannot perhaps see another coronation so conveniently as this, and I may see many young Percies, I beg your pardon for staying till this great ceremony is over, after which I purpose to pass some time with you, though I cannot flatter myself that I can even then long enjoy the pleasure which your company always gives me, and which is likewise expected from that of Mrs. Percy, by,

        Sir,
              Your most affectionate

Sept. 12, 1761.   Sam: Johnson.

140. To Dr. Staunton

Dear Sir

I make haste to answer your kind letter, in hope of hearing again from you before you leave us. I cannot but regret that a man of your qualifications should find it necessary to seek an establishment in Guadaloupe, which if a peace should restore to the French, I shall think it some alleviation of the loss, that it must restore likewise Dr. Staunton to the English.

It is a melancholy consideration, that so much of our time is necessarily to be spent upon the care of living, and that we can seldom obtain ease in one respect but by resigning it in another; yet I suppose we are by this dispensation not less happy in the whole, than if the spontaneous bounty of Nature poured all that we want into our hands. A few, if they were thus left to themselves, would, perhaps, spend their time in laudable pursuits; but the greater part would prey upon the quiet of each other, or, in the want of other objects, would prey upon themselves.

This, however, is our condition, which we must improve and solace as we can: and though we cannot choose always our place of residence, we may in every place find rational amusements, and possess in every place the comforts of piety and a pure conscience.

In America there is little to be observed except natural curiosities. The new world must have many vegetables and animals with which philosophers are but little acquainted. I hope you will furnish yourself with some books of natural history, and some glasses and other instruments of observation. Trust as little as you can to report : examine all you can by your own senses. I do not doubt but you will be able to add much to knowledge, and, perhaps, to medicine. Wild nations trust to simples ; and, perhaps, the Peruvian bark is not the only specifick which those extensive regions may afford us.

Wherever you are, and whatever be your fortune, be certain, dear Sir, that you carry with you my kind wishes ; and that whether you return hither, or stay in the other hemisphere, to hear that you are happy will give pleasure to,

    Sir, your most affectionate humble servant,
June 1, 1762.   Sam: Johnson.

141. To a Lady

Madam

I hope you will believe that my delay in answering your letter could proceed only from my unwillingness to destroy any hope that you had formed. Hope is itself a species of happiness, and, perhaps, the chief happiness which this world affords : but, like all other pleasures immoderately enjoyed, the excesses of hope must be expiated by pain ; and expectations improperly indulged, must end in disappointment. If it be asked, what is the improper expectation which it is dangerous to indulge, experience will quickly answer, that it is such expectation as is dictated not by reason, but by desire ; expectation raised, not by the common occurrences of life, but by the wants of the expectant ; an expectation that requires the common course of things to be changed, and the general rules of action to be broken.

When you made your request to me, Madam, you should have considered, Madam, what you were asking. You ask me to solicit a great man, to whom I never spoke, for a young person whom I had never seen, upon a supposition which I had no means of knowing to be true. There is no reason why, amongst all the great, I should chuse to supplicate the Archbishop, nor why, among all the possible objects of his bounty, the Archbishop should chuse your son. I know, Madam, how unwillingly conviction is admitted, when interest opposes it; but surely, Madam, you must allow, that there is no reason why that should be done by me, which every other man may do with equal reason, and which, indeed no man can do properly, without some very particular relation both to the Archbishop and to you. If I could help you in this exigence by any proper means, it would give me pleasure; but this proposal is so very remote from all usual methods, that I cannot comply with it, but at the risk of such answer and suspicions as I believe you do not wish me to undergo.

I have seen your son this morning; he seems a pretty youth, and will, perhaps, find some better friend than I can procure him; but, though he should at last miss the University, he may still be wise, useful, and happy.

I am, Madam, your most humble servant,
June 8, 1762.   SAM: JOHNSON.

142. TO MR. JOSEPH BARETTI, AT MILAN

Sir   London, July 20, 1762.

However justly you may accuse me for want of punctuality in correspondence, I am not so far lost in negligence as to omit the opportunity of writing to you, which Mr. Beauclerk's passage through Milan affords me.

I suppose you received the *Idlers*, and I intend that you shall soon receive *Shakspeare*, that you may explain his works to the ladies of Italy, and tell them the story of the editor, among the other strange narratives with which your long residence in this unknown region has supplied you.

As you have now been long away, I suppose your curiosity may pant for some news of your old friends. Miss Williams and I live much as we did. Miss Cotterel still continues to cling to Mrs. Porter, and Charlotte is now big of the fourth child. Mr. Reynolds gets six thousands a year. Levet is lately married, not without much suspicion that he has been wretchedly cheated in his match. Mr. Chambers is gone this day, for the first time, the circuit with the Judges. Mr. Richardson is dead of an apoplexy, and his second daughter has married a merchant.

My vanity, or my kindness, makes me flatter myself, that you would rather hear of me than of those whom I have mentioned; but of myself I have very little which I care to tell. Last winter I went down to my native town, where I found the streets much narrower and shorter than I thought I had left them, inhabited by a new race of people, to whom I was very little known. My play-fellows were grown old, and forced me to suspect that I was no longer young. My only remaining friend has changed his principles, and was become the tool of the predominant faction. My daughter-in-law, from whom I expected most, and whom I met with sincere benevolence, has lost the beauty and gaiety of youth, without having gained much of the wisdom of age. I wandered about for five days, and took the first convenient opportunity of returning to a place, where, if there is not much happiness, there is, at least, such a diversity of good and evil, that slight vexations do not fix upon the heart.[1]

I think in a few weeks to try another excursion; though to what end? Let me know, my Baretti, what has been the result of your return to your own country: whether time has made any alteration for

[1] This is a very just account of the relief which London affords to melancholy minds. BOSWELL.

the better, and whether, when the first raptures of salutation were over, you did not find your thoughts confessed their disappointment.

Moral sentences appear ostentatious and tumid, when they have no greater occasions than the journey of a wit to his own town : yet such pleasures and such pains make up the general mass of life ; and as nothing is little to him that feels it with great sensibility, a mind able to see common incidents in their real state, is disposed by very common incidents to very serious contemplations. Let us trust that a time will come, when the present moment shall be no longer irksome ; when we shall not borrow all our happiness from hope, which at last is to end in disappointment.

I beg that you will shew Mr. Beauclerk all the civilities which you have in your power ; for he has always been kind to me.

I have lately seen Mr. Stratico, Professor of Padua, who has told me of your quarrel with an Abbot of the Celestine order ; but had not the particulars very ready in his memory. When you write to Mr. Marsili, let him know that I remember him with kindness.

May you, my Baretti, be very happy at Milan, or some other place nearer to,

Sir, your most affectionate humble servant,

SAM: JOHNSON.

143. TO THE RIGHT HONOURABLE THE EARL OF BUTE

My Lord

When the bills were yesterday delivered to me by Mr. Wedderburne, I was informed by him of the future favours which his Majesty has, by your Lordship's recommendation, been induced to intend for me.

Bounty always receives part of its value from the manner in which it is bestowed ; your Lordship's kindness includes every circumstance that can gratify delicacy, or enforce obligation. You have conferred your favours on a man who has neither alliance nor interest, who has not merited them by services, nor courted them by officiousness; you have spared him the shame of solicitation, and the anxiety of suspense.

What has been thus elegantly given, will, I hope, not be reproachfully enjoyed; I shall endeavour to give your Lordship the only recompense which generosity desires,—the gratification of finding that your benefits are not improperly bestowed.

    I am, my Lord, your Lordship's most obliged,
     most obedient, and most humble servant,
July 20, 1762.   Sam: Johnson.

149. To George Strahan

Dear Sir   March 26, 1763.

You did not very soon answer my letter, and therefore cannot complain that I make no great haste to answer yours. I am well enough satisfied with the proficiency that you make, and hope that you will not relax the vigour of your diligence. I hope you begin now to see that all is possible which was professed. Learning is a wide field, but six years spent in close application are a long time; and I am still of opinion, that if you continue to consider knowledge as the most pleasing and desirable of all acquisitions, and do not suffer your course to be interrupted, you may take your degree not only without deficiency, but with great distinction.

You must still continue to write Latin. This is the most difficult part, indeed the only part that is very difficult of your undertaking. If you can exemplify the rules of syntax, I know not whether it will be worth while to trouble yourself with any more translations. You will more increase your number of words, and advance your skill in phraseology, by making a short theme or two every day; and when you have construed properly a stated number of verses, it will be pleasing to go from reading to composition, and from composition to reading. But do not be very particular about method; any method will do, if there be but diligence. Let me know, if you please, once a week what you are doing.

>I am,
>>Dear George,
>>>Your humble servant,
>>>>SAM: JOHNSON.

155. To GEORGE STRAHAN

Dear George

To give pain ought always to be painful, and I am sorry that I have been the occasion of any uneasiness to you, to whom I hope never to do any thing but for your benefit or your pleasure. Your uneasiness was without any reason on your part, as you had written with sufficient frequency to me, and I had only neglected to answer them, because as nothing new had been proposed to your study, no new direction or incitement could be offered you. But if it had happened that you had omitted what you did not omit, and that I had for an hour, or a week, or a much longer time, thought myself put out of your mind by something to which presence gave that prevalence, which presence will sometimes give even where there is the most prudence and experience, you are not to imagine that my friendship is light enough to be blown away by the first cross blast, or that my regard or kindness hangs by so slender a hair as to be broken off by the unfelt weight of a petty offence. I love you, and hope to love you long. You have hitherto done nothing to diminish my good will, and though you had done much more than you have supposed imputed to you, my good will would not have been diminished.

I write thus largely on this suspicion, which you have suffered to enter your mind, because in youth we are apt to be too rigorous in our expectations, and to suppose that the duties of life are to be performed with unfailing exactness and regularity; but in our progress through life we are forced to abate much of our demands, and to take friends such as we can find them, not as we would make them.

These concessions every wise man is more ready to make to others, as he knows that he shall often want them for himself; and when he remembers how often he fails in the observance or cultivation of his best friends, is willing to suppose that his friends may in their turn neglect him, without any intention to offend him.

When therefore it shall happen, as happen it will, that you or I have disappointed the expectation of the other, you are not to suppose that you have lost me, or that I intended to lose you; nothing will remain but to repair the fault, and to go on as if it never had been committed.

    I am, Sir,
      Your affectionate servant,
         Sam: Johnson.

Thursday, July 14, 1763.

163. À Mr. Mr. Boswell, à la Cour de l'Empereur, Utrecht

Dear Sir

You are not to think yourself forgotten, or criminally neglected, that you have had yet no letter from me. I love to see my friends, to hear from them, to talk to them, and to talk of them; but it is not without a considerable effort of resolution that I prevail upon myself to write. I would not, however, gratify my own indolence by the omission of any important duty, or any office of real kindness.

To tell you that I am or am not well, that I have or have not been in the country, that I drank your health in the room in which we sat last together, and that your acquaintance continue to speak of you with their former kindness, topicks with which those letters are commonly filled which are written only for the sake of writing, I seldom shall think worth communicating; but if I can have it in my power to calm any harassing disquiet, to excite any virtuous desire, to rectify any important opinion, or fortify any generous resolution, you need not doubt but I shall at least wish to prefer the pleasure of gratifying a friend much less esteemed than yourself, before the gloomy calm of idle vacancy. Whether I shall easily arrive at an exact punctuality of correspondence, I cannot tell. I shall, at present, expect that you will receive this in return for two which I have had from you. The first, indeed, gave me an account so hopeless of the state of your mind, that it hardly admitted or deserved an answer; by the second I was much better pleased: and the pleasure will still be increased by such a narrative of the progress of your studies, as may evince the continuance of an equal and rational application of your mind to some useful enquiry.

You will, perhaps, wish to ask, what study I would recommend. I shall not speak of theology, because it ought not to be considered as a question whether you shall endeavour to know the will of GOD.

I shall therefore, consider only such studies as we are at liberty to pursue or to neglect; and of these I know not how you will make a better choice, than by studying the civil law, as your father advises, and the ancient languages, as you had determined for yourself; at least resolve, while you remain in any settled residence, to spend a certain number of hours every day amongst your books. The dissipation of thought, of which you complain, is nothing more than the vacillation of a mind suspended between different motives, and changing its direction as any motive gains or loses strength. If you can but kindle in your mind any strong desire, if you can but keep predominant any wish for some particular excellence or attainment, the gusts of imagination will break away, without any effect upon your conduct, and commonly without any traces left upon the memory.

There lurks, perhaps, in every human heart a desire of distinction, which inclines every man first to hope, and then to believe, that Nature has given him something peculiar to himself. This vanity makes one mind nurse aversion, and another actuate desires, till they rise by art much above their original state of power; and as affectation, in time, improves to habit, they at last tyrannise over him who at first encouraged them only for show. Every desire is a viper in the bosom, who, while he was chill, was harmless; but when warmth gave him strength, exerted it in poison. You know a gentleman, who, when first he set his foot in the gay world, as he prepared himself to whirl in the vortex of pleasure, imagined a total indifference and universal negligence to be the most agreeable concomitants of youth, and the strongest indication of an airy temper and a quick apprehension. Vacant to every object, and sensible of every impulse, he thought that all appearance of diligence would deduct something from the reputation of genius; and hoped that he should appear to attain, amidst all the ease of carelessness, and all the tumult of diversion, that knowledge and those accomplishments which mortals of the common fabrick obtain only by mute abstraction and solitary drudgery. He tried this scheme of life awhile, was made weary of it by his sense and his virtue; he then wished to return to his studies; and finding long habits of idleness and pleasure harder to be cured than he expected, still willing to retain his claim to some extraordinary prerogatives, resolved the common consequences of irregularity into an unalterable decree of destiny, and concluded that Nature had originally formed him incapable of rational employment.

Let all such fancies, illusive and destructive, be banished henceforward from your thoughts for ever. Resolve, and keep your resolution; choose, and pursue your choice. If you spend this day in study, you will find yourself still more able to study to-morrow; not that you are to expect that you shall at once obtain a complete victory. Depravity is not very easily overcome. Resolution will sometimes relax, and diligence will sometimes be interrupted; but let no accidental surprize or deviation, whether short or long, dispose you to despondency. Consider these failings as incident to all mankind. Begin again where you left off, and endeavour to avoid the seducements that prevailed over you before.

This, my dear Boswell, is advice which, perhaps, has been often given you, and given you without effect. But this advice, if you will not take from others, you must take from your own reflections, if you purpose to do the duties of the station to which the bounty of Providence has called you.

Let me have a long letter from you as soon as you can. I hope you continue your journal, and enrich it with many observations upon the country in which you reside. It will be a favour if you can get me any books in the Frisick language, and can enquire how the poor are maintained in the Seven Provinces.

I am, dear Sir, your most affectionate servant,
London, Dec. 8, 1763.   SAM: JOHNSON.

172. To MRS. THRALE

Madam   London, Aug. 13, 1765.

If you have really so good an opinion of me as you express, it will not be necessary to inform you how unwillingly I miss the opportunity of coming to Brighthelmston in Mr. Thrale's company; or, since I cannot do what I wish first, how eagerly I shall catch the second degree of pleasure, by coming to you and him, as soon as I can dismiss my work from my hands.[1]

I am afraid to make promises even to myself, but I hope that the week after the next will be the end of my present business. When business is done, what remains but pleasure? and where should pleasure be sought but under Mrs. Thrale's influence?

Do not blame me for a delay by which I must suffer so much, and by which I suffer alone. If you cannot think I am good, pray think I am mending, and that in time I may deserve to be,

Dear Madam,
Your most obedient and
most humble servant,
SAM: JOHNSON.

[1] [His edition of Shakespeare.]

181. *A Mr. Mr.* Boswell, *chez Mr.* Waters, *Banquier, à Paris*

Dear Sir

Apologies are seldom of any use. We will delay till your arrival the reasons, good or bad, which have made me such a sparing and ungrateful correspondent. Be assured, for the present, that nothing has lessened either the esteem or love with which I dismissed you at Harwich. Both have been increased by all that I have been told of you by yourself or others; and when you return, you will return to an unaltered, and, I hope, unalterable friend.

All that you have to fear from me is the vexation of disappointing me. No man loves to frustrate expectations which have been formed in his favour; and the pleasure which I promise myself from your journals and remarks is so great, that perhaps no degree of attention or discernment will be sufficient to afford it.

Come home, however, and take your chance. I long to see you, and to hear you; and hope that we shall not be so long separated again. Come home, and expect such a welcome as is due to him whom a wise and noble curiosity has led, where perhaps no native of this country ever was before.

I have no news to tell you that can deserve your notice; nor would I willingly lessen the pleasure that any novelty may give you at your return. I am afraid we shall find it difficult to keep among us a mind which has been so long feasted with variety. But let us try what esteem and kindness can effect.

As your father's liberality has indulged you with so long a ramble, I doubt not but you will think his sickness, or even his desire to see you, a sufficient reason for hastening your return. The longer we live, and the more we think, the higher value we learn to put on the friendship and tenderness of parents and of friends. Parents we can have but once; and he promises himself too much, who enters life with the expectation of finding many friends. Upon some motive, I hope that you will be here soon ; and am willing to think that it will be an inducement to your return, that it is sincerely desired by,

dear Sir, your affectionate humble servant,

SAM : JOHNSON.

Johnson's Court, Fleet-street, January 14, 1766.

183. TO BENNET LANGTON

Dear Sir

In supposing that I should be more than commonly affected by the death of Peregrine Langton,[1] you were not mistaken ; he was one of those whom I loved at once by instinct and by reason. I have seldom indulged more hope of any thing than of being able to improve our acquaintance to friendship. Many a time have I placed myself again at Langton, and imagined the pleasure with which I should walk to Partney[2] in a summer morning ; but this is no longer possible. We must now endeavour to preserve what is left us,—his example of piety and œconomy. I hope you make what enquiries you can, and write down what is told you. The little things which distinguish domestick characters are soon forgotten : if you delay to enquire, you will have no information ; if you neglect to write, information will be vain.

His art of life certainly deserves to be known and studied. He lived in plenty and elegance upon an income which to many would appear indigent, and to most, scanty. How he lived, therefore, every man has an interest in knowing. His death, I hope, was peaceful ; it was surely happy.

I wish I had written sooner, lest, writing now, I should renew your grief ; but I would not forbear saying what I have now said.

This loss is, I hope, the only misfortune of a family

[1] Mr. Langton's uncle. BOSWELL.

[2] The place of residence of Mr. Peregrine Langton. BOSWELL.

to whom no misfortune at all should happen, if my wishes could avert it. Let me know how you all go on. Has Mr. Langton got him the little horse that I recommended ? It would do him good to ride about his estate in fine weather.

Be pleased to make my compliments to Mrs. Langton, and to dear Miss Langton, and Miss Di, and Miss Juliet, and to every body else.

THE CLUB holds very well together. Monday is my night.[1] I continue to rise tolerably well, and read more than I did. I hope something will yet come on it.

    I am, Sir, your most affectionate servant,
May 10, 1766,   SAM: JOHNSON.

Johnson's-court, Fleet-street.

185. TO JAMES BOSWELL

Dear Sir

The reception of your Thesis put me in mind of my debt to you. Why did you * * * * * * * * * * * * *.[2] I will punish you for it, by telling you that your Latin wants correction. In the beginning, *Spei alteræ*, not to urge that it should be *primæ*, is not grammatical: *alteræ* should be *alteri*. In the next line you seem to use *genus* absolutely, for what we call *family*, that is, for *illustrious extraction*, I doubt without authority. *Homines nullius originis*, for *Nullis orti majoribus*, or, *Nullo loco nati*, is, I am afraid, barbarous.—Ruddiman is dead.

I have now vexed you enough, and will try to please you. Your resolution to obey your father I sincerely approve ; but do not accustom yourself to enchain your volatility by vows : they will sometime leave a thorn in your mind, which you will, perhaps, never

---

[1] Of his being in the chair of THE LITERARY CLUB, which at this time met once a week in the evening. BOSWELL.

[2] The passage omitted alluded to a private transaction. BOSWELL.

be able to extract or eject. Take this warning, it is of great importance.

The study of the law is what you very justly term it, copious and generous; and in adding your name to its professors, you have done exactly what I always wished, when I wished you best. I hope that you will continue to pursue it vigorously and constantly. You gain, at least, what is no small advantage, security from those troublesome and wearisome discontents, which are always obtruding themselves upon a mind vacant, unemployed, and undetermined.

You ought to think it no small inducement to diligence and perseverance, that they will please your father. We all live upon the hope of pleasing somebody; and the pleasure of pleasing ought to be greatest, and at last always will be greatest, when our endeavours are exerted in consequence of our duty.

Life is not long, and too much of it must not pass in idle deliberation how it shall be spent; deliberation, which those who begin it by prudence, and continue it with subtilty, must, after long expence of thought, conclude by chance. To prefer one future mode of life to another, upon just reasons, requires faculties which it has not pleased our Creator to give us.

If, therefore, the profession you have chosen has some unexpected inconveniencies, console yourself by reflecting that no profession is without them; and that all the importunities and perplexities of business are softness and luxury, compared with the incessant cravings of vacancy, and the unsatisfactory expedients of idleness.

Hæc sunt quæ nostrâ potui te voce monere;
Vade, age.

As to your *History of Corsica*, you have no materials which others have not, or may not have. You have, somehow or other, warmed your imagination. I wish there were some cure, like the lover's leap, for all heads of which some single idea has obtained an unreasonable and irregular possession. Mind your own affairs, and leave the Corsicans to theirs.

I am, dear Sir, your most humble servant,
London, Aug. 21, 1766.   SAM: JOHNSON.

184. To WILLIAM DRUMMOND
Sir

I did not expect to hear that it could be, in an assembly convened for the propagation of Christian knowledge, a question whether any nation uninstructed in religion should receive instruction; or whether that instruction should be imparted to them by a translation of the holy books into their own language. If obedience to the will of GOD be necessary to happiness, and knowledge of his will be necessary to obedience, I know not how he that with-holds this knowledge, or delays it, can be said to love his neighbour as himself. He that voluntarily continues ignorance, is guilty of all the crimes which ignorance produces; as to him that should extinguish the tapers of a light-house, might justly be imputed the calamities of shipwrecks. Christianity is the highest perfection of humanity; and as no man is good but as he wishes the good of others, no man can be good in the highest degree who wishes not to others the largest measures of the greatest good. To omit for a year, or for a day, the most efficacious method of advancing Christianity, in compliance with any purposes that terminate on this side of the grave, is a crime of which I know not that the world has yet had an example, except in the practice of the planters of America, a race of mortals whom, I suppose, no other man wishes to resemble.

The Papists have, indeed, denied to the laity the use of the bible; but this prohibition, in few places now very rigorously enforced, is defended by arguments, which have for their foundation the care of souls. To obscure, upon motives merely political, the light of revelation, is a practice reserved for the reformed; and, surely, the blackest midnight of popery is meridian sunshine to such a reformation. I am not very willing that any language should be totally extinguished. The similitude and derivation of languages afford the most indubitable proof of the traduction of nations, and the genealogy of mankind. They add often physical certainty to historical evidence; and often supply the only evidence of ancient migrations, and of the revolutions of ages which left no written monuments behind them.

Every man's opinions, at least his desires, are a little influenced by his favourite studies. My zeal for languages may seem, perhaps, rather over-heated, even to those by whom I desire to be well-esteemed. To those who have nothing in their thoughts but trade or policy, present power, or present money, I should not think it necessary to defend my opinions; but with men of letters I would not unwillingly compound, by wishing the continuance of every language, however narrow in its extent, or however incommodious for common purposes, till it is reposited in some version of a known book, that it may be always hereafter examined and compared with other languages, and then permitting its disuse. For this purpose, the translation of the bible is most to be desired. It is not certain that the same method will not preserve the Highland language, for the purposes of learning, and abolish it from daily use. When the Highlanders read the Bible, they will naturally wish to have its obscurities cleared, and to know the history, collateral or appendant. Knowledge always desires increase: it is like fire, which must first be kindled by some external agent, but which will afterwards propagate itself. When they once desire to learn, they will naturally have recourse to the nearest language by which that desire can be gratified; and one will tell another that if he would attain knowledge, he must learn English.

This speculation may, perhaps, be thought more subtle than the grossness of real life will easily admit. Let it, however, be remembered, that the efficacy of ignorance has been long tried, and has not produced the consequence expected. Let knowledge, therefore, take its turn; and let the patrons of privation stand awhile aside, and admit the operation of positive principles.

You will be pleased, Sir, to assure the worthy man who is employed in the new translation, that he has my wishes for his success; and if here or at Oxford I can be of any use, that I shall think it more than honour to promote his undertaking.

I am sorry that I delayed so long to write.

I am, Sir, your most humble servant,
Johnson's-court, Fleet-street, SAM: JOHNSON.
Aug. 13, 1766.

194. To MRS. ASTON

Nov. 17, 1767.

Madam

If you impute it to disrespect or inattention, that I took no leave when I left Lichfield, you will do me great injustice. I know you too well not to value your friendship.

When I came to Oxford I inquired after the product of our walnut-tree, but it had, like other trees this year, but very few nuts, and for those few I came too late. The tree, as I told you, Madam, we cannot find to be more than thirty years old, and, upon measuring it, I found it, at about one foot from the ground, seven feet in circumference, and at the height of about seven feet, the circumference is five feet and a half; it would have been, I believe, still bigger, but that it has been lopped. The nuts are small, such as they call single nuts; whether this nut is of quicker growth than better I have not yet inquired; such as they are, I hope to send them next year.

You know, dear Madam, the liberty I took of hinting that I did not think your present mode of life very pregnant with happiness. Reflection has not yet changed my opinion. Solitude excludes pleasure, and does not always secure peace. Some communication of sentiments is commonly necessary to give vent to the imagination, and discharge the mind of its own flatulencies. Some lady surely might be found, in whose conversation you might delight, and in whose fidelity you might repose. *The World,* says Locke, *has people of all sorts.* You will forgive me this obtrusion of my opinion; I am sure I wish you well.

Poor Kitty has done what we have all to do, and Lucy has the world to begin anew: I hope she will find some way to more content than I left her possessing.

Be pleased to make my compliments to Mrs. Hinckley and Miss Turton.

I am, Madam,
Your most obliged and most humble servant,
SAM: JOHNSON.

200. To JAMES BOSWELL

My Dear Boswell

I have omitted a long time to write to you, without knowing very well why. I could now tell why I should not write; for who would write to men who publish the letters of their friends, without their leave? Yet I write to you in spite of my caution, to tell you that I shall be glad to see you, and that I wish you would empty your head of Corsica, which I think has filled it rather too long. But, at all events, I shall be glad, very glad to see you.

I am, Sir, yours affectionately,
Oxford, March 23, 1768.   SAM: JOHNSON.

203. To MRS. THRALE

Madam   Oxford, April 19, 1768.

If I should begin with telling you what is very true, that I have of late been very much disordered, you might perhaps think that in the next line I should impute this disorder to my distance from you; but I am not yet well enough to contrive such stratagems of compliment. I have been really very bad, and am glad that I was not at Streatham, where I should have been troublesome to you, and you could have given no help to me.

I am not, however, without hopes of being better, and therefore hear with great pleasure of the welfare of those from whom I always expect to receive pleasure when I am capable of receiving it, and think myself much favoured that you made so much haste to tell me of your recovery.

I design to love little Miss Nanny very well; but you must let us have a Bessy some other time. I suppose the Borough bells rung for the young lady's arrival. I hope she will be happy. I will not welcome her with any words of ill-omen. She will certainly be happy, if she be as she and all friends are wished to be by, Madam,

Your, &c.,
SAM: JOHNSON.

205. To MRS. THRALE

Madam [Oxford], May 23, 1768.

Though I purpose to come home to-morrow, I would not omit even so long, to tell you how much I think myself favoured by your notice. Every man is desirous to keep those friends whom he is proud to have gained, and I count the friendship of your house among the felicities of life.

I thank God that I am better, and am at least within hope of being as well as you have ever known me. Let me have your prayers.

I am, &c.,
SAM: JOHNSON.

206. To F. A. BARNARD

Sir May 28, 1768.

It is natural for a scholar to interest himself in an expedition, undertaken, like yours, for the importation of literature ; and therefore, though, having never travelled myself, I am very little qualified to give advice to a traveller ; yet, that I may not seem inattentive to a design so worthy of regard, I will try whether the present state of my health will suffer me to lay before you what observation or report have suggested to me, that may direct your inquiries, or facilitate your success. Things of which the mere rarity makes the value, and which are prized at a high rate by a wantonness rather than by use, are always passing from poorer to richer countries ; and therefore, though Germany and Italy were principally productive of typographical curiosities, I do not much imagine that they are now to be found therein great abundance. An eagerness for scarce books and early editions, which prevailed among the English about half a century ago, filled our shops with all the splendour and nicety of literature ; and when the Harleian Catalogue was published, many of the books were bought for the library of the King of France.

I believe, however, that by the diligence with which you have enlarged the library under your care, the present stock is so nearly exhausted, that, till new purchases supply the booksellers with new stores, you will not be able to do much more than glean up single books, as accident shall produce them ; this, therefore, is the time for visiting the continent.

What addition you can hope to make by ransacking other countries we will now consider. English literature you will not seek in any place but in England. Classical learning is diffused everywhere, and is not, except by accident, more copious in one part of the polite world than in another. But every country has literature of its own, which may be best gathered in its native soil. The studies of the learned are influenced by forms of government and modes of religion ; and, therefore, those books are necessary and common in some places, which, where different opinions or different manners prevail, are of little use, and for that reason rarely to be found.

Thus in Italy you may expect to meet with canonists and scholastic divines, in Germany with writers on the feudal laws, and in Holland with civilians. The schoolmen and canonists must not be neglected, for they are useful to many purposes; nor too anxiously sought, for their influence among us is much lessened by the Reformation. Of the canonists at least a few eminent writers may be sufficient. The schoolmen are of more general value. But the feudal and civil law I cannot but wish to see complete. The feudal constitution is the original of the law of property, over all the civilised part of Europe; and the civil law, as it is generally understood to include the law of nations, may be called with great propriety a regal study. Of these books, which have been often published, and diversified by various modes of impression, a royal library should have at least the most curious edition, the most splendid, and the most useful. The most curious edition is commonly the first, and the most useful may be expected among the last. Thus, of Tully's Offices, the edition of Fust is the most curious, and that of Graevius the most useful. The most splendid the eye will discern. With the old printers you are now become well acquainted; if you can find any collection of their productions to be sold, you will undoubtedly buy it; but this can scarcely be hoped, and you must catch up single volumes where you can find them. In every place things often occur where they are least expected. I was shown a Welsh grammar written in Welsh, and printed at Milan, I believe, before any grammar of that language had been printed here. Of purchasing entire libraries, I know not whether the inconvenience may not overbalance the advantage. Of libraries connected with general views, one will have many books in common with another. When you have bought two collections, you will find that you have bought many books twice over, and many in each which you have left at home, and, therefore, did not want; and when you have selected a small number, you will have the rest to sell at a great loss, or to transport hither at perhaps a greater. It will generally be more commodious to buy the few that you want, at a price somewhat advanced, than to encumber yourself with useless books. But libraries collected for particular studies will be very valuable acquisitions. The collection of an eminent civilian, feudist, or mathematician, will perhaps have very few superfluities. Topography or local history prevails much in many parts of the continent. I have been told that scarcely a village of Italy wants its historian. These books may be generally neglected, but some will deserve attention by the celebrity of the place, the eminence of the authors, or the beauty of the sculptures. Sculpture has always been more cultivated among other nations than among us. The old art of cutting on wood, which decorated the books of ancient impression, was never carried here to any excellence; and the practice of engraving on copper, which succeeded, has never been much employed among us in adorning books. The old books with wooden cuts are to be diligently sought; the designs were often made by great masters, and the prints are such as cannot be made by any artist now living. It will be of great use to collect in every place maps of the adjacent country, and plans of towns, buildings, and gardens. By this care you will form a more valuable body of geography than can otherwise be had. Many countries have been very exactly surveyed, but it must not be expected that the exactness of actual mensuration will be preserved, when the maps are reduced by a contracted scale, and incorporated into a general system.

The king of Sardinia's Italian dominions are not large, yet the maps made of them in the reign of Victor fill two Atlantic folios. This part of your design will deserve particular regard, because, in this, your success will always be proportioned to your diligence. You are too well acquainted with literary history not to know that many books derive their value from the reputation of the printers. Of the celebrated printers

you do not need to be informed, and if you did, might
consult Baillet, Jugemens des Sçavans. The productions of Aldus are enumerated in the Bibliotheca
Graeca, so that you may know when you have them
all; which is always of use, as it prevents needless
search. The great ornaments of a library, furnished
for magnificence as well as use, are the first editions,
of which, therefore, I would not willingly neglect the
mention. You know, sir, that the annals of typography
begin with the Codex, 1457; but there is great reason
to believe, that there are latent, in obscure corners,
books printed before it. The secular feast, in memory
of the invention of printing, is celebrated in the
fortieth year of the century; if this tradition, therefore, is right, the art had in 1457 been already exercised
nineteen years.

There prevails among typographical antiquaries a
vague opinion, that the Bible had been printed three
times before the edition of 1462, which Calmet calls
' La première édition bien avérée.' One of these
editions has been lately discovered in a convent, and
transplanted into the French king's library. Another
copy has likewise been found, but I know not whether
of the same impression, or another. These discoveries
are sufficient to raise hope and instigate inquiry. In
the purchase of old books, let me recommend to you
to inquire with great caution, whether they are perfect.
In the first edition the loss of a leaf is not easily observed. You remember how near we both were to
purchasing a mutilated Missal at a high price.

All this perhaps you know already, and, therefore,
my letter may be of no use. I am, however, desirous
to show you, that I wish prosperity to your undertaking. One advice more I will give, of more importance than all the rest, of which I, therefore, hope you
will have still less need. You are going into a part of
the world divided, as it is said, between bigotry and
atheism: such representations are always hyperbolical,
but there is certainly enough of both to alarm any
mind solicitous for piety and truth; let not the

contempt of superstition precipitate you into infidelity, or the horror of infidelity ensnare you in superstition.—
I sincerely wish you successful and happy, for
    I am, Sir,
        Your affectionate humble servant,
            SAM: JOHNSON.

213. To MISS FLINT

Mademoiselle   A Londres, Mars 31, 1769.

Il faut avouer que la lettre que vous m'avez fait l'honeur de m'ecrire, a eté long-tems sans rêponse. Voici mon apologie. J'ai eté affligé d'une maladie de violence peu supportable, & d'un lenteur bien ennuiant. Tout êtat a ses droits particuliers. On compte parmi les droits d'un malade ce de manquer aux offices de respect, at aux devoirs de reconoissance. Géné par ses douleurs, il ne scait veiller qu'à soi-même. Il ne pense qu'à se soulager, et à se retablir, peu attentif à tout autre soin, et peu sensible à la gloire d'etre traduit d'une main telle que la vôtre.

Neanmoins, Mademoiselle, votre merite auroit exigé que je m'efforcasse à vous rendre graces de vos egards, si je l'aurois pu faire sans y meler des querelles. Mais comment m'empescher de me plaindre de ces appas par lesquelles vous avez gagné sur l'esprit de Mademoiselle Reynolds jusqu'a ce qu'elle ne se souvient plus ni de sa patrie ni de ses amis. C'est peu de nous louer, c'est peu de repandre nos ouvrages par des traductions les plus belles, pendant que vous nous privez du plaisir de voir Mademoiselle Reynolds & de l'ecouter. Enfin, Mademoiselle, il faut être moins aimable, afin que nous vous aimions plus.
    Je suis,
        Mademoiselle,
            Vôtre tres humble &
            Obeissant Serviteur,
                SAM: JOHNSON.

217. To Mrs. Thrale

Madam Oxford, June 29, 1769.

Hesiod, who was very wise in his time, though nothing to such wise people as we, says, that the evil of the worst times has some good mingled with it. Hesiod was in the right. These times are not much to my mind; I am not well; but in these times you are safe, and have brought a pretty little Miss. I always wished it might be a Miss, and now that wish is gratified, nothing remains but that I entreat you to take care of yourself; for whatever number of girls or boys you may give us, we are far from being certain that any of them will ever do for us what you can do; it is certain that they cannot now do it, and the ability which they want, they are not likely to gain but by your precepts and your example; by an example of excellence, and by the admonitions of truth.

Mr. Thrale tells me, that my furlough is shortened; I am always ready to obey orders; I have not yet found any place from which I shall not willingly depart to come back to you.

I am, dearest Lady,
Your, &c.,
Sam: Johnson.

220. To Mrs. Thrale

Madam Lichfield, August 14, 1769.

I set out on Thursday morning, and found my companion, to whom I was very much a stranger, more agreeable than I expected. We went cheerfully forward, and passed the night at Coventry. We came in late, and went out early; and therefore I did not send for my cousin Tom; but I design to make him some amends for the omission.

Next day we came early to Lucy, who was, I believe, glad to see us. She had saved her best gooseberries upon the tree for me; and, as Steele says, *I was neither too proud nor too wise* to gather them. I have rambled a very little *inter fontes et flumina nota,* but I am not yet well. They have cut down the trees in George Lane. Evelyn, in his book of Forest Trees, tells us of wicked men that cut down trees, and never prospered afterwards; yet nothing has deterred these audacious aldermen from violating the Hamadryads of George Lane. As an impartial traveller I must however tell, that in Stow-street, where I left a draw-well, I have found a pump; but the lading-well in this ill-fated George Lane lies shamefully neglected.

I am going to-day or to-morrow to Ashbourne; but I am at a loss how I shall get back in time to London. Here are only chance coaches, so that there is no certainty of a place. If I do not come, let it not hinder your journey. I can be but a few days behind you; and I will follow in the Brighthelmstone coach. But I hope to come.

I took care to tell Miss Porter, that I have got another Lucy. I hope she is well. Tell Mrs. Salusbury, that I beg her stay at Streatham, for little Lucy's sake.

I am, &c.,

SAM: JOHNSON.

221. To MRS. ASTON

Brighthelmstone, August 26, 1769.

Madam

I suppose you have received the mill: the whole apparatus seemed to be perfect, except that there is wanting a little tin spout at the bottom, and some ring or knob, on which the bag that catches the meal is to be hung. When these are added, I hope you will be able to grind your own bread, and treat me with a cake made by yourself, of meal from your own corn of your own grinding.

I was glad, Madam, to see you so well, and hope your health will long increase, and then long continue.

I am, Madam,

Your most obedient servant,

SAM: JOHNSON.

222. To James Boswell

Dear Sir

Why do you charge me with unkindness? I have omitted nothing that could do you good, or give you pleasure, unless it be that I have forborne to tell you my opinion of your *Account of Corsica*. I believe my opinion, if you think well of my judgement, might have given you pleasure; but when it is considered how much vanity is excited by praise, I am not sure that it would have done you good. Your History is like other histories, but your Journal is in a very high degree curious and delightful. There is between the History and the Journal that difference which there will always be found between notions borrowed from without, and notions generated within. Your History was copied from books; your Journal rose out of your own experience and observation. You express images which operated strongly upon yourself, and you have impressed them with great force upon your readers. I know not whether I could name any narrative by which curiosity is better excited, or better gratified.

I am glad that you are going to be married; and as I wish you well in things of less importance, wish you well with proportionate ardour in this crisis of your life. What I can contribute to your happiness, I should be very unwilling to with-hold; for I have always loved and valued you, and shall love you and value you still more, as you become more regular and useful: effects which a happy marriage will hardly fail to produce.

I do not find that I am likely to come back very soon from this place. I shall, perhaps, stay a fortnight longer; and a fortnight is a long time to a lover absent from his mistress. Would a fortnight ever have an end?

I am, dear Sir,
your most affectionate humble servant,
Brighthelmstone, Sept. 9, 1769. Sam: Johnson.

233. To Mrs. Thrale

Madam Lichfield, July 11, 1770.

Since my last letter nothing extraordinary has happened. Rheumatism, which has been very troublesome, is grown better. I have not yet seen Dr. Taylor, and July runs fast away. I shall not have much time for him, if he delays much longer to come or send. Mr. Grene, the apothecary, has found a book, which tells who paid levies in our parish, and how much they paid, above an hundred years ago. Do you not think we study this book hard ? Nothing is like going to the bottom of things. Many families that paid the parish rates are now extinct, like the race of Hercules. *Pulvis et umbra sumus.* What is nearest us touches us most. The passions rise higher at domestic than at imperial tragedies. I am not wholly unaffected by the revolutions of Sadler-street; nor can forbear to mourn a little when old names vanish away, and new come into their place.

Do not imagine, Madam, that I wrote this letter for the sake of these philosophical meditations; for when I began it, I had neither Mr. Grene, nor his book, in my thoughts; but was resolved to write, and did not know what I had to send, but my respects to Mrs. Salusbury, and Mr. Thrale, and Harry, and the Misses.

I am, dearest Madam,
Yours, &c.,
Sam: Johnson.

235. To Mrs. Thrale

Dear Madam Lichfield, July, [1770].

Do not say that I never write to you, and do not think that I expected to find any friends here that could make me wish to prolong my stay. For your strawberries, however, I have no care. Mrs. Cobb has strawberries, and will give me as long as they last; and she has cherries too. Of the strawberries at Streatham I consign my part to Miss and Harry. I hope Susy grows, and Lucy begins to walk. Though this rainy weather confines us all in the house, I have neither frolicked nor fretted.

In the tumult, whatever it was, at your house, I hope my countrywomen either had no part, or behaved well. I told Mr. Heartwell, about three days ago, how well Warren was liked in her place.

I have passed one day at Birmingham with my old friend Hector—there's a name—and his sister, an old love. My mistress is grown much older than my friend.

>
——O, quid habes illius, illius
> Quæ spirabat amores,
> Quæ me surpuerat mihi.[1]

Time will impair the body, and uses us well if it spares the mind.

I am, &c.,
Sam: Johnson.

237. To Mrs. Thrale

Dearest Madam   Ashbourne, July 23, 1770.

There had not been so long an interval between my two last letters, but that when I came hither I did not at first understand the hours of the post.

I have seen the great bull; and very great he is. I have seen likewise his heir apparent, who promises to inherit all the bulk and all the virtues of his sire. I have seen the man who offered an hundred guineas for the young bull, while he was yet little better than a calf. Matlock, I am afraid, I shall not see, but I purpose to see Dovedale; and after all this seeing, I hope to see you.

I am, &c.,
Sam: Johnson.

---

[1] [Of her, of her what now remains,
Who breathed the loves, who charmed the swains,
And snatched me from my heart ?

Francis's Horace.]

244. To RICHARD FARMER

Sir

Some time ago Mr. Steevens and I took the liberty of sending a catalogue in hope of some improvement and augmentation. Mr. Steevens, who undertakes the whole care of this impression,[1] begins to fancy that he wants it.

I have done very little to the book; but by the plunder of your pamphlet, and the authorities which Mr. Steevens has very diligently collected, I think it will be somewhat improved. If you could spare us any thing we should think your communication a great favour. I hope amongst us all Shakespeare will be better understood. You have already done your part, and when you have finished what I am told you are now projecting will leave I believe much fewer difficulties to future criticks.

I am, Sir,

Your most humble servant,

SAM: JOHNSON.

Johnson's Court, Fleet Street, Feb. 18, 1771.

250. To JAMES BOSWELL

Dear Sir

If you are now able to comprehend that I might neglect to write without diminution of affection, you have taught me, likewise, how that neglect may be uneasily felt without resentment. I wished for your letter a long time, and when it came, it amply recompensed the delay. I never was so much pleased as now with your account of yourself; and sincerely hope, that between publick business, improving studies, and domestick pleasures, neither melancholy nor caprice

---

[1] [Johnson's Shakespeare was published in 1765 and again in 1768. In 1773 appeared a new edition, with 'Notes by Samuel Johnson and George Steevens'. The 'plundered' pamphlet was Farmer's *Essay on the Learning of Shakespeare.*]

will find any place for entrance. Whatever philosophy may determine of material nature, it is certainly true of intellectual nature, that it *abhors a vacuum*: our minds cannot be empty; and evil will break in upon them, if they are not pre-occupied by good. My dear Sir, mind your studies, mind your business, make your lady happy, and be a good Christian. After this,

> ——————— *tristitiam et metus*
> *Trades protervis in mare Creticum*
> *Portare ventis.*[1]

If we perform our duty, we shall be safe and steady, '*Sive per*,' &c., whether we climb the Highlands, or are tost among the Hebrides; and I hope the time will come when we may try our powers both with cliffs and water. I see but little of Lord Elibank, I know not why; perhaps by my own fault. I am this day going into Staffordshire and Derbyshire for six weeks.

I am, dear Sir,
 your most affectionate, and most humble servant,
London, June 20, 1771.   SAM: JOHNSON.

251. To MRS. THRALE

Dear Madam   Thursday, June 20, 1771.

This night, at nine o'clock, Sam. Johnson and Francis Barber Esquires, set out in the Lichfield stage; Francis is indeed rather upon it. What adventures we may meet with who can tell?

I shall write when I come to Lichfield, and hope to hear in return, that you are safe, and Mrs. Salusbury better, and all the rest as well as I left them.

I am, &c.,
 SAM: JOHNSON.

---

[1] [Nor fear, nor grief, shall break my rest;
 Bear them, ye vagrant winds, away,
 And drown them in the Cretan Sea.
         Francis's Horace.]

253. To Mrs. Thrale

Dear Madam [Lichfield], June 25, 1771.

All your troubles, I hope, are now past, and the little stranger safe in the cradle. You have then nothing to do but survey the lawn from your windows, and see Lucy try to run after Harry.

Here things go wrong. They have cut down another tree, but they do not yet grow very rich. I enquired of my barber after another barber; that barber, says he, is dead, and his son has left off, to turn maltster. Maltsters, I believe, do not get much money. The price of barley and the king's duty are known, and their profit is never suffered to rise high.—But there is often a rise upon stock.—There may as well be a fall.—Very seldom. There are those in this town that have not a farthing less this year than fifty pounds by the rise upon stock. Did you think there had been yet left a city in England, where the gain of fifty pounds in a year would be mentioned with emphasis?

I am, &c.,
Sam: Johnson.

254. To Mrs. Thrale

Dear Madam Ashbourne, July 3, 1771.

Last Saturday I came to Ashbourne; the dangers or the pleasures of the journey I have at present no disposition to recount; else might I paint the beauties of my native plains; might I tell of 'the smiles of nature, and the charms of art:' else might I relate how I crossed the Staffordshire canal, one of the great efforts of human labour, and human contrivance; which, from the bridge on which I viewed it, passed away on either side, and loses itself in distant regions, uniting waters that nature had divided, and dividing lands which nature had united. I might tell how these reflections fermented in my mind till the chaise stopped at Ashbourne, at Ashbourne in the Peak. Let not

the barren name of the Peak terrify you ; I have never
wanted strawberries and cream. The great bull has
no disease but age. I hope in time to be like the great
bull ; and hope you will be like him too a hundred
years hence.

I am, &c.,
SAM: JOHNSON.

260. To MRS. THRALE

Ashbourne, July 17, 1771.

Madam

At Lichfield I found little to please me. One more
of my few school-fellows is dead ; upon which I might
make a new reflection, and say, *Mors omnibus com-
munis.* Miss Porter was rather better than last year ;
but I think Miss Aston grows rather worse. I took
a walk in quest of juvenile images, but caught a cloud
instead of Juno.

I longed for Taylor's chaise ; but I think Lucy did
not long for it, though she was not sorry to see it.
Lucy is a philosopher ; and considers me as one of
the external and accidental things that are to be taken
and left without emotion. If I could learn of Lucy
would it be better ? Will you teach me ?

I would not have it thought that I forget Mrs.
Salusbury ; but nothing that I can say will be of use ;
and what comfort she can have, your duty will not
fail to give her.

What is the matter that Queeney uses me no better ?
I should think she might have written to me ; but she
has neither sent a message nor a compliment. I thank
Harry for remembering me.

Rheumatism teazes me yet.

I m, &c.,
SAM: JOHNSON.

266. To MRS. THRALE

Lichfield, Sat. Aug. 3, 1771.

Dear Madam

If you were well enough to write last Tuesday,

you will surely be well enough to read on Monday; and therefore I will now write to you as before.

Having stayed my month with Taylor, I came away on Wednesday, leaving him, I think, in a disposition of mind not very uncommon, at once weary of my stay, and grieved at my departure.

My purpose was to have made haste to you and Streatham; and who would have expected that I should be stopped by Lucy? Hearing me give Francis orders to take us places, she told me that I should not go till after next week. I thought it proper to comply; for I was pleased to find that I could please, and proud of shewing you that I do not come an universal outcast. Lucy is likewise a very peremptory maiden; and if I had gone without permission, I am not very sure that I might have been welcome at another time.

When we meet, we may compare our different uses of this interval. I shall charge you with having lingered away, in expectation and disappointment, two months, which are both physically and morally considered as analogous to the fervid and vigorous part of human life; two months, in which Nature exerts all her powers of benefaction, and graces the liberality of her hand by the elegance of her smile; two months, which, as Doodle says, ' you never saw before,' and which, as La Bruyere says, ' you shall never see again.'

But complaints are vain; we will try to do better another time.—To-morrow and to-morrow.—A few designs and a few failures, and the time of designing will be past.

Mr. Seward left Lichfield yesterday, I am afraid, not much mended by his opium. He purposes to wait on you; and if envy could do much mischief, he would have much to dread, since he will have the pleasure of seeing you sooner than,

Dear Madam,
Your, &c.,
SAM: JOHNSON.

269. To David Garrick

Streatham, Dec. 12, 1771.

Dear Sir

I have thought upon your epitaph but without much effect. An epitaph is no easy thing.

Of your three stanzas, the third is utterly unworthy of you. The first and third together give no discriminative character. If the first alone were to stand, Hogarth would not be distinguished from any other man of intellectual eminence. Suppose you worked upon something like this:

> The Hand of Art here torpid lies
>   That traced the essential form of Grace:
> Here Death has closed the curious eyes
>   That saw the manners in the face.
>
> If Genius warm thee, Reader, stay,
>   If Merit touch thee, shed a tear;
> Be Vice and Dulness far away!
>   Great Hogarth's honour'd dust is here.

In your second stanza, *pictured morals* is a beautiful expression, which I would wish to retain; but *learn* and *mourn* cannot stand for rhymes. *Art and nature* have been seen together too often. In the first stanza is *feeling*, in the second *feel*. *Feeling* for *tenderness* or *sensibility* is a word merely colloquial, of late introduction, not yet sure enough of its own existence to claim a place upon a stone. *If thou hast neither*, is quite prose, and prose of the familiar kind. Thus easy is it to find faults, but it is hard to make an Epitaph.

When you have reviewed it, let me see it again: you are welcome to any help that I can give, on condition that you make my compliments to Mrs. Garrick.

        I am, dear Sir,
          Your most, &c.,
            Sam: Johnson.

275. To Dr. Taylor

Dear Sir

When I promised to dine with you to-morrow I did not sufficiently consider what I was promising. On the last day of Lent I do not willingly go out, and shall be glad to change to-morrow for Monday, or any other day except Thursday next week.

I am, Sir,

Your most, &c.,

April 17, 1772.   SAM: JOHNSON.

277. To Dr. Taylor

Dear Sir

I am sorry to find both from your own letter and from Mr. Langley that your health is in a state so different from what might be wished. The Langleys impute a great part of your complaints to a mind unsettled and discontented. I know that you have disorders, though I hope not very formidable, independent of the mind, and that your complaints do not arise from the mere habit of complaining. Yet there is no distemper, not in the highest degree acute, on which the mind has not some influence, and which is not better resisted by a cheerful than a gloomy temper. I would have you read when you can force your attention, but that perhaps will be not so often as is necessary to encrease the general cheerfulness of Life. If you could get a little apparatus for chimistry or experimental philosophy it would offer you some diversion, or if you made some little purchase at a small distance, or took some petty farm into your own hands, it would break your thoughts when they become tyrannous and troublesome, and supply you at once with exercise and amusement.

You tell me nothing of Kedlestone, which you went down with a design of visiting, nor of Dr. Butler, who seems to be a very rational man, and who told you with great honesty that your cure must in the greatest measure depend upon yourself.

Your uneasiness at the misfortunes of your Relations, I comprehend perhaps too well. It was an irresistible obtrusion of a disagreeable image, which you always wished away but could not dismiss, an incessant persecution of a troublesome thought neither to be pacified nor ejected. Such has of late been the state of my own mind. I had formerly great command of my attention, and what I did not like could forbear to think on. But of this power, which is of the highest importance to the tranquillity of life, I have been so much exhausted, that I do not go into a company towards night, in which I foresee any thing disagreeable, nor enquire after any thing to which I am not indifferent, lest something, which I know to be nothing, should fasten upon my imagination, and hinder me from sleep. Thus it is that the progress of life brings often with it diseases, not of the body only, but of the mind. We must endeavour to cure both the one and the other. In our bodies we must ourselves do a great part, and for the mind it is very seldom that any help can be had, but what prayer and reason shall supply.

I have got my work [1] so far forward that I flatter myself with concluding it this month, and then shall do nothing so willingly as come down to Ashbourne. We will try to make October a pleasant month.

I am, Sir.

Yours affectionately,

August 31, 1772. SAM: JOHNSON.

I wish we could borrow of Dr. Bentley the Preces in usum Sarum.

284. TO MRS. THRALE

Dear Madam   Ashbourne, Nov. 7, 1772.

So many days and never a letter!—*Fugere fides, pietasque pudorque.* This is Turkish usage. And I have been hoping and hoping. But you are so glad to have me out of your mind

[1] [A revised edition of the Dictionary.]

I think you were quite right in your advice about the thousand pounds, for the payment could not have been delayed long; and a short delay would have lessened credit, without advancing interest. But in great matters you are hardly ever mistaken.

We have here very rainy weather; but it makes the grass grow, and makes our waterfall roar. I wish Queeney heard it; she would think it very pretty. I go down to it every day, for I have not much to do; and have not been very well; but by physick am grown better. You and all your train may be supposed to keep me company in my walks. I wish I could know how you brew, and how you go on; but you tell me nothing.

I am, &c.,
SAM: JOHNSON.

295. To JAMES BOSWELL

Dear Sir

I have read your kind letter much more than the elegant *Pindar* which it accompanied. I am always glad to find myself not forgotten; and to be forgotten by you would give me great uneasiness. My northern friends have never been unkind to me: I have from you, dear Sir, testimonies of affection, which I have not often been able to excite; and Dr. Beattie rates the testimony which I was desirous of paying to his merit, much higher than I should have thought it reasonable to expect.

I have heard of your masquerade.[1] What says your synod to such innovations? I am not studiously scrupulous, nor do I think a masquerade either evil in itself, or very likely to be the occasion of evil; yet as the world thinks it a very licentious relaxation of manners, I would not have been one of the *first* masquers in a country where no masquerade had ever been before.[2]

[1] Given by a lady at Edinburgh. BOSWELL.
[2] There had been masquerades in Scotland; but not for a very long time. BOSWELL.

A new edition of my great *Dictionary* is printed, from a copy which I was persuaded to revise; but having made no preparation, I was able to do very little. Some superfluities I have expunged, and some faults I have corrected, and here and there have scattered a remark; but the main fabrick of the work remains as it was. I had looked very little into it since I wrote it, and, I think, I found it full as often better, as worse, than I expected.

Baretti and Davies have had a furious quarrel; a quarrel, I think, irreconcileable. Dr. Goldsmith has a new comedy, which is expected in the spring. No name is yet given it. The chief diversion arises from a stratagem by which a lover is made to mistake his future father-in-law's house for an inn. This, you see, borders upon farce. The dialogue is quick and gay, and the incidents are so prepared as not to seem improbable.

I am sorry that you lost your cause of Intromission, because I yet think the arguments on your side unanswerable. But you seem, I think, to say that you gained reputation even by your defeat; and reputation you will daily gain, if you keep Lord Auchinleck's precept in your mind, and endeavour to consolidate in your mind a firm and regular system of law, instead of picking up occasional fragments.

My health seems in general to improve; but I have been troubled for many weeks with a vexatious catarrh, which is sometimes sufficiently distressful. I have not found any great effects from bleeding and physick; and am afraid, that I must expect help from brighter days and softer air.

Write to me now and then; and whenever any good befalls you, make haste to let me know it, for no one will rejoice at it more than,

dear Sir,
your most humble servant,

London, Feb. 24, 1773.   SAM: JOHNSON.

You continue to stand very high in the favour of Mrs. Thrale.

297. To Mr. B——d [1]

Sir

That in the hurry of a sudden departure you should yet find leisure to consult my convenience, is a degree of kindness, and an instance of regard, not only beyond my claims, but above my expectation. You are not mistaken in supposing that I set a high value on my American friends, and that you should confer a very valuable favour upon me by giving me an opportunity of keeping myself in their memory.

I have taken the liberty of troubling you with a packet, to which I wish a safe and speedy conveyance, because I wish a safe and speedy voyage to him that conveys it.

I am, Sir,
your most humble servant,
London, Johnson's-court,   SAM: JOHNSON.
Fleet-street, March 4, 1773.

298. To the Reverend Mr. White [2]

Dear Sir

Your kindness for your friends accompanies you across the Atlantick. It was long since observed by Horace, that no ship could leave care behind; you have been attended in your voyage by other powers,—by benevolence and constancy; and I hope care did not often shew her face in their company.

---

[1] This gentleman, who now resides in America in a publick character of considerable dignity, desired that his name might not be transcribed at full length. BOSWELL.

[2] Now Doctor White, and Bishop of the Episcopal Church in Pennsylvania. During his first visit to England in 1771, as a candidate for holy orders, he was several times in company with Dr. Johnson, who expressed a wish to see the edition of his *Rasselas*, which Dr. White told him had been printed in America. Dr. White, on his return, immediately sent him a copy. BOSWELL.

I received the copy of *Rasselas*. The impression is not magnificent, but it flatters an authour, because the printer seems to have expected that it would be scattered among the people. The little book has been well received, and is translated into Italian, French, German, and Dutch. It has now one honour more by an American edition.

I know not that much has happened since your departure that can engage your curiosity. Of all publick transactions the whole world is now informed by the news-papers. Opposition seems to despond; and the dissenters, though they have taken advantage of unsettled times, and a government much enfeebled, seem not likely to gain any immunities.

Dr. Goldsmith has a new comedy in rehearsal at Covent-Garden, to which the manager predicts ill success. I hope he will be mistaken. I think it deserves a very kind reception.

I shall soon publish a new edition of my large *Dictionary*; I have been persuaded to revise it, and have mended some faults, but added little to its usefulness.

No book has been published since your departure, of which much notice is taken. Faction only fills the town with pamphlets, and greater subjects are forgotten in the noise of discord.

Thus have I written, only to tell you how little I have to tell. Of myself I can only add, that having been afflicted many weeks with a very troublesome cough, I am now recovered.

I take the liberty which you give me of troubling you with a letter, of which you will please to fill up the direction.

I am, Sir,
your most humble servant,
Johnson's-court, Fleet-street,   SAM: JOHNSON.
London, March 4, 1773.

299. To Dr. William Samuel Johnson of Connecticut

Sir

Of all those whom the various accidents of life have brought within my notice, there is scarce any man whose acquaintance I have more desired to cultivate than yours. I cannot indeed charge you with neglecting me, yet our mutual inclination could never gratify itself with opportunities. The current of the day always bore us away from one another, and now the Atlantic is between us.

Whether you carried away an impression of me as pleasing as that which you left me of yourself, I know not; if you did, you have not forgotten me, and will be glad that I do not forget you. Merely to be remembered is indeed a barren pleasure, but it is one of the pleasures which is more sensibly felt as human nature is more exalted.

To make you wish that I should have you in my mind, I would be glad to tell you something which you do not know; but all public affairs are printed; and as you and I have no common friend, I can tell you no private history.

The Government, I think, grow stronger; but I am afraid the next general election will be a time of uncommon turbulence, violence, and outrage.

Of Literature no great product has appeared, or is expected; the attention of the people has for some years been otherwise employed.

I was told a day or two ago of a design which must excite some curiosity. Two ships are in preparation, which are under the command of Captain Constantine Phipps, to explore the Northern Ocean; not to seek the north-east or the north-west passage, but to sail directly north, as near the pole as they can go. They hope to find an open ocean, but I suspect it is one mass of perpetual congelation. I do not much wish well to discoveries, for I am always afraid they will end in conquest and robbery.

I have been out of order this winter, but am grown better. Can I never hope to see you again, or must I be always content to tell you that in another hemisphere,

>I am, Sir
>>Your most humble servant,
>>>SAM: JOHNSON.

Johnson's Court, Fleet Street, London,
  March 4, 1773.

T. W. S. Johnson, LL.D., Stratford, Connecticut.

302. To MRS. THRALE

[Johnson's Court], March 17, 1773.

Dear Madam

To tell you that I am sorry both for the poor lady and for you is useless. I cannot help either of you. The weakness of mind is perhaps only a casual interruption or intermission of the attention, such as we all suffer when some weighty care or urgent calamity has possession of the mind. She will compose herself. She is unwilling to die, and the first conviction of approaching death raised great perturbation. I think she has but very lately thought death close at hand. She will compose herself to do that as well as she can, which must at last be done. May she not want the Divine assistance.

You, Madam, will have a great loss; a greater than is common in the loss of a parent. Fill your mind with hope of her happiness, and turn your thoughts first to Him who gives and takes away, in whose presence the living and dead are standing together. Then remember, that when this mournful duty is paid, others yet remain of equal obligation, and, we may hope, of less painful performance. Grief is a species of idleness, and the necessity of attention to the present preserves us, by the merciful disposition of Providence, from being lacerated and devoured by sorrow for the past. You must think on your husband and your children, and do for them what this dear lady has done for you.

Not to come to town while the great struggle continues is undoubtedly well resolved. But do not harass yourself into danger; you owe the care of your health to all that love you, at least to all whom it is your duty to love. You cannot give such a mother too much, if you do not give her what belongs to another.

I am, &c.,

SAM: JOHNSON.

305. To OLIVER GOLDSMITH

Sir

I beg that you will excuse my Absence to the Club. I am going this evening to Oxford.

I have another favour to beg. It is that I may be considered as proposing Mr. Boswel for a candidate of our Society, and that he may be considered as regularly nominated.

I am, Sir,

Your most humble servant,

April 23, 1773.   SAM: JOHNSON.

308. To MRS. THRALE

Madam   [Johnson's Court], May 17, 1773.

Never imagine that your letters are long; they are always too short for my curiosity. I do not know that I was ever content with a single perusal.

Of dear Mrs. Salusbury I never expect much better news than you send me; *de pis en pis* is the natural and certain course of her dreadful malady. I am content when it leaves her ease enough for the exercise of her mind.

Why should Mr. Thrale suppose, that what I took the liberty of suggesting was concerted with you? He does not know how much I revolve his affairs, and how honestly I desire his prosperity. I hope he has let the hint take some hold of his mind.

Your declaration to Miss Fanny is more general than my opinions allow. I think an unlimited promise of acting by the opinion of another so wrong, that nothing, or hardly any thing, can make it right. All unnecessary vows are folly, because they suppose a prescience of the future which has not been given us. They are, I think, a crime, because they resign that life to chance which God has given us to be regulated by reason; and superinduce a kind of fatality, from which it is the great privilege of our nature to be free. Unlimited obedience is due only to the Universal Father of Heaven and Earth. My parents may be mad or foolish; may be wicked and malicious; may be erroneously religious, or absurdly scrupulous. I am not bound to compliance with mandates either positive or negative, which either religion condemns, or reason rejects. There wanders about the world a wild notion, which extends over marriage more than over any other transaction. If Miss Fanny followed a trade, would it be said that she was bound in conscience to give or refuse credit at her father's choice? And is not marriage a thing in which she is more interested, and has therefore more right of choice? When I may suffer for my own crimes, when I may be sued for my own debts, I may judge by parity of reason for my own happiness. The parent's moral right can arise only from his kindness, and his civil right only from his money.

Conscience cannot dictate obedience to the wicked, or compliance with the foolish; and of interest mere prudence is the judge.

If the daughter is bound without a promise, she promises nothing; and if she is not bound, she promises too much.

What is meant by tying up money in trade I do not understand. No money is so little tied as that which is employed in trade. Mr. * * * * perhaps only means, that in consideration of money to be advanced, he will oblige his son to be a trader. This is reasonable enough. Upon ten thousand pounds diligently occupied, they may live in great plenty and splendour, without the mischiefs of idleness.

I can write a long letter as well as my mistress; and shall be glad that my long letters may be as welcome as her's.

My nights are grown again very uneasy and troublesome. I know not that the country will mend them; but I hope your company will mend my days. Though I cannot now expect much attention, and would not wish for more than can be spared from the poor dear lady, yet I shall see you and hear you every now and then; and to see and hear you, is always to hear wit, and to see virtue.

I shall, I hope, see you to-morrow, and a little on the two next days; and with that little I must for the present try to be contented.

I am, Madam,

Your most obedient and most humble servant
SAM: JOHNSON.

319. To JAMES BOSWELL

Mr. Johnson sends his compliments to Mr. Boswell, being just arrived at Boyd's.—Saturday night.

320. To MRS. THRALE

Dear Madam   Edinburgh, August 17, 1773.

On the 13th, I left Newcastle, and in the afternoon came to Alnwick, where we were treated with great civility by the Duke: I went through the apartments, walked on the wall, and climbed the towers. That night we lay at Belford, and on the next night came to Edinburgh. On Sunday (15th) I went to the English chapel. After dinner, Dr. Robertson came in, and promised to shew me the place. On Monday I saw their public buildings: the cathedral, which I told Robertson I wished to see because it had once been a church, the courts of justice, the parliament-house, the advocates' library, the repository of records, the college and its library, and the palace, particularly the old tower where the king of Scotland seized David

Rizzio in the queen's presence. Most of their buildings are very mean; and the whole town bears some resemblance to the old part of Birmingham.

Boswell has very handsome and spacious rooms; level with the ground on one side of the house, and on the other four stories high.

At dinner on Monday were the Duchess of Douglas, an old lady, who talks broad Scotch with a paralytick voice, and is scarce understood by her own countrymen; the Lord Chief Baron, Sir Adolphus Oughton, and many more. At supper there was such a conflux of company that I could scarcely support the tumult. I have never been well in the whole journey, and am very easily disordered.

This morning I saw at breakfast Dr. Blacklock, the blind poet, who does not remember to have seen light, and is read to, by a poor scholar, in Latin, Greek, and French. He was originally a poor scholar himself. I looked on him with reverence. To-morrow our journey begins; I know not when I shall write again. I am but poorly.

I am, &c.,
SAM: JOHNSON.

321. To MRS. THRALE

Dear Madam Banff, August 25, 1773.

It has so happened that though I am perpetually thinking on you, I could seldom find opportunity to write; I have in fourteen days sent only one letter; you must consider the fatigues of travel, and the difficulties encountered in a strange country.

August 18th, I passed, with Boswel, the Frith of Forth, and began our journey; in the passage we observed an island, which I persuaded my companions to survey. We found it a rock somewhat troublesome to climb, about a mile long, and half a mile broad; in the middle were the ruins of an old fort, which had on one of the stones—Maria Re. 1564. It had been only a blockhouse one story high. I measured two apartments, of which the walls were entire, and found them twenty-seven feet long, and twenty-three broad. The rock had some grass and many thistles, both cows and sheep were grazing. There was a spring of water. The name is Inchkeith. Look on your maps.

This visit took about an hour. We pleased ourselves with being in a country all our own, and then went back to the boat, and landed at Kinghorn, a mean town, and travelling through Kirkaldie, a very long town meanly built, and Cowpar, which I could not see because it was night, we came late to St. Andrew's, the most ancient of the Scotch universities, and once the see of the Primate of Scotland. The inn was full, but lodgings were provided for us at the house of the professor of rhetorick, a man of elegant manners, who showed us, in the morning, the poor remains of a stately cathedral, demolished in Knox's reformation, and now only to be imaged by tracing its foundation, and contemplating the little ruins that are left. Here was once a religious house. Two of the vaults or cellars of the subprior are yet entire. In one of them lives an old woman, who claims an hereditary residence in it, boasting that her husband was the sixth tenant of this gloomy mansion, in a lineal descent, and claiming by her marriage with this lord of the cavern an alliance with the Bruces. Mr. Boswel staid a while to interrogate her, because he understood her language; she told him, that she and her cat lived together; that she had two sons some where, who might perhaps be dead; that when there were quality in the town notice was taken of her, and that now she was neglected, but did not trouble them. Her habitation contained all that she had; her turf for fire was laid in one place, and her balls of coal dust in another, but her bed seemed to be clean. Boswell asked her if she never heard any noises, but she could tell him of nothing supernatural, though she sometimes wandered in the night among the graves and ruins, only she had some notice by dreams of the death of her relations.

We then viewed the remains of a castle on the margin

of the sea, in which the archbishops resided, and in which Cardinal Beatoun was killed.

The professors who happened to be resident in the vacation made a public dinner, and treated us very kindly and respectfully. They shewed us their colleges, in one of which there is a library that for luminousness and elegance may vie at least with the new edifice at Streatham. But learning seems not to prosper among them ; one of their colleges has been lately alienated, and one of their churches lately deserted. An experiment was made of planting a shrubbery in the church, but it did not thrive.

Why the place should thus fall to decay I know not ; for education, such as is here to be had, is sufficiently cheap. Their term, or, as they call it, their session, lasts seven months in the year, which the students of the highest rank and greatest expence may pass here for twenty pounds, in which are included board, lodging, books, and the continual instruction of three professors.

20th, We left St. Andrew's, well satisfied with our reception, and, crossing the Firth of Tay, came to Dundee, a dirty, despicable town. We passed afterwards through Aberbrothick, famous once for an abbey, of which there are only a few fragments left, but those fragments testify that the fabrick was once of great extent, and stupendous magnificence. Two of the towers are yet standing, though shattered ; into one of them Boswel climbed, but found the stairs broken : the way into the other we did not see, and had not time to search ; I believe it might be ascended, but the top, I think, is open.

We lay at Montrose, a neat place, with a spacious area for the market. and an elegant town-house.

21st, We travelled towards Aberdeen, another University, and in the way dined at Lord Monboddo's, the Scotch judge who has lately written a strange book about the origin of language, in which he traces monkeys up to men, and says that in some countries the human species have tails like other beasts. He enquired for these long-tailed men of Banks, and was not well pleased that they had not been found in all his peregrination. He talked nothing of this to me, and I hope we parted friends; for we agreed pretty well, only we differed in adjusting the claims of merit between a shopkeeper of London, and a savage of the American wildernesses. Our opinions were, I think, maintained on both sides without full conviction; Monboddo declared boldly for the savage, and I, perhaps for that reason, sided with the citizen.

We came late to Aberdeen, where I found my dear mistress's letter, and learned that all our little people were happily recovered of the measles. Every part of your letter was pleasing.

There are two cities of the name of Aberdeen: the old town, built about a mile inland, once the see of a bishop, which contains the King's College, and the remains of the cathedral, and the new town, which stands, for the sake of trade, upon a firth or arm of the sea, so that ships rest against the key.

The two cities have their separate magistrates, and the two colleges are in effect two universities, which confer degrees independently on each other.

New Aberdeen is a large town, built almost wholly of that granite which is used for the new pavement in London, which, hard as it is, they square with very little difficulty. Here I first saw the women in plaids. The plaid makes at once a hood and cloak, without cutting or sewing, merely by the manner of drawing the opposite sides over the shoulders. The maids at the inns run over the house barefoot, and children, not dressed in rags, go without shoes or stockings. Shoes are indeed not yet in universal use, they came late into this country. One of the professors told us, as we were mentioning a fort built by Cromwell, that the country owed much of its present industry to Cromwell's soldiers. They taught us, said he, to raise cabbage and make shoes. How they lived without shoes may yet be seen; but in the passage through villages, it seems to him that surveys their gardens, that when they had not cabbage they had nothing.

Education is here of the same price as at St. Andrews, only the session is but from the 1st of November to the 1st of April. The academical buildings seem rather to advance than decline. They shewed their libraries, which were not very splendid, but some manuscripts were so exquisitely penned that I wished my dear mistress to have seen them.

I had an unexpected pleasure, by finding an old acquaintance now professor of physick in the King's College : we were on both sides glad of the interview, having not seen nor perhaps thought on one another for many years ; but we had no emulation, nor had either of us risen to the other's envy, and our old kindness was easily renewed. I hope we shall never try the effect of so long an absence, and that I shall always be,

    Madam,
     Your most humble servant,
        SAM : JOHNSON.

322. TO MRS. THRALE

Dear Madam   Inverness, Aug. 28, 1773.

August 23rd, I had the honour of attending the Lord Provost of Aberdeen, and was presented with the freedom of the city, not in a gold box, but in good Latin. Let me pay Scotland one just praise ! there was no officer gaping for a fee ; this could have been said of no city on the English side of the Tweed. I wore my patent of freedom *pro more* in my hat, from the new town to the old, about a mile. I then dined with my friend the professor of physick at his house, and saw the King's College. Boswell was very angry that the Aberdeen professors would not talk. When I was at the English church in Aberdeen I happened to be espied by Lady Di. Middleton, whom I had sometime seen in London ; she told what she had seen to Mr. Boyd, Lord Errol's brother, who wrote us an invitation to Lord Errol's house, called Slanes Castle. We went thither on the next day (24th of August), and found a house, not old, except but one tower, built upon the margin of the sea upon a rock, scarce accessible from the sea; at one corner a tower makes a perpendicular continuation of the lateral surface of the rock, so that it is impracticable to walk round; the house inclosed a square court, and on all sides within the court is a piazza or gallery two stories high. We came in as we were invited to dinner, and after dinner offered to go; but Lady Errol sent us word by Mr. Boyd, that if we went before Lord Errol came home we must never be forgiven, and ordered out the coach to shew us two curiosities. We were first conducted by Mr. Boyd to Dunbuys, or the yellow rock. Dunbuys is a rock consisting of two protuberances, each perhaps one hundred yards round, joined together by a narrow neck, and separated from the land by a very narrow channel or gully. These rocks are the haunts of sea-fowl, whose clang, though this is not their season, we heard at a distance. The eggs and the young are gathered here in great numbers at the time of breeding. There is a bird here called a coote, which though not much bigger than a duck lays a larger egg than a goose. We went then to see the Buller or Boulloir of Buchan: Buchan is the name of the district, and the Buller is a small creek or gulf into which the sea flows through an arch of the rock. We walked round it, and saw it black at a great depth. It has its name from the violent ebullition of the water, when high winds or high tides drive it up the arch into the bason. Walking a little further I spied some boats, and told my companions that we would go into the Buller and examine it. There was no danger; all was calm; we went through the arch, and found ourselves in a narrow gulf surrounded by craggy rocks, of height not stupendous, but to a Mediterranean visitor uncommon. On each side was a cave, of which the fishermen knew not the extent, in which smugglers hide their goods, and sometimes parties of pleasure take a dinner.

I am, &c.,
SAM: JOHNSON.

I think I grow better.

323. To Mrs. Thrale

Dearest Madam   Skie, Sept. 6, 1773.

I am now looking on the sea from a house of Sir Alexander Macdonald in the isle of Skie. Little did I once think of seeing this region of obscurity, and little did you once expect a salutation from this verge of European life. I have now the pleasure of going where nobody goes, and seeing what nobody sees. Our design is to visit several of the smaller islands, and then pass over to the south-west of Scotland.

I returned from the sight of Buller's Buchan to Lord Errol's, and, having seen his library, had for a time only to look upon the sea, which rolled between us and Norway. Next morning, August 25th, we continued our journey through a country not uncultivated, but so denuded of its woods, that in all this journey I had not travelled an hundred yards between hedges, or seen five trees fit for the carpenter. A few small plantations may be found, but I believe scarcely any thirty years old; at least, as I do not forget to tell, they are all posteriour to the Union. This day we dined with a country gentleman, who has in his grounds the remains of a Druid's temple, which when it is complete is nothing more than a circle or double circle of stones, placed at equal distances, with a flat stone, perhaps an altar, at a certain point, and a stone taller than the rest at the opposite point. The tall stone is erected I think at the south. Of these circles there are many in all the unfrequented parts of the island. The inhabitants of these parts respect them as memorials of the sepulture of some illustrious person. Here I saw a few trees. We lay at Banff.

August 26th, We dined at Elgin, where we saw the ruins of a noble cathedral; the chapter-house is yet standing. A great part of Elgin is built with small piazzas to the lower story. We went on to Foris, over the heath where Macbeth met the witches, but had no adventure; only in the way we saw for the first time some houses with fruit trees about them. The improvements of the Scotch are for immediate profit, they do not yet think it quite worth their while to plant what will not produce something to be eaten or sold in a very little time. We rested at Foris.

A very great proportion of the people are barefoot, and if one may judge by the rest of the dress, to send out boys without shoes into the streets or ways[1]; there are however more beggars than I have ever seen in England, they beg if not silently yet very modestly.

Next day we came to Nairn, a miserable town, but a royal burgh, of which the chief annual magistrate is styled Lord Provost. In the neighbourhood we saw the castle of the old Thane of Cawdor. There is one ancient tower with its battlements and winding stairs yet remaining; the rest of the house is, though not modern, of later erection.

On the 28th, we went to Fort George, which is accounted the most regular fortification in the island. The major of artillery walked with us round the walls, and shewed us the principles upon which every part was constructed, and the way in which it could be defended. We dined with the Governor Sir Eyre Coote and his officers. It was a very pleasant and instructive day, but nothing puts my honoured Mistress out of my mind.

At night we came to Inverness, the last considerable town in the north, where we staid all the next day, for it was Sunday, and saw the ruins of what is called Macbeth's castle. It never was a large house, but was strongly situated. From Inverness we were to travel on horseback.

August 30th, we set out with four horses. We had two Highlanders to run by us, who were active, officious, civil, and hardy. Our journey was for many miles along a military way made upon the banks of Lough Ness, a water about eighteen miles long, but not I think half a mile broad. Our horses were not bad, and the way was very pleasant; the rock out of

[1] [The sentence is obviously defective.]

which the road was cut was covered with birch trees, fern, and heath. The lake below was beating its bank by a gentle wind, and the rocks beyond the water on the right stood sometimes horrid and wild, and sometimes opened into a kind of bay, in which there was a spot of cultivated ground yellow with corn. In one part of the way we had trees on both sides for perhaps half a mile.—Such a length of shade perhaps Scotland cannot shew in any other place.

You are not to suppose that here are to be any more towns or inns. We came to a cottage which they call the general's hut, where we alighted to dine, and had eggs and bacon, and mutton, with wine, rum, and whiskey. I had water.

At a bridge over the river, which runs into the Ness, the rocks rise on three sides, with a direction almost perpendicular, to a great height; they are in part covered with trees, and exhibit a kind of dreadful magnificence;—standing like the barriers of nature placed to keep different orders of being in perpetual separation. Near this bridge is the Fall of Fiers, a famous cataract, of which, by clambering over the rocks, we obtained a view. The water was low, and therefore we had only the pleasure of knowing that rain would make it at once pleasing and formidable; there will then be a mighty flood, foaming along a rocky channel, frequently obstructed by protuberances and exasperated by reverberation, at last precipitated with a sudden descent, and lost in the depth of a gloomy chasm.

We came somewhat late to Fort Augustus, where the lieutenant governor met us beyond the gates, and apologised that at that hour he could not, by the rules of a garrison, admit us otherwise than at a narrow door which only one can enter at a time. We were well entertained and well lodged, and next morning, after having viewed the fort, we pursued our journey.

Our way now lay over the mountains, which are not to be passed by climbing them directly, but by traversing, so that as we went forward we saw our baggage following us below in a direction exactly contrary. There is in these ways much labour but little danger, and perhaps other places of which very terrifick representations are made are not in themselves more formidable. These roads have all been made by hewing the rock away with pickaxes, or bursting it with gunpowder. The stones so separated are often piled loose as a wall by the wayside. We saw an inscription importing the year in which one of the regiments made two thousand yards of the road eastward.

After tedious travel of some hours we came to what I believe we must call a village, a place where there were three huts built of turf, at one of which we were to have our dinner and our bed, for we could not reach any better place that night. This place is called Enock in Glenmorrison. The house in which we lodged was distinguished by a chimney, the rest had only a hole for the smoke. Here we had eggs, and mutton, and a chicken, and a sausage, and rum. In the afternoon tea was made by a very decent girl in a printed linen; she engaged me so much, that I made her a present of Cocker's arithmetick.

I am, &c.,
Sam: Johnson.

324. To Mrs. Thrale

Dearest Madam　　　　　　　　Skie, Sept. 14, 1773.

The post, which comes but once a week into these parts, is so soon to go that I have not time to go on where I left off in my last letter. I have been several days in the island of Raarsa, and am now again in the isle of Skie, but at the other end of it.

Skie is almost equally divided between the two great families of Macdonald and Macleod, other proprietors having only small districts. The two great lords do not know within twenty square miles the contents of their own territories.

—— kept up but ill the reputation of Highland

hospitality; we are now with Macleod, quite at the other end of the island, where there is a fine young gentleman and fine ladies. The ladies are studying Earse. I have a cold, and am miserably deaf, and am troublesome to Lady Macleod; I force her to speak loud, but she will seldom speak loud enough.

Raarsa is an island about fifteen miles long and two broad, under the dominion of one gentleman who has three sons and ten daughters; the eldest is the beauty of this part of the world, and has been polished at Edinburgh: they sing and dance, and without expence have upon their table most of what sea, air, or earth can afford. I intended to have written about Raarsa, but the post will not wait longer than while I send my compliments to my dear master and little mistresses.

I am, &c.,

SAM: JOHNSON.

326. TO MRS. THRALE

Dearest Madam   Skie, Sept. 21, 1773.

I am so vexed at the necessity of sending yesterday so short a letter, that I purpose to get a long letter beforehand by writing something every day, which I may the more easily do, as a cold makes me now too deaf to take the usual pleasure in conversation. Lady Macleod is very good to me, and the place at which we now are is equal in strength of situation, in the wildness of the adjacent country, and in the plenty and elegance of the domestick entertainment, to a castle in Gothick romance. The sea with a little island is before us; cascades play within view. Close to the house is the formidable skeleton of an old castle probably Danish, and the whole mass of building stands upon a protuberance of rock, inaccessible till of late but by a pair of stairs on the sea side, and secure in ancient times against any enemy that was likely to invade the kingdom of Skie.

Macleod has offered me an island; if it were not too far off I should hardly refuse it: my island would be pleasanter than Brighthelmstone, if you and my master could come to it; but I cannot think it pleasant to live quite alone

Oblitusque meorum, obliviscendus et illis.[1]

That I should be elated by the dominion of an island to forgetfulness of my friends at Streatham I cannot believe, and I hope never to deserve that they should be willing to forget me.

It has happened that I have been often recognised in my journey where I did not expect it. At Aberdeen I found one of my acquaintance professor of physick; turning aside to dine with a country gentleman, I was owned at table by one who had seen me at a philosophical lecture; at Macdonald's I was claimed by a naturalist, who wanders about the islands to pick up curiosities; and I had once in London attracted the notice of Lady Macleod. I will now go on with my account.

The Highland girl made tea, and looked and talked not inelegantly; her father was by no means an ignorant or a weak man; there were books in the cottage, among which were some volumes of Prideaux's Connection: this man's conversation we were glad of while we staid. He had been *out*, as they call it, in forty five, and still retained his old opinions. He was going to America, because his rent was raised beyond what he thought himself able to pay.

At night our beds were made, but we had some difficulty in persuading ourselves to lie down in them, though we had put on our own sheets; at last we ventured, and I slept very soundly in the vale of Glenmorrison, amidst the rocks and mountains. Next morning our landlord liked us so well, that he walked some miles with us for our company, through a country so wild and barren that the proprietor does not, with all his pressure upon his tenants, raise more than four hundred pounds a-year for near one hundred square

---

[1] [Your friends forgetting, by your friends forgot.
Francis's Horace.]

miles, or sixty thousand acres. He let us know that
he had forty head of black cattle, an hundred goats,
and an hundred sheep, upon a farm that he remembered let at five pounds a-year, but for which he now
paid twenty. He told us some stories of their march
into England. At last he left us, and we went forward,
winding among mountains, sometimes green and sometimes naked, commonly so steep as not easily to be
climbed by the greatest vigour and activity: our way
was often crossed by little rivulets, and we were entertained with small streams trickling from the rocks,
which after heavy rains must be tremendous torrents.

About noon we came to a small glen, so they call
a valley, which compared with other places appeared
rich and fertile; here our guides desired us to stop,
that the horses might graze, for the journey was very
laborious, and no more grass would be found. We
made no difficulty of compliance, and I sat down to
take notes on a green bank, with a small stream running
at my feet, in the midst of savage solitude, with
mountains before me, and on either hand, covered with
heath. I looked around me, and wondered that I was
not more affected, but the mind is not at all times
equally ready to be put in motion; if my mistress and
master and Queeney had been there we should have
produced some reflections among us, either poetical
or philosophical, for though *solitude be the nurse of woe*,
conversation is often the parent of remarks and
discoveries.

In about an hour we remounted, and pursued our
journey. The lake by which we had travelled for
some time ended in a river, which we passed by a
bridge, and came to another glen, with a collection
of huts, called Auknashealds; the huts were generally
built of clods of earth, held together by the inter-
texture of vegetable fibres, of which earth there are
great levels in Scotland which they call mosses. Moss
in Scotland is bog in Ireland, and moss-trooper is bog-
trotter: there was, however, one hut built of loose
stones, piled up with great thickness into a strong

though not solid wall. From this house we obtained some great pails of milk, and having brought bread with us, were very liberally regaled. The inhabitants, a very coarse tribe, ignorant of any language but Earse, gathered so fast about us, that if we had not had Highlanders with us, they might have caused more alarm than pleasure; they are called the Clan of Macrae.

We had been told that nothing gratified the Highlanders so much as snuff and tobacco, and had accordingly stored ourselves with both at Fort Augustus. Boswell opened his treasure, and gave them each a piece of tobacco roll. We had more bread than we could eat for the present, and were more liberal than provident. Boswell cut it in slices, and gave them an opportunity of tasting wheaten bread for the first time. I then got some halfpence for a shilling, and made up the deficiencies of Boswell's distribution, who had given some money among the children. We then directed that the mistress of the stone house should be asked what we must pay her: she, who perhaps had never before sold any thing but cattle, knew not, I believe, well what to ask, and referred herself to us: we obliged her to make some demand, and one of the Highlanders settled the account with her at a shilling. One of the men advised her, with the cunning that clowns never can be without, to ask more; but she said that a shilling was enough. We gave her half a crown, and she offered part of it again. The Macraes were so well pleased with our behaviour, that they declared it the best day they had seen since the time of the old Laird of Macleod, who, I suppose, like us, stopped in their valley, as he was travelling to Skie.

We were mentioning this view of the Highlander's life at Macdonald's, and mentioning the Macraes with some degree of pity, when a Highland lady informed us that we might spare our tenderness, for she doubted not but the woman who supplied us with milk was mistress of thirteen or fourteen milch cows.

I cannot forbear to interrupt my narrative. Boswell,

with some of his troublesome kindness, has informed this family and reminded me that the 18th of September is my birth-day. The return of my birth-day, if I remember it, fills me with thoughts which it seems to be the general care of humanity to escape. I can now look back upon threescore and four years, in which little has been done, and little has been enjoyed; a life diversified by misery, spent part in the sluggishness of penury, and part under the violence of pain, in gloomy discontent or importunate distress. But perhaps I am better than I should have been if I had been less afflicted. With this I will try to be content.

In proportion as there is less pleasure in retrospective considerations, the mind is more disposed to wander forward into futurity; but at sixty-four what promises, however liberal of imaginary good, can futurity venture to make ? yet something will be always promised, and some promises will always be credited. I am hoping and I am praying that I may live better in the time to come, whether long or short, than I have yet lived, and in the solace of that hope endeavour to repose. Dear Queeney's day is next, I hope she at sixty-four will have less to regret.

I will now complain no more, but tell my mistress of my travels.

After we left the Macraes we travelled on through a country like that which we passed in the morning. The Highlands are very uniform, for there is little variety in universal barrenness; the rocks, however, are not all naked, some have grass on their sides, and birches and alders on their tops, and in the vallies are often broad and clear streams, which have little depth, and commonly run very quick: the channels are made by the violence of the wintry floods; the quickness of the stream is in proportion to the declivity of the descent, and the breadth of the channel makes the water shallow in a dry season.

There are red deer and roebucks in the mountains, but we found only goats in the road, and had very little entertainment as we travelled either for the eye or ear. There are, I fancy, no singing birds in the Highlands.

Towards night we came to a very formidable hill called Rattiken, which we climbed with more difficulty than we had yet experienced, and at last came to Glenelg, a place on the sea-side opposite to Skie. We were by this time weary and disgusted, nor was our humour much mended by our inn, which, though it was built of lime and slate, the Highlander's description of a house which he thinks magnificent, had neither wine, bread, eggs, nor any thing that we could eat or drink. When we were taken up stairs, a dirty fellow bounced out of the bed where one of us was to lie. Boswell blustered, but nothing could be got. At last a gentleman in the neighbourhood, who heard of our arrival, sent us rum and white sugar. Boswell was now provided for in part, and the landlord prepared some mutton chops, which we could not eat, and killed two hens, of which Boswell made his servant broil a limb, with what effect I know not. We had a lemon and a piece of bread, which supplied me with my supper. When the repast was ended, we began to deliberate upon bed; Mrs. Boswell had warned us that we should *catch something*, and had given us *sheets* for our *security*, for —— and ——, she said, came back from Skie, so scratching themselves. I thought sheets a slender defence against the confederacy with which we were threatened, and by this time our Highlanders had found a place where they could get some hay: I ordered hay to be laid thick upon the bed, and slept upon it in my great coat: Boswell laid sheets upon his bed, and reposed in linen like a gentleman. The horses were turned out to grass, with a man to watch them. The hill Rattiken and the inn at Glenelg were the only things of which we, or travellers yet more delicate, could find any pretensions to complain.

Sept. 2nd, I rose rustling from the hay, and went to tea, which I forget whether we found or brought. We saw the isle of Skie before us, darkening the horizon with its rocky coast. A boat was procured, and we launched into one of the straits of the Atlantick ocean. We had a passage of about twelve miles to the point where Sir Alexander Macdonald resided, having come from his seat in the middle of the island to a small house on the shore, as we believe, that he might with less reproach entertain us meanly. If he aspired to meanness, his retrograde ambition was completely gratified, but he did not succeed equally in escaping reproach. He had no cook, nor I suppose much provision, nor had the Lady the common decencies of her tea-table: we picked up our sugar with our fingers. Boswell was very angry, and reproached him with his improper parsimony; I did not much reflect upon the conduct of a man with whom I was not likely to converse as long at any other time.

You will now expect that I should give you some account of the isle of Skie, of which, though I have been twelve days upon it, I have little to say. It is an island perhaps fifty miles long, so much indented by inlets of the sea that there is no part of it removed from the water more than six miles. No part that I have seen is plain; you are always climbing or descending, and every step is upon rock or mire. A walk upon ploughed ground in England is a dance upon carpets compared to the toilsome drudgery of wandering in Skie. There is neither town nor village in the island, nor have I seen any house but Macleod's, that is not much below your habitation at Brighthelmstone. In the mountains there are stags and roebucks, but no hares, and few rabbits; nor have I seen any thing that interested me as a zoologist, except an otter, bigger than I thought an otter could have been.

You are perhaps imagining that I am withdrawn from the gay and the busy world into regions of peace and pastoral felicity, and am enjoying the reliques of the golden age; that I am surveying nature's magnificence from a mountain, or remarking her minuter beauties on the flowery bank of a winding rivulet; that I am invigorating myself in the sunshine, or delighting my imagination with being hidden from the invasion of human evils and human passions in the darkness of a thicket; that I am busy in gathering shells and pebbles on the shore, or contemplative on a rock, from which I look upon the water, and consider how many waves are rolling between me and Streatham.

The use of travelling is to regulate imagination by reality, and instead of thinking how things may be, to see them as they are. Here are mountains which I should once have climbed, but to climb steeps is now very laborious, and to descend them dangerous; and I am now content with knowing, that by scrambling up a rock, I shall only see other rocks, and a wider circuit of barren desolation. Of streams, we have here a sufficient number, but they murmur not upon pebbles, but upon rocks. Of flowers, if Chloris herself were here, I could present her only with the bloom of heath. Of lawns and thickets, he must read that would know them, for here is little sun and no shade. On the sea I look from my window, but am not much tempted to the shore; for since I came to this island, almost every breath of air has been a storm, and what is worse, a storm with all its severity, but without its magnificence, for the sea is here so broken into channels that there is not a sufficient volume of water either for lofty surges or a loud roar.

On Sept. 6th, we left Armidale to visit Raarsa, the island which I have already mentioned. We were to cross part of Skie on horseback; a mode of travelling very uncomfortable, for the road is so narrow, where any road can be found, that only one can go, and so craggy that the attention can never be remitted; it allows, therefore, neither the gaiety of conversation, nor the laxity of solitude; nor has it in itself the amusement of much variety, as it affords only all the possible transpositions of bog, rock, and rivulet. Twelve miles, by computation, make a reasonable journey for a day.

At night we came to a tenant's house, of the first

rank of tenants, where we were entertained better than at the landlord's. There were books both English and Latin. Company gathered about us, and we heard some talk of the second sight, and some talk of the events of forty-five; a year which will not soon be forgotten among the islanders. The next day we were confined by a storm. The company, I think, encreased, and our entertainment was not only hospitable but elegant. At night, a minister's sister, in very fine brocade, sung Earse songs; I wished to know the meaning, but the Highlanders are not much used to scholastick questions, and no translations could be obtained.

Next day, Sept. 8th, the weather allowed us to depart; a good boat was provided us, and we went to Raarsa under the conduct of Mr. Malcolm Macleod, a gentleman who conducted Prince Charles through the mountains in his distresses. The Prince, he says, was more active than himself; they were, at least, one night without any shelter.

The wind blew enough to give the boat a kind of dancing agitation, and in about three or four hours we arrived at Raarsa, where we were met by the Laird and his friends upon the shore. Raarsa, for such is his title, is master of two islands; upon the smaller of which, called Rona, he has only flocks and herds. Rona gives title to his eldest son. The money which he raises annually by rent from all his dominions, which contain at least fifty thousand acres, is not believed to exceed two hundred and fifty pounds; but as he keeps a large farm in his own hands, he sells every year great numbers of cattle, which add to his revenue, and his table is furnished from the farm and from the sea, with very little expence, except for those things this country does not produce, and of those he is very liberal. The wine circulates vigorously, and the tea, chocolate, and coffee, however they are got, are always at hand.

I am, &c.,
SAM: JOHNSON.

We are this morning trying to get out of Skie.

327. To Mrs. Thrale

Dear Madam   Skie, Sept. 24, 1773.

I am still in Skie. Do you remember the song?

> Ev'ry island is a prison,
> Strongly guarded by the sea.

We have at one time no boat, and at another may have too much wind; but of our reception here we have no reason to complain. We are now with Colonel Macleod, in a more pleasant place than I thought Skie could afford. Now to the narrative.

We were received at Raarsa on the sea-side, and after clambering with some difficulty over the rocks, a labour which the traveller, wherever he reposes himself on land, must in these islands be contented to endure, we were introduced into the house, which one of the company called the Court of Raarsa, with politeness which not the Court of Versailles could have thought defective. The house is not large, though we were told in our passage that it had eleven fine rooms, nor magnificently furnished, but our utensils were most commonly silver. We went up into a dining room, about as large as your blue room, where we had something given us to eat, and tea and coffee.

Raarsa himself is a man of no inelegant appearance, and of manners uncommonly refined. Lady Raarsa makes no very sublime appearance for a sovereign, but is a good housewife, and a very prudent and diligent conductress of her family. Miss Flora Macleod is a celebrated beauty; has been admired at Edinburgh; dresses her head very high; and has manners so lady like, that I wish her head-dress was lower. The rest of the nine girls are all pretty; the youngest is between Queeney and Lucy. The youngest boy, of four years old, runs barefoot, and wandered with us over the rocks to see a mill. I believe he would walk on that rough ground without shoes ten miles in a day.

The Laird of Raarsa has sometimes disputed the chieftainry of the clan with Macleod of Skie, but being much inferior in extent of possessions, has, I suppose, been forced to desist. Raarsa and its provinces have descended to its present possessor through a succession of four hundred years, without any increase or diminution. It was indeed lately in danger of forfeiture, but the old Laird joined some prudence with his zeal, and when Prince Charles landed in Scotland, made over his estate to his son, the present Laird, and led one hundred men of Raarsa into the field, with officers of his own family. Eighty-six only came back after the last battle. The Prince was hidden, in his distress, two nights at Raarsa, and the king's troops burnt the whole country, and killed some of the cattle.

You may guess at the opinions that prevail in this country; they are, however, content with fighting for their king; they do not drink for him. We had no foolish healths. At night, unexpectedly to us who were strangers, the carpet was taken up; the fiddler of the family came up, and a very vigorous and general dance was begun. As I told you, we were two-and-thirty at supper; there were full as many dancers; for though all who supped did not dance, some danced of the young people who did not sup. Raarsa himself danced with his children, and old Malcolm, in his filibeg, was as nimble as when he led the Prince over the mountains. When they had danced themselves weary, two tables were spread, and I suppose at least twenty dishes were upon them. In this country some preparations of milk are always served up at supper, and sometimes in the place of tarts at dinner. The table was not coarsely heaped, but at once plentiful and elegant. They do not pretend to make a loaf; there are only cakes, commonly of oats or barley, but they made me very nice cakes of wheat flour. I always sat at the left hand of Lady Raarsa, and young Macleod of Skie, the chieftain of the clan, sat on the right.

After supper a young lady, who was visiting, sung

Earse songs, in which Lady Raarsa joined prettily enough, but not gracefully; the young ladies sustained the chorus better. They are very little used to be asked questions, and not well prepared with answers. When one of the songs was over, I asked the princess that sat next me, *What is that about?* I question if she conceived that I did not understand it. For the entertainment of the company, said she. But, Madam, what is the meaning of it? It is a love song. This was all the intelligence that I could obtain; nor have I been able to procure the translation of a single line of Earse.

At twelve it was bed time. I had a chamber to myself, which, in eleven rooms to forty people, was more than my share. How the company and the family were distributed is not easy to tell. Macleod the chieftain, and Boswell, and I, had all single chambers on the first floor. There remained eight rooms only for at least seven-and-thirty lodgers. I suppose they put up temporary beds in the dining room, where they stowed all the young ladies. There was a room above stairs with six beds, in which they put ten men. The rest in my next.

SAM: JOHNSON.

328. To MACLEOD OF MACLEOD

Dear Sir

We are now on the margin of the sea, waiting for a boat and a wind. Boswell grows impatient; but the kind treatment which I find wherever I go, makes me leave, with some heaviness of heart, an island which I am not very likely to see again. Having now gone as far as horses can carry us, we thankfully return them. My steed will, I hope, be received with kindness; he has borne me, heavy as I am, over ground both rough and steep, with great fidelity; and for the use of him, as for your other favours, I hope you will believe me thankful, and willing, at whatever distance we may be placed, to show my sense of your kindness, by any offices of friendship that may fall within my power.

Lady Macleod and the young ladies have, by their hospitality and politeness, made an impression on my mind, which will not easily be effaced. Be pleased to tell them, that I remember them with great tenderness, and great respect.

> I am, Sir,
> Your most obliged
> and most humble servant,
> SAM: JOHNSON.

We passed two days at Talisker very happily, both by the pleasantness of the place and elegance of our reception.

Ostig, Sept. 28, 1773.

329. TO MRS. THRALE

Ostich in Skie, Sept. 30, 1773.

Dearest Madam

I am still confined in Skie. We were unskilful travellers, and imagined that the sea was an open road which we could pass at pleasure; but we have now learned with some pain, that we may still wait for a long time the caprices of the equinoctial winds, and sit reading or writing as I now do, while the tempest is rolling the sea, or roaring in the mountains. I am now no longer pleased with the delay; you can hear from me but seldom, and I cannot at all hear from you. It comes into my mind that some evil may happen, or that I might be of use while I am away. But these thoughts are vain; the wind is violent and adverse, and our boat cannot yet come. I must content myself with writing to you, and hoping that you will sometime receive my letter. Now to my narrative.

Sept. 9th: Having passed the night as is usual, I rose, and found the dining room full of company; we feasted and talked, and when the evening came it brought musick and dancing. Young Macleod, the great proprietor of Skie and head of his clan, was very distinguishable; a young man of nineteen; bred a while at St. Andrews, and afterwards at Oxford; a pupil of G. Strahan. He is a young man of a mind as much advanced as I have ever known; very elegant of manners, and very graceful in his person. He has the full spirit of a feudal chief; and I was very ready to accept his invitation to Dunvegan. All Raarsa's children are beautiful. The ladies, all except the eldest, are in the morning dressed in their hair. The true Highlander never wears more than a riband on her head till she is married.

On the third day Boswell went out with old Malcolm to see a ruined castle, which he found less entire than was promised, but he saw the country. I did not go, for the castle was perhaps ten miles off, and there is no riding at Raarsa, the whole island being rock or mountain, from which the cattle often fall and are destroyed. It is very barren, and maintains, as near as I could collect, about seven hundred inhabitants, perhaps ten to a square mile. In these countries you are not to suppose that you shall find villages or inclosures. The traveller wanders through a naked desart, gratified sometimes, but rarely, with the sight of cows, and now and then finds a heap of loose stones and turf in a cavity between rocks, where a being born with all those powers which education expands, and all those sensations which culture refines, is condemned to shelter itself from the wind and rain. Philosophers there are who try to make themselves believe that this life is happy; but they believe it only while they are saying it, and never yet produced conviction in a single mind; he, whom want of words or images sunk into silence, still thought, as he thought before, that privation of pleasure can never please, and that content is not to be much envied, when it has no other principle than ignorance of good.

This gloomy tranquillity, which some may call fortitude, and others wisdom, was, I believe, for a long time to be very frequently found in these dens

of poverty: every man was content to live like his
neighbours, and never wandering from home, saw no
mode of life preferable to his own, except at the house
of the laird, or the laird's nearest relations, whom he
considered as a superior order of beings, to whose
luxuries or honours he had no pretensions. But the
end of this reverence and submission seems now
approaching; the Highlanders have learned that there
are countries less bleak and barren than their own,
where, instead of working for the laird, every man
may till his own ground, and eat the produce of his
own labour. Great numbers have been induced by
this discovery to go every year for some time past to
America. Macdonald and Macleod of Skie have lost
many tenants and many labourers, but Raarsa has
not yet been forsaken by a single inhabitant.

Rona is yet more rocky and barren than Raarsa,
and though it contains perhaps four thousand acres,
is possessed only by a herd of cattle and the keepers.

I find myself not very able to walk upon the mountains, but one day I went out to see the walls yet
standing of an ancient chapel. In almost every island
the superstitious votaries of the Romish church erected
places of worship, in which the drones of convents or
cathedrals performed the holy offices, but by the
active zeal of Protestant devotion, almost all of them
have sunk into ruin. The chapel at Raarsa is now only
considered as the burying-place of the family, and
I suppose of the whole island.

We would now have gone away and left room for
others to enjoy the pleasures of this little court, but
the wind detained us till the 12th, when, though it
was Sunday, we thought it proper to snatch the
opportunity of a calm day. Raarsa accompanied us
in his six-oared boat, which he said was his coach and
six. It is indeed the vehicle in which the ladies take
the air and pay their visits, but they have taken very
little care for accommodations. There is no way in
or out of the boat for a woman, but by being carried;
and in the boat thus dignified with a pompous name,

there is no seat but an occasional bundle of straw. Thus we left Raarsa; the seat of plenty, civility, and cheerfulness.

We dined at a publick house at Port Re; so called because one of the Scottish kings landed there, in a progress through the western isles. Raarsa paid the reckoning privately. We then got on horseback, and by a short but very tedious journey came to Kingsburgh, at which the same king lodged after he landed. Here I had the honour of saluting the far famed Miss Flora Macdonald, who conducted the Prince, dressed as her maid, through the English forces from the island of Lewes; and, when she came to Skie, dined with the English officers, and left her maid below. She must then have been a very young lady; she is now not old; of a pleasing person, and elegant behaviour. She told me that she thought herself honoured by my visit; and I am sure that whatever regard she bestowed on me was liberally repaid. 'If thou likest her opinions, thou wilt praise her virtue.' She was carried to London, but dismissed without a trial, and came down with Malcolm Macleod, against whom sufficient evidence could not be procured. She and her husband are poor, and are going to try their fortune in America.

Sic rerum volvitur orbis.

At Kingsburgh we were very liberally feasted, and I slept in the bed on which the Prince reposed in his distress; the sheets which he used were never put to any meaner offices, but were wrapped up by the lady of the house, and at last, according to her desire, were laid round her in her grave. These are not Whigs.

On the 13th, travelling partly on horseback where we could not row, and partly on foot where we could not ride, we came to Dunvegan, which I have described already. Here, though poor Macleod had been left by his grandfather overwhelmed with debts, we had another exhibition of feudal hospitality. There were two stags in the house, and venison came to the table every day in its various forms. Macleod, besides his estate in Skie, larger I suppose than some English counties, is proprietor of nine inhabited isles; and of his islands uninhabited I doubt if he very exactly knows the number. I told him that he was a mighty monarch. Such dominions fill an Englishman with envious wonder; but when he surveys the naked mountain, and treads the quaking moor, and wanders over the wild regions of gloomy barrenness, his wonder may continue, but his envy ceases. The unprofitableness of these vast domains can be conceived only by the means of positive instances. The heir of *Col*, an island not far distant, has lately told me how wealthy he should be if he could let *Rum*, another of his islands, for twopence half-penny an acre; and Macleod has an estate, which the surveyor reports to contain eighty thousand acres, rented at six hundred pounds a-year.

While we were at Dunvegan, the wind was high, and the rain violent, so that we were not able to put forth a boat to fish in the sea, or to visit the adjacent islands, which may be seen from the house; but we filled up the time as we could, sometimes by talk, sometimes by reading. I have never wanted books in the isle of Skie.

We were visited one day by the Laird and Lady of Muck, one of the western islands, two miles long, and three quarters of a mile high. He has half his island in his own culture, and upon the other half live one hundred and fifty dependents, who not only live upon the product, but export corn sufficient for the payment of their rent.

Lady Macleod has a son and four daughters; they have lived long in England, and have the language and manners of English ladies. We lived with them very easily. The hospitality of this remote region is like that of the golden age. We have found ourselves treated at every house as if we came to confer a benefit.

We were eight days at Dunvegan, but we took the first opportunity which the weather afforded, after the first days, of going away, and on the 21st, went to Ulinish, where we were well entertained, and wandered a little after curiosities. In the afternoon an interval of calm sunshine courted us out to see a cave on the shore famous for its echo. When we went into the boat, one of our companions was asked in Earse, by the boatmen, who they were that came with him? He gave us characters, I suppose, to our advantage, and was asked, in the spirit of the Highlands, whether I could recite a long series of ancestors? The boatmen said, as I perceived afterwards, that they heard the cry of an English ghost. This, Boswell says, disturbed him. We came to the cave, and clambering up the rocks, came to an arch, open at one end, one hundred and eighty feet long, thirty broad in the broadest part, and about thirty high. There was no echo; such is the fidelity of report; but I saw what I had never seen before, muscles and whilks in their natural state. There was another arch in the rock, open at both ends.

Sept. 23rd: We removed to Talisker, a house occupied by Mr. Macleod, a Lieutenant-Colonel in the Dutch service. Talisker has been long in the possession of gentlemen, and therefore has a garden well cultivated; and, what is here very rare, is shaded by trees: a place where the imagination is more amused cannot easily be found. The mountains about it are of great height, with waterfalls succeeding one another so fast, that as one ceases to be heard another begins. Between the mountains there is a small valley extending to the sea, which is not far off, beating upon a coast very difficult of access.

Two nights before our arrival two boats were driven upon this coast by the tempest; one of them had a pilot that knew the passage, the second followed, but a third missed the true course, and was driven forward with great danger of being forced into the vast ocean, but, however, gained at last some other island. The crews crept to Talisker, almost lifeless with wet, cold, fatigue, and terrour, but the lady took care of them. She is a woman of more than common qualifications;

having travelled with her husband, she speaks four languages.

You find that all the islanders, even in these recesses of life, are not barbarous. One of the ministers who has adhered to us almost all the time is an excellent scholar. We have now with us the young Laird of Col, who is heir, perhaps, to two hundred square miles of land. He has first studied at Aberdeen, and afterwards gone to Hertfordshire to learn agriculture, being much impressed with desire of improvement: he likewise has the notions of a chief, and keeps a piper. At Macleod's the bagpipe always played while we were dining.

Col has undertaken, by the permission of the waves and wind, to carry us about several of the islands, with which he is acquainted enough to shew us whatever curious is given by nature or left by antiquity; but we grew afraid of deviating from our way home, lest we should be shut up for months upon some little protuberance of rock, that just appears above the sea, and perhaps is scarcely marked upon a map.

You remember the Doge of Genoa, who being asked what struck him most at the French court, answered, 'Myself.' I cannot think many things here more likely to affect the fancy than to see Johnson ending his sixty-fourth year in the wilderness of the Hebrides. But now I am here, it will gratify me very little to return without seeing, or doing my best to see what those places afford. I have a desire to instruct myself in the whole system of pastoral life; but I know not whether I shall be able to perfect the idea. However, I have many pictures in my mind, which I could not have had without this journey, and should have passed it with great pleasure had you, and Master, and Queeney been in the party. We should have excited the attention and enlarged the observation of each other, and obtained many pleasing topicks of future conversation. As it is, I travel with my mind too much at home, and perhaps miss many things worthy of observation, or pass them with transient notice;

so that the images, for want of that re-impression which discussion and comparison produce, easily fade away; but I keep a book of remarks, and Boswell writes a regular journal of our travels, which, I think, contains as much of what I say and do as of all other occurrences together; 'for such a faithful chronicler as Griffith.'

I hope, dearest Madam, you are equally careful to reposite proper memorials of all that happens to you and your family, and then when we meet we shall tell our stories. I wish you had gone this summer in your usual splendour to Brighthelmstone.

Mr. Thrale probably wonders how I live all this time without sending to him for money. Travelling in Scotland is dear enough, dearer in proportion to what the country affords than in England, but residence in the isles is unexpensive. Company is, I think, considered as a supply of pleasure, and a relief of that tediousness of life which is felt in every place, elegant or rude. Of wine and punch they are very liberal, for they get them cheap; but as there is no customhouse on the island, they can hardly be considered as smugglers. Their punch is made without lemons, or any substitute.

Their tables are very plentiful; but a very nice man would not be pampered. As they have no meat but as they kill it, they are obliged to live while it lasts upon the same flesh. They kill a sheep, and set mutton boiled and roast on the table together. They have fish both of the sea and of the brooks; but they can hardly conceive that it requires any sauce. To sauce in general they are strangers; now and then butter is melted, but I dare not always take, lest I should offend by disliking it. Barley-broath is a constant dish, and is made well in every house. A stranger, if he is prudent, will secure his share, for it is not certain that he will be able to eat any thing else.

Their meat being often newly killed is very tough, and as nothing is sufficiently subdued by the fire, is not easily to be eaten. Carving is here a very laborious employment, for the knives are never whetted. Table-knives are not of long subsistence in the Highlands; every man, while arms were a regular part of dress, had his knife and fork appendant to his dirk. Knives they now lay upon the table, but the handles are apt to shew that they have been in other hands, and the blades have neither brightness nor edge.

Of silver there is no want; and it will last long, for it is never cleaned. They are a nation just rising from barbarity; long contented with necessaries, now somewhat studious of convenience, but not yet arrived at delicate discriminations. Their linen is, however, both clean and fine. Bread, such as we mean by that name, I have never seen in the isle of Skie. They have ovens, for they bake their pies, but they never ferment their meal, nor mould a loaf. Cakes of oats and barley are brought to the table, but I believe wheat is reserved for strangers. They are commonly too hard for me, and therefore I take potatoes to my meat, and am sure to find them on almost every table.

They retain so much of the pastoral life, that some preparation of milk is commonly one of the dishes both at dinner and supper. Tea is always drunk at the usual times; but in the morning the table is polluted with a plate of slices of strong cheese. This is peculiar to the Highlands; at Edinburgh there are always honey and sweet-meats on the morning tea-table.

Strong liquors they seem to love. Every man, perhaps woman, begins the day with a dram; and the punch is made both at dinner and supper.

They have neither wood nor coal for fuel, but burn peat or turf in their chimnies. It is dug out of the moors or mosses, and makes a strong and lasting fire, not always very sweet, and somewhat apt to smoke the pot.

The houses of inferior gentlemen are very small, and every room serves many purposes. In the bed-rooms, perhaps, are laid up stores of different kinds; and the parlour of the day is a bed-room at night. In the room which I inhabited last, about fourteen feet square, there were three chests of drawers, a long chest for larger clothes, two closet cupboards, and the bed. Their rooms are commonly dirty, of which they seem to have little sensibility, and if they had more, clean floors would be difficultly kept, where the first step from the door is into the dirt. They are very much inclined to carpets, and seldom fail to lay down something under their feet, better or worse as they happen to be furnished.

The Highland dress, being forbidden by law, is very little used; sometimes it may be seen, but the English traveller is struck with nothing so much as the *nudité des pieds* of the common people.

Skie is the greatest island, or the greatest but one, among the Hebrides. Of the soil I have already given some account, it is generally barren, but some spots are not wholly unfruitful. The gardens have apples and pears, cherries, strawberries, raspberries, currants, and gooseberries, but all the fruit that I have seen is small. They attempt to sow nothing but oats and barley. Oats constitute the bread corn of the place. Their harvest is about the beginning of October; and being so late, is very much subject to disappointments from the rains that follow the equinox. This year has been particularly disastrous. Their rainy season lasts from Autumn to Spring. They have seldom very hard frosts; nor was it ever known that a lake was covered with ice strong enough to bear a skater. The sea round them is always open. The snow falls but soon melts; only in 1771, they had a cold Spring in which the island was so long covered with it, that many beasts, both wild and domestick, perished, and the whole country was reduced to distress, from which I know not if it is even yet recovered.

The animals here are not remarkably small; perhaps they recruit their breed from the main land. The cows are sometimes without horns. The horned and unhorned cattle are not accidental variations, but different species, they will however breed together.

October 3d: The wind is now changed, and if we

snatch the moment of opportunity, an escape from this island is become practicable ; I have no reason to complain of my reception, yet I long to be again at home.

You and my master may perhaps expect, after this description of Skie, some account of myself. My eye is, I am afraid, not fully recovered ; my ears are not mended ; my nerves seem to grow weaker, and I have been otherwise not as well as I sometimes am, but think myself lately better. This climate perhaps is not within my degree of healthy latitude.

Thus I have given my most honoured mistress the story of me and my little ramble. We are now going to some other isle, to what we know not, the wind will tell us.

I am, &c.,
SAM: JOHNSON.

Compliments to Queeney, and Jack, and Lucy, and all.

332. To MRS. THRALE

Honoured Mistress   Inverary, Oct. 23, 1773.

My last letters to you and my dear master were written from Mull, the third island of the Hebrides in extent. There is no post, and I took the opportunity of a gentleman's passage to the main land.

In Mull we were confined two days by the weather ; on the third we got on horse-back, and after a journey difficult and tedious, over rocks naked and valleys untracked, through a country of barrenness and solitude, we came, almost in the dark, to the sea side, weary and dejected, having met with nothing but water falling from the mountains that could raise any image of delight. Our company was the young Laird of Col and his servant. Col made every Maclean open his house where we came, and supply us with horses when we departed ; but the horses of this country are small, and I was not mounted to my wish.

At the sea side we found the ferry-boat departed ;

if it had been where it was expected, the wind was against us, and the hour was late, nor was it very desirable to cross the sea in darkness with a small boat. The captain of a sloop that had been driven thither by the storms, saw our distress, and as we were hesitating and deliberating, sent his boat, which, by Col's order, transported us to the isle of Ulva. We were introduced to Mr. Macquarry, the head of a small clan, whose ancestors have reigned in Ulva beyond memory, but who has reduced himself, by his negligence and folly, to the necessity of selling this venerable patrimony.

On the next morning we passed the strait to Inch Kenneth, an island about a mile in length, and less than half a mile broad; in which Kenneth, a Scottish saint, established a small clerical college, of which the chapel walls are still standing. At this place I beheld a scene which I wish you and my master and Queeney had partaken.

The only family on the island is that of Sir Allan, the chief of the ancient and numerous clan of Maclean; the clan which claims the second place, yielding only to Macdonald in the line of battle. Sir Allan, a chieftain, a baronet, and a soldier, inhabits in this insulated desart a thatched hut with no chambers. Young Col, who owns him as his chief, and whose cousin was his lady, had, I believe, given him some notice of our visit; he received us with the soldier's frankness and the gentleman's elegance, and introduced us to his daughters, two young ladies who have not wanted education suitable to their birth, and who, in their cottage, neither forgot their dignity, nor affected to remember it. Do not you wish to have been with us?

Sir Allan's affairs are in disorder by the fault of his ancestors, and while he forms some scheme for retrieving them, he has retreated hither.

When our salutations were over, he showed us the island. We walked uncovered into the chapel, and saw in the reverend ruin the effects of precipitate reformation. The floor is covered with ancient gravestones, of which the inscriptions are not now legible; and without some of the chief families still continue the right of sepulture. The altar is not yet quite demolished; beside it, on the right side, is a bas-relief of the Virgin with her child, and an angel hovering over her. On the other side still stands a handbell, which, though it has no clapper, neither Presbyterian bigotry nor barbarian wantonness has yet taken away. The chapel is thirty-eight feet long, and eighteen broad. Boswell, who is very pious, went into it at night to perform his devotions, but came back in haste, for fear of spectres. Near the chapel is a fountain, to which the water, remarkably pure, is conveyed from a distant hill, through pipes laid by the Romish clergy, which still perform the office of conveyance, though they have never been repaired since Popery was suppressed.

We soon after went in to dinner, and wanted neither the comforts nor the elegancies of life. There were several dishes, and variety of liquours. The servants live in another cottage; in which, I suppose, the meat is dressed.

Towards evening, Sir Allan told us that Sunday never passed over him like another day. One of the ladies read, and read very well, the evening service;— and Paradise was opened in the wild.

Next day, 18th, we went and wandered among the rocks on the shore, while the boat was busy in catching oysters, of which there is a great bed. Oysters lie upon the sand, one I think sticking to another, and cockles are found a few inches under the sand.

We then went in the boat to Sondiland, a little island very near. We found it a wild rock, of about ten acres; part naked, part covered with sand, out of which we picked shells; and part clothed with a thin layer of mould, on the grass of which a few sheep are sometimes fed. We then came back and dined. I passed part of the afternoon in reading, and in the evening one of the ladies played on her harpsichord, and Boswell and Col danced a reel with the other.

1773 (aetat. 64)

On the 19th, we persuaded Sir Allan to launch his boat again, and go with us to Icolmkill, where the first great preacher of Christianity to the Scots built a church, and settled a monastery. In our way we stopped to examine a very uncommon cave on the coast of Mull. We had some difficulty to make our way over the vast masses of broken rocks that lie before the entrance, and at the mouth were embarrassed with stones, which the sea had accumulated, as at Brighthelmstone; but as we advanced, we reached a floor of soft sand, and as we left the light behind us, walked along a very spacious cavity, vaulted over head with an arch almost regular, by which a mountain was sustained, at least a very lofty rock. From this magnificent cavern went a narrow passage to the right hand, which we entered with a candle, and though it was obstructed with great stones, clambered over them to a second expansion of the cave, in which there lies a great square stone, which might serve as a table. The air here was very warm, but not oppressive, and the flame of the candle continued pyramidal. The cave goes onward to an unknown extent, but we were now one hundred and sixty yards under ground; we had but one candle, and had never heard of any that went further and came back; we therefore thought it prudent to return.

Going forward in our boat, we came to a cluster of rocks, black and horrid, which Sir Allan chose for the place where he would eat his dinner. We climbed till we got seats. The stores were opened, and the repast taken.

We then entered the boat again; the night came upon us; the wind rose; the sea swelled; and Boswell desired to be set on dry ground: we, however, pursued our navigation, and passed by several little islands, in the silent solemnity of faint moonshine, seeing little, and hearing only the wind and the water. At last we reached the island; the venerable seat of ancient sanctity; where secret piety reposed, and where fallen greatness was reposited. The island has no house of entertainment, and we manfully made our bed in a farmer's barn. The description I hope to give you another time.

I am, &c.,
Sam: Johnson.

348. To James Boswell

Dear Sir

Dr. Webster's informations[1] were much less exact and much less determinate than I expected: they are, indeed, much less positive than, if he can trust his own book which he laid before me, he is able to give. But I believe it will always be found, that he who calls much for information will advance his work but slowly.

I am, however, obliged to you, dear Sir, for your endeavours to help me, and hope, that between us something will some time be done, if not on this, on some occasion.

Chambers is either married, or almost married, to Miss Wilton, a girl of sixteen, exquisitely beautiful, whom he has, with his lawyer's tongue, persuaded to take her chance with him in the East.

We have added to the club, Charles Fox, Sir Charles Bunbury, Dr. Fordyce, and Mr. Steevens.

Return my thanks to Dr. Webster. Tell Dr. Robertson I have not much to reply to his censure of my negligence; and tell Dr. Blair, that since he has written hither what I said to him, we must now consider ourselves as even, forgive one another, and begin again. I care not how soon, for he is a very pleasing man. Pay my compliments to all my friends, and remind Lord Elibank of his promise to give me all his works.

I hope Mrs. Boswell and little Miss are well.—When shall I see them again? She is a sweet lady, only she was so glad to see me go, that I have almost a mind to come again, that she may again have the same pleasure.

Enquire if it be practicable to send a small present of

[1] [About the Hebrides.]

a cask of porter to Dunvegan, Rasay, and Col. I would not wish to be thought forgetful of civilities.

I am, Sir, your humble servant,
March 5, 1774. SAM: JOHNSON.

352. To JAMES BOSWELL

Dear Sir [*Not dated, but written about the* 15*th of March,* 1774.]

I am ashamed to think that since I received your letter I have passed so many days without answering it.

I think there is no great difficulty in resolving your doubts. The reasons for which you are inclined to visit London, are, I think, not of sufficient strength to answer the objections. That you should delight to come once a year to the fountain of intelligence and pleasure, is very natural; but both information and pleasure must be regulated by propriety. Pleasure, which cannot be obtained but by unseasonable or unsuitable expence, must always end in pain; and pleasure, which must be enjoyed at the expence of another's pain, can never be such as a worthy mind can fully delight in.

What improvement you might gain by coming to London, you may easily supply, or easily compensate, by enjoining yourself some particular study at home, or opening some new avenue to information. Edinburgh is not yet exhausted; and I am sure you will find no pleasure here which can deserve either that you should anticipate any part of your future fortune, or that you should condemn yourself and your lady to penurious frugality for the rest of the year.

I need not tell you what regard you owe to Mrs. Boswell's entreaties; or how much you ought to study the happiness of her who studies yours with so much diligence, and of whose kindness you enjoy such good effects. Life cannot subsist in society but by reciprocal concessions. She permitted you to ramble last year, you must permit her now to keep you at home.

Your last reason is so serious, that I am unwilling to oppose it. Yet you must remember, that your image of worshipping once a year in a certain place, in imitation of the Jews, is but a comparison; and *simile non est idem*; if the annual resort to Jerusalem was a duty to the Jews, it was a duty because it was commanded; and you have no such command, therefore no such duty. It may be dangerous to receive too readily, and indulge too fondly, opinions, from which, perhaps, no pious mind is wholly disengaged, of local sanctity and local devotion. You know what strange effects they have produced over a great part of the Christian world. I am now writing, and you, when you read this, are reading under the Eye of Omnipresence.

To what degree fancy is to be admitted into religious offices, it would require much deliberation to determine. I am far from intending totally to exclude it. Fancy is a faculty bestowed by our Creator, and it is reasonable that all His gifts should be used to His glory, that all our faculties should co-operate in His worship; but they are to co-operate according to the will of Him that gave them, according to the order which His wisdom has established. As ceremonies prudential or convenient are less obligatory than positive ordinances, as bodily worship is only the token to others or ourselves of mental adoration, so Fancy is always to act in subordination to Reason. We may take Fancy for a companion, but must follow Reason as our guide. We may allow Fancy to suggest certain ideas in certain places; but Reason must always be heard, when she tells us, that those ideas and those places have no natural or necessary relation. When we enter a church we habitually recall to mind the duty of adoration, but we must not omit adoration for want of a temple; because we know, and ought to remember, that the Universal Lord is every where present; and that, therefore, to come to Jona, or to Jerusalem, though it may be useful, cannot be necessary.

Thus I have answered your letter, and have not

answered it negligently. I love you too well to be careless when you are serious.

I think I shall be very diligent next week about our travels, which I have too long neglected.

I am, dear Sir, your most, &c.,
SAM: JOHNSON.

Compliments to Madam and Miss.

353. TO WARREN HASTINGS

Sir

Though I have had but little personal knowledge of you, I have had enough to make me wish for more; and though it be now a long time since I was honoured by your visit, I had too much pleasure from it to forget it. By those whom we delight to remember, we are unwilling to be forgotten; and therefore I cannot omit this opportunity of reviving myself in your memory by a letter which you will receive from the hands of my friend Mr. Chambers;[1] a man, whose purity of manners and vigour of mind are sufficient to make every thing welcome that he brings.

That this is my only reason for writing, will be too apparent by the uselessness of my letter to any other purpose. I have no questions to ask; not that I want curiosity after either the ancient or present state of regions in which have been seen all the power and splendour of wide-extended empire; and which, as by some grant of natural superiority, supply the rest of the world with almost all that pride desires and luxury enjoys. But my knowledge of them is too scanty to furnish me with proper topicks of inquiry; I can only wish for information; and hope, that a mind comprehensive like yours will find leisure, amidst the cares of your important station, to inquire into many subjects of which the European world either thinks not at all, or thinks with deficient intelligence and uncertain conjecture. I shall hope, that he who once intended

[1] Afterwards Sir Robert Chambers, one of his Majesty's Judges in India. BOSWELL.

to increase the learning of his country by the introduction of the Persian language, will examine nicely the traditions and histories of the East; that he will survey the wonders of its ancient edifices, and trace the vestiges of its ruined cities; and that, at his return, we shall know the arts and opinions of a race of men, from whom very little has been hitherto derived.

You, Sir, have no need of being told by me, how much may be added by your attention and patronage to experimental knowledge and natural history. There are arts of manufacture practised in the countries in which you preside, which are yet very imperfectly known here, either to artificers or philosophers. Of the natural productions, animate and inanimate, we yet have so little intelligence, that our books are filled, I fear, with conjectures about things which an Indian peasant knows by his senses.

Many of those things my first wish is to see; my second to know, by such accounts as a man like you will be able to give.

As I have not skill to ask proper questions, I have likewise no such access to great men as can enable me to send you any political information. Of the agitations of an unsettled government, and the struggles of a feeble ministry, care is doubtless taken to give you more exact accounts than I can obtain. If you are inclined to interest yourself much in publick transactions, it is no misfortune to you to be so distant from them.

That literature is not totally forsaking us, and that your favourite language is not neglected, will appear from the book,[1] which I should have pleased myself more with sending, if I could have presented it bound: but time was wanting. I beg, however, Sir, that you will accept it from a man very desirous of your regard; and that if you think me able to gratify you by any thing more important you will employ me.

I am now going to take leave, perhaps a very long leave, of my dear Mr. Chambers. That he is going to live where you govern, may justly alleviate the regret

[1] Jones's *Persian Grammar.* BOSWELL.

1774 (aetat. 64)

of parting; and the hope of seeing both him and you again, which I am not willing to mingle with doubt, must at present comfort as it can,

     Sir, your most humble servant,
March 30, 1774.   Sam: Johnson.

358. To Bennet Langton

Dear Sir

You have reason to reproach me that I have left your last letter so long unanswered, but I had nothing particular to say. Chambers, you find, is gone far, and poor Goldsmith is gone much further. He died of a fever, exasperated, as I believe, by the fear of distress. He had raised money and squandered it, by every artifice of acquisition, and folly of expence. But let not his frailties be remembered; he was a very great man.

I have just begun to print my *Journey to the Hebrides*, and am leaving the press to take another journey into Wales, whither Mr. Thrale is going, to take possession of, at least, five hundred a year, fallen to his lady. All at Streatham, that are alive, are well.

I have never recovered from the last dreadful illness, but flatter myself that I grow gradually better; much, however, yet remains to mend. Κυριε ελέησον.[1]

If you have the Latin version of *Busy, curious, thirsty fly*, be so kind as to transcribe and send it; but you need not be in haste, for I shall be I know not where, for at least five weeks. I wrote the following tetrastick on poor Goldsmith :—

Τὸν τάφον εἰσοράας τὸν Ὀλιβάροιο. κονίην
Ἄφροσι μὴ σεμνὴν, Ξεῖνε, πόδεσσι πάτει·
Οἷσι μέμηλε φύσις, μέτρων χάρις, ἔργα παλαιῶν,
Κλαίετε ποιητὴν, ἱστορικὸν, φυσικόν.

Please to make my most respectful compliments to all the ladies, and remember me to young George and his sisters. I reckon George begins to shew a pair of heels.

[1] [*Lord have mercy.* For the epitaph see p. 267.]

Do not be sullen now, but let me find a letter when I come back.

> I am, dear Sir,
> your affectionate, humble servant,
July 5, 1774. SAM: JOHNSON.

362. To JAMES BOSWELL

Dear Sir

There has appeared lately in the papers an account of a boat overset between Mull and Ulva, in which many passengers were lost, and among them Maclean of Col. We, you know, were once drowned;[1] I hope, therefore, that the story is either wantonly or erroneously told. Pray satisfy me by the next post.

I have printed two hundred and forty pages. I am able to do nothing much worth doing to dear Lord Hailes's book. I will, however, send back the sheets; and hope, by degrees, to answer all your reasonable expectations.

Mr. Thrale has happily surmounted a very violent and acrimonious opposition; but all joys have their abatement: Mrs. Thrale has fallen from her horse, and hurt herself very much. The rest of our friends, I believe, are well. My compliments to Mrs. Boswell.

> I am, Sir, your most affectionate servant,
London, Octob. 27, 1774. SAM: JOHNSON.

364. To WILLIAM STRAHAN

Sir

I waited on you this morning having forgotten your new engagement; for this you must not reproach me, for if I had looked upon your present station[2] with malignity I could not have forgotten it.

I came to consult you upon a little matter that gives me some uneasiness. In one of the pages there is

[1] In the news-papers. BOSWELL.
[2] [He had been elected Member for Malmesbury.]

a severe censure of the clergy of an English Cathedral[1] which I am afraid is just, but I have since recollected that from me it may be thought improper, for the Dean did me a kindness about forty years ago. He is now very old, and I am not young. Reproach can do him no good, and in myself I know not whether it is zeal or wantonness.

Can a leaf be cancelled without too much trouble ? tell me what I shall do. I have no settled choice, but I would not refuse to allow the charge. To cancel it seems the surer side. Determine for me.

    I am, Sir, Your most humble servant,
Nov. 30, 1774.   SAM: JOHNSON.

Tell me your mind : if you will cancel it I will write something to fill up the vacuum. Please to direct to the borough.

373

Mr. James Macpherson

I received your foolish and impudent note. Whatever insult is offered me I will do my best to repel; and what I cannot do for myself, the law will do for me. I will not desist from detecting what I think a cheat, from any fear of the menaces of a ruffian.

You want me to retract. What shall I retract ? I thought your book an imposture from the beginning ; I think it upon yet surer reasons an imposture still. For this opinion I give the publick my reasons, which I here dare you to refute. But however I may despise you, I reverence truth, and if you can prove the genuineness of the work I will confess it. Your rage I defy. Your abilities, since your Homer, are not so

---

[1] [The reference is to p. 48 of the first edition of *A Journey to the Western Islands*, in which, in its uncancelled state, Johnson had described the Dean and Chapter (of Lichfield) as 'longing to melt the lead of an English Cathedral. What they shall melt, it were just that they should swallow'. This leaf was cancelled, and a harmless generalization substituted.]

formidable; and what I hear of your morals, inclines me to pay regard not to what you shall say, but to what you shall prove. You may print this if you will.

SAM: JOHNSON.

378. TO JAMES BOSWELL, ESQ.

My Dear Boswell

I am surprized that, knowing as you do the disposition of your countrymen to tell lies in favour of each other,[1] you can be at all affected by any reports that circulate among them. Macpherson never in his life offered me a sight of any original or of any evidence of any kind; but thought only of intimidating me by noise and threats, till my last answer,—that I would not be deterred from detecting what I thought a cheat, by the menaces of a ruffian—put an end to our correspondence.

The state of the question is this. He, and Dr. Blair, whom I consider as deceived, say, that he copied the poem from old manuscripts. His copies, if he had them, and I believe him to have none, are nothing. Where are the manuscripts? They can be shewn if they exist, but they were never shewn. *De non existentibus et non apparentibus*, says our law, *eadem est ratio*. No man has a claim to credit upon his own word, when better evidence, if he had it, may be easily produced. But, so far as we can find, the Erse language was never written till very lately for the purposes of religion. A nation that cannot write, or a language that was never written, has no manuscripts.

But whatever he has he never offered to show. If old manuscripts should now be mentioned, I should, unless there were more evidence than can be easily had, suppose them another proof of Scotch conspiracy in national falsehood.

[1] My friend has, in this letter, relied upon my testimony, with a confidence, of which the ground has escaped my recollection. BOSWELL.

Do not censure the expression; you know it to be true.

Dr. Memis's question is so narrow as to allow no speculation; and I have no facts before me but those which his advocate has produced against you.

I consulted this morning the President of the London College of Physicians, who says, that with us, *Doctor of Physick* (we do not say *Doctor of Medicine*) is the highest title that a practicer of physick can have; that *Doctor* implies not only *Physician*, but teacher of physick; that every *Doctor* is legally a *Physician*; but no man, not a *Doctor*, can *practice physick* but by *licence* particularly granted. The Doctorate is a licence of itself. It seems to us a very slender cause of prosecution. . . .

I am now engaged, but in a little time I hope to do all you would have. My compliments to Madam and Veronica.

   I am, Sir, your most humble servant,
February 7, 1775.   SAM: JOHNSON.

380. To JAMES BOSWELL

Dear Sir

I am sorry that I could get no books for my friends in Scotland. Mr. Strahan has at last promised to send two dozen to you. If they come, put the names of my friends into them; you may cut them out,[1] and paste them with a little starch in the book.

You then are going wild about Ossian. Why do you think any part can be proved? The dusky manuscript of Egg is probably not fifty years old; if it be an hundred, it proves nothing. The tale of Clanranald has no proof. Has Clanranald told it? Can he prove it? There are, I believe, no Erse manuscripts. None of the old families had a single letter in Erse that we heard of. You say it is likely that they could write. The learned, if any learned there were, could;

---

[1] From a list in his hand-writing. BOSWELL.

but knowing by that learning, some written language, in that language they wrote, as letters had never been applied to their own. If there are manuscripts, let them be shewn, with some proof that they are not forged for the occasion. You say many can remember parts of Ossian. I believe all those parts are versions of the English; at least there is no proof of their antiquity.

Macpherson is said to have made some translations himself; and having taught a boy to write it, ordered him to say that he had learnt it of his grandmother. The boy, when he grew up, told the story. This Mrs. Williams heard at Mr. Strahan's table. Don't be credulous; you know how little a Highlander can be trusted. Macpherson is, so far as I know, very quiet. Is not that proof enough? Every thing is against him. No visible manuscript; no inscription in the language: no correspondence among friends: no transaction of business, of which a single scrap remains in the ancient families. Macpherson's pretence is, that the character was Saxon. If he had not talked unskilfully of *manuscripts*, he might have fought with oral tradition much longer. As to Mr. Grant's information, I suppose he knows much less of the matter than ourselves.

In the mean time, the bookseller says that the sale[1] is sufficiently quick. They printed four thousand. Correct your copy wherever it is wrong, and bring it up. Your friends will all be glad to see you. I think of going myself into the country about May.

I am sorry that I have not managed to send the book sooner. I have left four for you, and do not restrict you absolutely to follow my directions in the distribution. You must use your own discretion.

Make my compliments to Mrs. Boswell: I suppose she is now just beginning to forgive me.

    I am, dear Sir, your humble servant,
Feb. 25, 1775.   SAM: JOHNSON.

Of his *Journey to the Western Islands of Scotland*. BOSWELL.

386. To Mrs. Thrale

[Johnson's Court, London], April 1, 1775.

Madam

I had mistaken the day on which I was to dine with Mr. Bruce, and hear of Abissinia, and therefore am to dine this day with Mr. Hamilton.

The news from Oxford is, that no tennis-court can be hired at any price; and that the Vice-Chancellor will not write to the Clarendon trustees without some previous intimation that his request will not be unacceptable. We must therefore find some way of applying to Lord Mansfield, who with the Archbishop of York and the Bishop of Chester holds the trust. Thus are we thrown to a vexatious distance. Poor Carter! do not tell him.

The other Oxford news is, that they have sent me a degree of Doctor of Laws, with such praises in the diploma as, perhaps, ought to make me ashamed; they are very like your praises. I wonder whether I shall ever shew them to you.

Boswel will be with you. Please to ask Murphy the way to Lord Mansfield. Dr. Wetherell, who is now here, and will be here for some days, is very desirous of seeing the brewhouse; I hope Mr. Thrale will send him an invitation. He does what he can for Carter.

To-day I dine with Hamilton; to-morrow with Hoole; on Monday with Paradise; on Tuesday with master and mistress; on Wednesday with Dilly; but come back to the Tower.

Sic nunquam rediturus labitur annus.

I am, Madam,
Your most humble servant,
Sam: Johnson.

Poor Mrs. Williams is very bad, worse than I ever saw her.

390. To Mrs. Thrale

May 12, 1775.

And so, my dearest Mistress, you lie a bed hatching suspicions. I did not mean to reproach you, nor meant any thing but respect, and impatience to know how you did.

I wish I could say or send any thing to divert you; but I have done nothing and seen nothing. I dined one day with Paoli, and yesterday with Mrs. Southwell, and called on Congreve. Mr. Twiss, hearing that you talked of despoiling his book of the fine print, has sent you a copy to frame. He is going to Ireland, and I have given him letters to Dr. Leland and Mr. Falkner.

Mr. M—— is so ill that the Lady is not visible; but yesterday I had I know not how much kiss of Mrs. Abington, and very good looks from Miss * * * the maid of honour.

Boswell has made me promise not to go to Oxford till he leaves London; I had no great reason for haste, and therefore might as well gratify a friend. I am always proud and pleased to have my company desired. Boswell would have thought my absence a loss, and I knew not who else would have considered my presence as profit. He has entered himself at the Temple, and I joined in his bond. He is to plead before the Lords, and hopes very nearly to gain the cost of his journey. He lives much with his friend Paoli, who says, a man must see Wales to enjoy England.

The book which is now most read, but which, as far as I have gone, is but dull, is Gray's letters, prefixed by Mr. Mason to his poems. I have borrowed mine, and therefore cannot lend it, and I can hardly recommend the purchase.

I have offended; and, what is stranger, have justly offended the nation of Rasay. If they could come hither, they would be as fierce as the Americans. Rasay has written to Boswell an account of the injury done him, by representing his house as subordinate to that of Dunvegan. Boswell has his letter, and I believe copied my answer. I have appeased him, if a degraded chief can possibly be appeased; but it will be thirteen days, days of resentment and discontent, before my recantation can reach him. Many a dirk will imagination, during that interval, fix in my heart. I really question if at this time my life would not be in danger, if distance did not secure it.

Boswell will find his way to Streatham before he goes, and will detail this great affair. I would have come on Saturday, but that I am engaged to do Dr. Lawrence a little service on Sunday. Which day shall I come next week? I hope you will be well enough to see me often.

I am, dearest Madam,
Your, &c.,
SAM: JOHNSON.

398. To JAMES BOSWELL

Dear Sir

I make no doubt but you are now safely lodged in your own habitation, and have told all your adventures to Mrs. Boswell and Miss Veronica. Pray teach Veronica to love me. Bid her not mind mamma.[1]

Mrs. Thrale has taken cold, and been very much disordered, but I hope is grown well. Mr. Langton went yesterday to Lincolnshire, and has invited Nicolaida [2] to follow him. Beauclerk talks of going to Bath. I am to set out on Monday; so there is nothing but dispersion.

I have returned Lord Hailes's entertaining sheets, but must stay till I come back for more, because it will be inconvenient to send them after me in my vagrant state.

I promised Mrs. Macaulay [3] that I would try to serve

[1] [See No. 348.]

[2] A learned Greek. BOSWELL.

[3] Wife of the Rev. Mr. Kenneth Macaulay, authour of *The History of St. Kilda*. BOSWELL.

her son at Oxford. I have not forgotten it, nor am
unwilling to perform it. If they desire to give him an
English education, it should be considered whether
they cannot send him for a year or two to an English
school. If he comes immediately from Scotland, he
can make no figure in our Universities. The schools
in the north, I believe, are cheap; and, when I was
a young man, were eminently good.

There are two little books published by the Foulis,
Telemachus and Collins's *Poems*, each a shilling: I
would be glad to have them.

Make my compliments to Mrs. Boswell, though she
does not love me. You see what perverse things ladies
are, and how little fit to be trusted with feudal estates.
When she mends and loves me, there may be more hope
of her daughters.

I will not send compliments to my friends by name,
because I would be loath to leave any out in the enu-
meration. Tell them, as you see them, how well
I speak of Scotch politeness, and Scotch hospitality,
and Scotch beauty, and of every thing Scotch, but
Scotch oat-cakes, and Scotch prejudices.

Let me know the answer of Rasay, and the decision
relating to Sir Allan.[1]

I am, my dearest Sir, with great affection, your
  most obliged, and most humble servant,
May 27, 1775.   SAM: JOHNSON.

408. To MRS. THRALE

Dear Madam   Lichfield, June 19, 1775.

I hope it is very true that Ralph mends, and wish
you were gone to see him, that you might come back
again.

Queeney revenges her long task upon Mr. Baretti's
hen, who must sit on duck eggs a week longer than on

[1] A law-suit carried on by Sir Allan Maclean, Chief
of his Clan, to recover certain parts of his family estates
from the Duke of Argyle. BOSWELL.

her own. I hope she takes great care of my hen, and the Guinea hen, and her pretty little brood.

I was afraid Mawbey would succeed, and have little hope from the scrutiny. Did you ever know a scrutiny change the account ?

Miss A—— does not run after me, but I do not want her, here are other ladies.

Invenies alium, si te hic fastidit Alexis.[1]

Miss * * * * grows old, and Miss Vyse has been ill, but I believe she came to me as soon as she got out. And I can always go to Stowhill. So never grieve about me. Only flatulencies are come again.

Your dissertation upon Queeney is very deep. I know not what to say to the chief question. Nature probably has some part in human characters, and accident has some part; which has most we will try to settle when we meet.

Small letters will undoubtedly gain room for more words, but words are useless if they cannot be read. The lines need not all be kept distinct, and some words I shall wish to leave out, though very few. It must be revised before it is engraved. I always told you that Mr. Thrale was a man, take him for all in all, you ne'er will look upon his like ; but you never mind him nor me, till time forces conviction into your steely bosom. You will, perhaps, find all right about the house and the windows.

Pray always suppose that I send my respects to Master, and Queeney, and Harry, and Susey, and Sophy.

Poor Lucy mends very slowly, but she is very good-humoured, while I do just as she would have me.

Lady Smith has got a new post-chaise, which is not nothing to talk on at Lichfield. Little things here serve for conversation. Mrs. Aston's parrot pecked my leg, and I heard of it some time after at Mrs. Cobb's.

———We deal in nicer things
Than routing armies and dethroning kings.

[1] And find an easier love though not so fair.
    Dryden's Virgil.

A week ago Mrs. Cobb gave me sweetmeats to breakfast, and I heard of it last night at Stowhill.

If you are for small talk :

——Come on, and do the best you can,
I fear not you, nor yet a better man.

I could tell you about Lucy's two cats, and Brill her brother's old dog, who is gone deaf; but the day would fail me. *Suadentque cadentia sidera somnum.*[1] So said Æneas. But I have not yet had my dinner. I have begun early, for what would become of the nation if a letter of this importance should miss the post ? Pray write to, dearest Madam,

Your, &c.,
SAM : JOHNSON.

410. TO MRS. THRALE

Dear Madam June 23, 1775.

So now you have been at the regatta, for I hope you got tickets somewhere, else you wanted me, and I shall not be sorry, because you fancy you can do so well without me ; but however I hope you got tickets, and were dressed fine and fanciful, and made a fine part of the fine show, and heard musick, and said good things, and staid on the water four hours after midnight, and came well home, and slept, and dreamed of the regatta, and waked, and found yourself in bed, and thought now it is all over, only I must write about it to Lichfield.

We make a hard shift here to live on without a regatta. The cherries are ripe at Stowhill, and the currants are ripening, and the ladies are very kind to me. I wish, however, you would go to Surry, and come back, though I think it wiser to stay till the improvement in Ralph may become perceptible, else you will be apt to judge by your wishes and your imagination.

---

[1] *somnos.* Virgil, *Æneid*, ii. 'The setting stars to kindly rest invite.' Dryden's Virgil.

Let us in the mean time hope the best. Let me but know when you go, and when you come back again.

If you or Mr. Thrale would write to Dr. Wetherell about Mr. Carter, it will please Wetherell, and keep the business in motion. They know not otherwise how to communicate news if they have it.

As to my hopes and my wishes, I can keep them to myself. They will perhaps grow less if they are laughed at. I needed not tell them, but that I have little else to write, and I needed not write, but that I do not like to be without hearing from you, because I love the Thrales and the Thralites.

I am, &c.,
Sam: Johnson.

414. To Mrs. Thrale

[Ashbourne, July 1775.]

Now, thinks my dearest Mistress to herself, sure I am at last gone too far to be pestered every post with a letter : he knows that people go into the country to be at quiet ; he knows too that when I have once told the story of Ralph, the place where I am affords me nothing that I shall delight to tell, or he will wish to be told ; he knows how troublesome it is to write letters about nothing ; and he knows that he does not love trouble himself, and therefore ought not to force it upon others.

But, dearest Lady, you may see once more how little knowledge influences practice, notwithstanding all this knowledge, you see, here is a letter.

Every body says the prospect of harvest is uncommonly delightful; but this has been so long the Summer talk, and has been so often contradicted by Autumn, that I do not suffer it to lay much hold on my mind. Our gay prospects have now for many years together ended in melancholy retrospects. Yet I am of opinion that there is much corn upon the ground. Every dear year encourages the farmer to sow more and more, and favourable seasons will be sent at last. Let us hope that they will be sent now.

The Doctor and Frank are gone to see the hay. It was cut on Saturday, and yesterday was well wetted; but to day has its fill of sunshine. I hope the hay at Streatham was plentiful, and had good weather.

Our lawn is as you left it, only the pool is so full of mud that the water-fowl have left it. Here are many calves, who, I suppose, all expect to be great bulls and cows.

Yesterday I saw Mrs. Diot at church, and shall drink tea with her some afternoon.

I cannot get free from this vexatious flatulence, and therefore have troublesome nights, but otherwise I am not very ill. Now and then a fit, and not violent. I am not afraid of the waterfall. I now and then take physick; and suspect that you were not quite right in omitting to let blood before I came away. But I do not intend to do it here.

You will now find the advantage of having made one at the regatta. You will carry with you the importance of a publick personage, and enjoy a superiority which, having been only local and accidental, will not be regarded with malignity. You have a subject by which you can gratify general curiosity, and amuse your company without bewildering them. You can keep the vocal machine in motion, without those seeming paradoxes that are sure to disgust; without that temerity of censure which is sure to provoke enemies; and that exuberance of flattery which experience has found to make no friends. It is the good of publick life that it supplies agreeable topicks and general conversation. Therefore wherever you are, and whatever you see, talk not of the Punick war; nor of the depravity of human nature; nor of the slender motives of human actions; nor of the difficulty of finding employment or pleasure; but talk, and talk, and talk of the regatta, and keep the rest for, dearest Madam,

      Your, &c.,
        SAM: JOHNSON.

415. To Mrs. Thrale

Dear Madam   Ashbourne, July 6, 1775.

Dr. Taylor says he shall be very glad to see you all here again, if you have a mind of retirement. But I told him that he must not expect you this summer; and he wants to know why?

I am glad you have read Boswell's journal, because it is something for us to talk about, and that you have seen the Hornecks,[1] because that is a publick theme. I would have you see, and read, and hear, and talk it all, as occasion offers.

Pray thank Queeney for her letter. I still hope good of poor Ralph; but sure never poor rogue was so troubled with his teeth. I hope occasional bathing, and keeping him about two minutes with his body immersed, may promote the discharge from his head, and set his little brain at liberty. Pray give my service to my dear friend Harry, and tell him that Mr. Murphy does not love him better than I do.

I am inclined to be of Mr. Thrale's mind about the changes in the state. A dissolution of the Parliament would, in my opinion, be little less than a dissolution of the government, by the encouragement which it would give to every future faction to disturb the publick tranquillity. Who would ever want places and power if perseverance in falsehood and violence of outrage were found to be certain and infallible means of procuring them? yet I have so little confidence in our present statesmen, that I know not whether any thing is less likely, for being either absurd or dangerous.

I am, dearest Lady,
Your, &c.,
Sam: Johnson.

[1] 'The Hornecks were and are still two Ladies no less beautiful than modest and sensible. Both have been my pupils; but Madam never liked them much, because few would take notice of her where they were.'—Baretti.

421. To Mrs. Thrale

Dear Madam
July 17, 1775.

The post is come without a letter; how could I be so sullen—but *he must be humble who would please.* Perhaps you are gone to Brighthelmstone, and so could not write; however it be, this I feel, that I have no letter; but then I have sometimes had two, and if I have as many letters as there come posts nobody will pity me if I were to complain.

How was your hay made? The Doctor has had one part well housed, another wetted and dried till it is hardly worth the carriage; and now many acres newly mown, that have hitherto had good weather. This may be considered as a foreign article; the domestick news is, that our bull-bitch has puppies, and that our six calves are no longer to be fed by hand, but to live on grass.

Mr. Langley has made some improvements in his garden. A rich man might do more; but what he has done is well.

You have never in all your letters touched but once upon my master's summer projects. Is he towering into the air, and tending to the centre? Is he excavating the earth, or covering its surface with edifices? Something he certainly is doing, and something he is spending. A genius never can be quite still. I do not murmur at his expences; a good harvest will supply them.

We talk here of Polish oats, and Siberian barley, of which both are said to be more productive, to ripen in less time, and to afford better grain than the English. I intend to procure specimens of both, which we will try in some spots of our own ground.

The Doctor has no great mind to let me go. Shall I teaze him, and plague him till he is weary of me? I am, I hope, pretty well, and fit to come home. I shall be expected by all my ladies to return through Lichfield, and to stay there a while; but if I thought you wanted me, I hope you know what would be done by,

Dearest, dearest Madam,
Your most humble servant,
Sam: Johnson.

427. To Mrs. Thrale

Dear Madam August 1, 1775.

I wonder how it could happen. I forgot that the post went out yesternight, and so omitted to write; I therefore sent this by the by-post, and hope it will come, that I may not lose my regular letter.

This was to have been my last letter from this place, but Lucy says I must not go this week. Fits of tenderness with Mrs. Lucy are not common; but she seems now to have a little paroxysm, and I was not willing to counteract it. When I am to go I shall take care to inform you. The lady at Stowhill says, how comes Lucy to be such a sovereign, all the town besides could not have kept you.

America now fills every mouth, and some heads, and a little of it shall come into my letter. I do not much like the news. Our troops have indeed the superiority; five-and-twenty hundred have driven five thousand from their intrenchment; but the Americans fought skilfully; had coolness enough in the battle to carry off their men; and seem to have retreated orderly, for they were not pursued. They want nothing but confidence in their leaders, and familiarity with danger. Our business is to pursue their main army, and disperse it by a decisive battle; and then waste the country till they sue for peace. If we make war by parties and detachments, dislodge them from one place, and exclude them from another, we shall by a local, gradual, and ineffectual war, teach them our own knowledge, harden their obstinacy, and strengthen their confidence, and at last come to fight on equal terms of skill and bravery, without equal numbers.

Mrs. Williams wrote me word, that you had honoured her with a visit, and *behaved lovely.*

Mr. Thrale left off digging his pool, I suppose, for want of water. The first thing to be done is by digging in three or four places, to try how near the springs will rise to the surface; for though we cannot hope to be always full, we must be sure never to be dry.

Poor * * * *! I am sorry for him. It is sad to give
a family of children no pleasure but by dying. It was
said of Otho : *Hoc tantum fecit nobile quod periit.*[1] It
may be changed to * * * * : *Hoc tantum fecit utile.*

If I could do Mr. Carter any good at Oxford, I could
easily stop there ; for through it, if I go by Birmingham, I am likely to pass ; but the place is now a sullen
solitude. Whatever can be done I am ready to do ; but
our operations must for the present be at London.

I am, &c.,
SAM: JOHNSON.

428. To MRS. THRALE

Madam Lichfield, August 2, 1775.

I dined to-day at Stowhill, and am come away to
write my letter. Never surely was I such a writer
before. Do you keep my letters ? I am not of your
opinion that I shall not like to read them hereafter ;
for though there is in them not much history of mind,
or any thing else, they will, I hope, always be in some
degree the records of a pure and blameless friendship,
and in some hours of languour and sadness may revive
the memory of more cheerful times.

Why you should suppose yourself not desirous hereafter to read the history of your own mind, I do not
see. Twelve years, on which you now look as on a vast
expanse of life, will probably be passed over uniformly
and smoothly, with very little perception of your
progress, and with very few remarks upon the way.
That accumulation of knowledge which you promise to
yourself, by which the future is to look back upon the
present, with the superiority of manhood to infancy,
will perhaps never be attempted, or never will be
made ; and you will find, as millions have found before
you, that forty-five has made little sensible addition to
thirty-three.

As the body after a certain time gains no increase of

[1] [His only noble action was his death.]

height, and little of strength, there is likewise a period, though more variable by external causes, when the mind commonly attains its stationary point, and very little advances its powers of reflection, judgment, and ratiocination. The body may acquire new modes of motion, or new dexterities of mechanick operations, but its original strength receives not improvement; the mind may be stored with new languages, or new sciences, but its power of thinking remains nearly the same, and unless it attains new subjects of meditation, it commonly produces thoughts of the same force and the same extent, at very distant intervals of life, as the tree, unless a foreign fruit be ingrafted, gives year after year productions of the same form and the same flavour.

By intellectual force or strength of thought is meant the degree of power which the mind possesses of surveying the subject of meditation, with its circuit of concomitants, and its train of dependence.

Of this power, which all observe to be very different in different minds, part seems the gift of nature, and part the acquisition of experience. When the powers of nature have attained their intended energy, they can be no more advanced. The shrub can never become a tree. And it is not unreasonable to suppose, that they are before the middle of life in their full vigour.

Nothing then remains but practice and experience; and perhaps why they do so little, may be worth enquiry.

But I have just now looked, and find it so late, that I will enquire against the next post-night.

I am, &c.,
SAM: JOHNSON.

429. To MRS. THRALE

Dear Madam Lichfield, August 5, 1775.

Instead of forty reasons for my return, one is sufficient,—that you wish for my company. I purpose to write no more till you see me. The ladies at Stowhill and

Greenhill[1] are unanimously of opinion, that it will be
best to take a post-chaise, and not be troubled with the
vexations of a common carriage. I will venture to
suppose the ladies at Streatham to be of the same mind.

You will now expect to be told why you will not be
so much wiser as you expect, when you have lived
twelve years longer.

It is said, and said truly, that experience is the best
teacher; and it is supposed, that as life is lengthened
experience is encreased. But a closer inspection of
human life will discover that time often passes without
any incident which can much enlarge knowledge or
rectify judgment. When we are young we learn much,
because we are universally ignorant; we observe every
thing, because every thing is new. But after some years,
the occurrences of daily life are exhausted; one day
passes like another, in the same scene of appearances,
in the same course of transactions; we have to do what
we have often done, and what we do not try, because
we do not wish to do much better; we are told what
we already know, and therefore what repetition cannot
make us know with greater certainty.

He that has early learned much, perhaps seldom
makes, with regard to life and manners, much addition
to his knowledge; not only because as more is known
there is less to learn, but because a mind stored with
images and principles turns inwards for its own entertainment, and is employed in sorting those ideas which
run into confusion, and in recollecting those which are
stealing away; practices by which wisdom may be
kept but not gained. The merchant who was at first
busy in acquiring money, ceases to grow richer, from
the time when he makes it his business only to count it.

Those who have families or employments are engaged
in business of little difficulty, but of great importance,
requiring rather assiduity of practice than subtilty
of speculation, occupying the attention with images
too bulky for refinement, and too obvious for research.

[1] [Mrs. Aston and Mrs. Gastrell.]

The right is already known, what remains is only to follow it. Daily business adds no more to wisdom, than daily lesson to the learning of the teacher. But of how few lives does not stated duty claim the greater part.

Far the greater part of human minds never endeavour their own improvement. Opinions once received from instruction, or settled by whatever accident, are seldom recalled to examination; having been once supposed to be right, they are never discovered to be erroneous, for no application is made of any thing that time may present, either to shake or to confirm them. From this acquiescence in preconceptions none are wholly free; between fear of uncertainty, and dislike of labour, every one rests while he might yet go forward; and they that were wise at thirty-three, are very little wiser at forty-five.

Of this speculation you are perhaps tired, and would rather hear of Sophy. I hope before this comes, that her head will be easier, and your head less filled with fears and troubles, which you know are to be indulged only to prevent evil, not to encrease it.

Your uneasiness about Sophy is probably unnecessary, and at worst your other children are healthful, and your affairs prosperous. Unmingled good cannot be expected; but as we may lawfully gather all the good within our reach, we may be allowed to lament after that which we lose. I hope your losses are at an end, and that as far as the condition of our present existence permits, your remaining life will be happy.

I am, Madam,
Your most obliged and most humble servant,
SAM: JOHNSON.

431. To JAMES BOSWELL

Dear Sir

I am returned from the annual ramble into the middle counties. Having seen nothing I had not seen before, I have nothing to relate. Time has left that part of the island few antiquities; and commerce has

left the people no singularities. I was glad to go
abroad, and, perhaps, glad to come home; which is,
in other words, I was, I am afraid, weary of being at
home, and weary of being abroad. Is not this the
state of life ? But, if we confess this weariness, let us
not lament it, for all the wise and all the good say, that
we may cure it.

For the black fumes which rise in your mind, I can
prescribe nothing but that you disperse them by honest
business or innocent pleasure, and by reading, sometimes easy and sometimes serious. Change of place is
useful; and I hope that your residence at Auchinleck
will have many good effects....

That I should have given pain to Rasay, I am
sincerely sorry; and am therefore very much pleased
that he is no longer uneasy. He still thinks that I have
represented him as personally giving up the Chieftain-
ship. I meant only that it was no longer contested
between the two houses, and supposed it settled,
perhaps, by the cession of some remote generation, in
the house of Dunvegan. I am sorry the advertisement
was not continued for three or four times in the paper.

That Lord Monboddo and Mr. Macqueen should
controvert a position contrary to the imaginary interest
of literary or national prejudice, might be easily
imagined; but of a standing fact there ought to be no
controversy: If there are men with tails, catch an
homo caudatus; if there was writing of old in the
Highlands or Hebrides, in the Erse language, produce
the manuscripts. Where men write, they will write to
one another, and some of their letters, in families
studious of their ancestry, will be kept. In Wales
there are many manuscripts.

I have now three parcels of Lord Hailes's history,
which I purpose to return all the next week: that his
respect for my little observations should keep his work
in suspense, makes one of the evils of my journey. It
is in our language, I think, a new mode of history,
which tells all that is wanted, and, I suppose, all that
is known, without laboured splendour of language, or

affected subtility of conjecture. The exactness of his dates raises my wonder. He seems to have the closeness of Henault without his constraint.

Mrs. Thrale was so entertained with your *Journal*,[1] that she almost read herself blind. She has a great regard for you.

Of Mrs. Boswell, though she knows in her heart that she does not love me, I am always glad to hear any good, and hope that she and the little dear ladies will have neither sickness nor any other affliction. But she knows that she does not care what becomes of me, and for that she may be sure that I think her very much to blame.

Never, my dear Sir, do you take it into your head to think that I do not love you; you may settle yourself in full confidence both of my love and my esteem; I love you as a kind man, I value you as a worthy man, and hope in time to reverence you as a man of exemplary piety. I hold you, as Hamlet has it, ' in my heart of hearts,' and therefore, it is little to say, that,

I am, Sir, your affectionate humble servant,
London, Aug. 27, 1775. SAM: JOHNSON.

437. To ROBERT LEVET

Dear Sir Sept. 18, 1775. Calais.

We are here in France, after a very pleasing passage of no more than six hours. I know not when I shall write again, and therefore I write now, though you cannot suppose that I have much to say. You have seen France yourself. From this place we are going to Rouen, and from Rouen to Paris, where Mr. Thrale designs to stay about five or six weeks. We have a regular recommendation to the English residents, so we shall not be taken for vagabonds. We think to go one way and return another, and see as much as we can. I will try to speak a little French; I tried hitherto

---

[1] My *Journal of a Tour to the Hebrides*, which that lady read in the original manuscript. BOSWELL.

but little, but I spoke sometimes. If I heard better, I suppose I should learn faster.

> I am, Sir, your humble servant,
> SAM: JOHNSON.

445. To Mrs. Montagu

Madam
Thursday, Dec. 21, 1775.

I know not when any letter has given me so much pleasure or vexation as that which I had yesterday the honour of receiving. That you, Madam, should wish for my company is surely a sufficient reason for being pleased;—that I should delay twice, what I had so little right to expect even once, has so bad an appearance, that I can only hope to have it thought that I am ashamed.—You have kindly allowed me to name a day. Will you be pleased, Madam, to accept of me any day after Tuesday? Till I am favoured with your answer, or despair of so much condescension, I shall suffer no engagement to fasten itself upon me.

I am, Madam,
> Your most obliged and most humble servant,
> SAM: JOHNSON.

451. To John Wesley

Sir
Feb. 6, 1776.

When I received your Commentary on the Bible, I durst not at first flatter myself that I was to keep it, having so little claim to so valuable a present; and when Mrs. Hall informed me of your kindness, was hindered from time to time from returning you those thanks which I now entreat you to accept. I have thanks likewise to return you for the addition of your important suffrage to my argument on the American question. To have gained such a mind as yours may justly confirm me in my own opinion.[1] What effect my

[1] ['The Americans', wrote Wesley, 'are not contend-

paper has upon the public, I know not; but I have no reason to be discouraged. The lecturer was surely in the right, who, though he saw his audience slinking away, refused to quit the chair while Plato staid.

> I am, reverend Sir,
> Your most humble servant,
> SAM: JOHNSON.

458. To JAMES BOSWELL

Dear Sir

I have not had your letter half an hour; as you lay so much weight upon my notions, I should think it not just to delay my answer.

I am very sorry that your melancholy should return, and should be sorry likewise if it could have no relief but from company. My counsel you may have when you are pleased to require it; but of my company you cannot in the next month have much, for Mr. Thrale will take me to Italy, he says, on the first of April.

Let me warn you very earnestly against scruples. I am glad that you are reconciled to your settlement, and think it a great honour to have shaken Lord Hailes's opinion of entails. Do not, however, hope wholly to reason away your troubles; do not feed them with attention, and they will die imperceptibly away. Fix your thoughts upon your business, fill your intervals with company, and sunshine will again break in upon your mind. If you will come to me, you must come very quickly; and even then I know not but we may scour the country together, for I have a mind to see Oxford and Lichfield, before I set out on this long journey. To this I can only add, that

> I am, dear Sir,
> your most affectionate humble servant,

March 5, 1776.   SAM: JOHNSON.

ing for liberty, but for the illegal privilege of being exempt from parliamentary taxation.']

463. To the Reverend Dr. Wetherell, Master of University College, Oxford

Dear Sir

Few things are more unpleasant than the transaction of business with men who are above knowing or caring what they have to do ; such as the trustees for Lord Cornbury's institution will, perhaps, appear, when you have read Dr. * * * * 's letter.

The last part of the Doctor's letter is of great importance. The complaint [1] which he makes I have heard long ago, and did not know but it was redressed. It is unhappy that a practice so erroneous has not yet been altered ; for altered it must be, or our press will be useless, with all its privileges. The booksellers, who, like all other men, have strong prejudices in their own favour, are enough inclined to think the practice of printing and selling books by any but themselves, an encroachment on the rights of their fraternity ; and have need of stronger inducements to circulate academical publications than those of one another ; for, of that mutual co-operation by which the general trade is carried on, the University can bear no part. Of those whom he neither loves nor fears, and from whom he expects no reciprocation of good offices, why should any man promote the interest but for profit ? I suppose, with all our scholastick ignorance of mankind, we are still too knowing to expect that the booksellers will erect themselves into patrons, and buy and sell under the influence of a disinterested zeal for the promotion of learning.

To the booksellers, if we look for either honour or profit from our press, not only their common profit, but something more must be allowed ; and if books, printed at Oxford, are expected to be rated at a high price, that

[1] I suppose the complaint was, that the trustees of the Oxford Press did not allow the London booksellers a sufficient profit upon vending their publications. BOSWELL. [*Bookseller* represents the modern *publisher*.]

price must be levied on the publick, and paid by the ultimate purchaser, not by the intermediate agents. What price shall be set upon the book, is, to the booksellers, wholly indifferent, provided that they gain a proportionate profit by negociating the sale.

Why books printed at Oxford should be particularly dear, I am, however, unable to find. We pay no rent; we inherit many of our instruments and materials; lodging and victuals are cheaper than at London; and, therefore, workmanship ought, at least, not to be dearer. Our expences are naturally less than those of booksellers; and, in most cases, communities are content with less profit than individuals.

It is, perhaps, not considered through how many hands a book often passes, before it comes into those of the reader; or what part of the profit each hand must retain, as a motive for transmitting it to the next.

We will call our primary agent in London, Mr. Cadell, who receives our books from us, gives them room in his warehouse, and issues them on demand; by him they are sold to Mr. Dilly a wholesale bookseller, who sends them into the country; and the last seller is the country bookseller. Here are three profits to be paid between the printer and the reader, or in the style of commerce, between the manufacturer and the consumer; and if any of these profits is too penuriously distributed, the process of commerce is interrupted.

We are now come to the practical question, what is to be done? You will tell me, with reason, that I have said nothing, till I declare how much, according to my opinion, of the ultimate price ought to be distributed through the whole succession of sale.

The deduction, I am afraid, will appear very great: but let it be considered before it is refused. We must allow, for profit, between thirty and thirty-five *per cent.*, between six and seven shillings in the pound; that is, for every book which costs the last buyer twenty shillings, we must charge Mr. Cadell with something less than fourteen. We must set the copies at fourteen shillings each, and superadd what is called the quarterly-book, or for every hundred books so charged we must deliver an hundred and four.

The profits will then stand thus :—

Mr. Cadell, who runs no hazard, and gives no credit, will be paid for warehouse room and attendance by a shilling profit on each book, and his chance of the quarterly-book.

Mr. Dilly, who buys the book for fifteen shillings, and who will expect the quarterly-book if he takes five and twenty, will send it to his country customer at sixteen and six, by which, at the hazard of loss, and the certainty of long credit, he gains the regular profit of ten *per cent.* which is expected in the wholesale trade.

The country bookseller, buying at sixteen and sixpence, and commonly trusting a considerable time, gains but three and sixpence, and if he trusts a year, not much more than two and sixpence ; otherwise than as he may, perhaps, take as long credit as he gives.

With less profit than this, and more you see he cannot have, the country bookseller cannot live ; for his receipts are small, and his debts sometimes bad.

Thus, dear Sir, I have been incited by Dr. * * * * 's letter to give you a detail of the circulation of books, which, perhaps, every man has not had opportunity of knowing ; and which those who know it, do not, perhaps, always distinctly consider.

I am, &c.,
March 12, 1776.   SAM : JOHNSON.[1]

465. To MRS. THRALE

Lichfield, March 25, 1776.

Dear Madam

This letter will not, I hope, reach you many days

---

[1] I am happy in giving this full and clear statement to the publick, to vindicate, by the authority of the greatest authour of his age, that respectable body of men, the Booksellers of London, from vulgar reflections, as if their profits were exorbitant, when, in truth, Dr. Johnson has here allowed them more than they usually demand. BOSWELL.

before me ; in a distress which can be so little relieved, nothing remains for a friend but to come and partake it.

Poor dear sweet little boy ! When I read the letter this day to Mrs. Aston, she said, ' Such a death is the next to translation.' Yet however I may convince myself of this, the tears are in my eyes, and yet I could not love him as you loved him, nor reckon upon him for a future comfort, as you and his father reckoned upon him.

He is gone, and we are going. We could not have enjoyed him long, and shall not long be separated from him. He has probably escaped many such pangs as you are now feeling.

Nothing remains, but that with humble confidence we resign ourselves to Almighty Goodness, and fall down, without irreverent murmurs, before the Sovereign Distributer of good and evil, with hope that though sorrow endureth for a night yet joy may come in the morning.

I have known you, Madam, too long to think that you want any arguments for submission to the Supreme Will ; nor can my consolations have any effect but that of showing that I wish to comfort you. What can be done you must do for yourself. Remember first, that your child is happy ; and then, that he is safe, not only from the ills of this world, but from those more formidable dangers which extend their mischief to eternity. You have brought into the world a rational being ; have seen him happy during the little life that has been granted him ; and can have no doubt but that his happiness is now permanent and immutable.

When you have obtained by prayer such tranquillity as nature will admit, force your attention, as you can, upon your accustomed duties and accustomed entertainments. You can do no more for our dear boy, but you must not therefore think less on those whom your attention may make fitter for the place to which he is gone.

I am, dearest, dearest Madam,
Your most affectionate humble servant,
SAM: JOHNSON.

481. To Mrs. Boswell

Madam

You must not think me uncivil in omitting to answer the letter with which you favoured me some time ago. I imagined it to have been written without Mr. Boswell's knowledge, and therefore supposed the answer to require, what I could not find, a private conveyance.

The difference with Lord Auchinleck is now over; and since young Alexander has appeared, I hope no more difficulties will arise among you; for I sincerely wish you all happy. Do not teach the young ones to dislike me, as you dislike me yourself; but let me at least have Veronica's kindness, because she is my acquaintance.

You will now have Mr. Boswell home; it is well that you have him; he has led a wild life. I have taken him to Lichfield, and he has followed Mr. Thrale to Bath. Pray take care of him, and tame him. The only thing in which I have the honour to agree with you is, in loving him; and while we are so much of a mind in a matter of so much importance, our other quarrels will, I hope, produce no great bitterness.

I am, Madam, your most humble servant,
May 16, 1776.   Sam: Johnson.

502. To James Boswell, Esq.

Dear Sir

I had great pleasure in hearing that you are at last on good terms with your father. Cultivate his kindness by all honest and manly means. Life is but short; no time can be afforded but for the indulgence of real sorrow, or contests upon questions seriously momentous. Let us not throw away any of our days upon useless resentment, or contend who shall hold out longest in stubborn malignity. It is best not to be angry; and best, in the next place, to be quickly reconciled. May you and your father pass the remainder of your time in reciprocal benevolence! . . .

Do you ever hear from Mr. Langton ? I visit him sometimes, but he does not talk. I do not like his scheme of life ; but as I am not permitted to understand it, I cannot set any thing right that is wrong. His children are sweet babies.

I hope my irreconcileable enemy, Mrs. Boswell, is well. Desire her not to transmit her malevolence to the young people. Let me have Alexander, and Veronica, and Euphemia, for my friends.

Mrs. Williams, whom you may reckon as one of your well-wishers, is in a feeble and languishing state, with little hope of growing better. She went for some part of the autumn into the country, but is little benefited ; and Dr. Lawrence confesses that his art is at an end. Death is, however, at a distance ; and what more than that can we say of ourselves ? I am sorry for her pain, and more sorry for her decay. Mr. Levett is sound, wind and limb.

I was some weeks this autumn at Brighthelmstone. The place was very dull, and I was not well ; the expedition to the Hebrides was the most pleasant journey that I ever made. Such an effort annually would give the world a little diversification.

Every year, however, we cannot wander, and must therefore endeavour to spend our time at home as well as we can. I believe it is best to throw life into a method, that every hour may bring its employment, and every employment have its hour. Xenophon observes, in his *Treatise of Oeconomy*, that if every thing be kept in a certain place, when any thing is worn out or consumed, the vacuity which it leaves will shew what is wanting ; so if every part of time has its duty, the hour will call into remembrance its proper engagement.

I have not practised all this prudence myself, but I have suffered much for want of it ; and I would have you, by timely recollection and steady resolution, escape from those evils which have lain heavy upon me.

I am, my dearest Boswell,
your most humble servant,

Bolt-court, Nov. 16, 1776.   SAM: JOHNSON

510. To JAMES BOSWELL

Dear Sir

I have been much pleased with your late letter, and am glad that my old enemy, Mrs. Boswell, begins to feel some remorse. As to Miss Veronica's Scotch, I think it cannot be helped. An English maid you might easily have; but she would still imitate the greater number, as they would be likewise those whom she must most respect. Her dialect will not be gross. Her Mamma has not much Scotch, and you have yourself very little. I hope she knows my name, and does not call me *Johnston*.[1]

The immediate cause of my writing is this:—One Shaw, who seems a modest and a decent man, has written an *Erse Grammar*, which a very learned Highlander, Macbean, has, at my request, examined and approved.

The book is very little, but Mr. Shaw has been persuaded by his friends to set it at half a guinea, though I advised only a crown, and thought myself liberal. You, whom the authour considers as a great encourager of ingenious men, will receive a parcel of his proposals and receipts. I have undertaken to give you notice of them, and to solicit your countenance. You must ask no poor man, because the price is really too high. Yet such a work deserves patronage.

It is proposed to augment our club from twenty to thirty, of which I am glad; for as we have several in it whom I do not much like to consort with,[2] I am for reducing it to a mere miscellaneous collection of conspicuous men, without any determinate character. . . .

I am, dear Sir, most affectionately your's,
March 11, 1777. SAM: JOHNSON.

My respects to Madam, to Veronica, to Alexander, to Euphemia, to David.

[1] John*son* is the most common English formation of the Sirname from *John*; John*ston* the Scotch. My illustrious friend observed that many North Britons pronounced his name in their own way. BOSWELL.

[2] On account of their differing from him as to religion and politicks. BOSWELL.

517. To Charles O'Connor

Sir

Having had the pleasure of conversing with Dr. Campbell about your character and your literary undertaking, I am resolved to gratify myself by renewing a correspondence [1] which began and ended a great while ago, and ended, I am afraid, by my fault; a fault which, if you have not forgotten it, you must now forgive.

If I have ever disappointed you, give me leave to tell you, that you have likewise disappointed me. I expected great discoveries in Irish antiquity, and large publications in the Irish language; but the world still remains as it was, doubtful and ignorant. What the Irish language is in itself, and to what languages it has affinity, are very interesting questions, which every man wishes to see resolved that has any philological or historical curiosity. Dr. Leland begins his history too late: the ages which deserve an exact enquiry are those times (for such there were) when Ireland was the school of the west, the quiet habitation of sanctity and literature. If you could give a history, though imperfect, of the Irish nation, from its conversion to Christianity to the invasion from England, you would amplify knowledge with new views and new objects. Set about it therefore, if you can: do what you can easily do without anxious exactness. Lay the foundation, and leave the superstructure to posterity.

I am, Sir, your most humble servant,
May 19, 1777. Sam: Johnson.

523. To the Reverend Dr. Dodd

Dear Sir

That which is appointed to all men is now coming upon you. Outward circumstances, the eyes and the thoughts of men, are below the notice of an immortal being about to stand the trial for eternity, before the

[1] [See above, No. 107.]

Supreme Judge of heaven and earth. Be comforted: your crime, morally or religiously considered, has no very deep dye of turpitude. It corrupted no man's principles; it attacked no man's life. It involved only a temporary and reparable injury. Of this, and of all other sins, you are earnestly to repent; and may GOD, who knoweth our frailty, and desireth not our death, accept your repentance, for the sake of his Son JESUS CHRIST our Lord.

In requital of those well-intended offices which you are pleased so emphatically to acknowledge, let me beg that you make in your devotions one petition for my eternal welfare.

       I am, dear Sir, your affectionate servant,
June 26, 1777.   SAM: JOHNSON.

525. TO BENNET LANGTON

Dear Sir

I have lately been much disordered by a difficulty of breathing, but am now better. I hope your house is well.

You know we have been talking lately of St. Cross, at Winchester; I have an old acquaintance whose distress makes him very desirous of an hospital, and I am afraid I have not strength enough to get him into the Chartreux. He is a painter, who never rose higher than to get his immediate living, and from that, at eighty-three, he is disabled by a slight stroke of the palsy, such as does not make him at all helpless on common occasions, though his hand is not steady enough for his art.

My request is, that you will try to obtain a promise of the next vacancy, from the Bishop of Chester. It is not a great thing to ask, and I hope we shall obtain it. Dr. Warton has promised to favour him with his notice, and I hope he may end his days in peace.

       I am, Sir, your most humble servant,
June 29, 1777.   SAM: JOHNSON.

526. To W. Sharp

Sir

To the collection of *English Poets*, I have recommended the volume of Dr. Watts to be added; his name has long been held by me in veneration, and I would not willingly be reduced to tell of him only that he was born and died. Yet of his life I know very little, and therefore must pass him in a manner very unworthy of his character, unless some of his friends will favour me with the necessary information; many of them must be known to you; and by your influence, perhaps I may obtain some instruction. My plan does not exact much; but I wish to distinguish Watts, a man who never wrote but for a good purpose. Be pleased to do for me what you can.

I am, Sir, your humble servant,
Sam: Johnson.

Bolt-Court, Fleet-street, July 7, 1777.

527. To Dr. Vyse

Sir

I doubt not but you will readily forgive me for taking the liberty of requesting your assistance in recommending an old friend to his Grace the Archbishop, as Governour of the Charter-house.

His name is De Groot; he was born at Gloucester; I have known him many years. He has all the common claims to charity, being old, poor, and infirm, in a great degree. He has likewise another claim, to which no scholar can refuse attention; he is by several descents the nephew of Hugo Grotius; of him, from whom perhaps every man of learning has learnt something. Let it not be said that in any lettered country a nephew of Grotius asked a charity and was refused.

I am, reverend Sir, your most humble servant,
July 9, 1777.   Sam: Johnson.

528. To JAMES BOSWELL

Dear Sir

Your notion of the necessity of an yearly interview is very pleasing to both my vanity and tenderness. I shall, perhaps, come to Carlisle another year; but my money has not held out so well as it used to do. I shall go to Ashbourne, and I purpose to make Dr. Taylor invite you. If you live awhile with me at his house, we shall have much time to ourselves, and our stay will be no expence to us or him. I shall leave London the 28th; and after some stay at Oxford and Lichfield, shall probably come to Ashbourne about the end of your Session, but of all this you shall have notice. Be satisfied we will meet somewhere.

What passed between me and poor Dr. Dodd you shall know more fully when we meet.

Of lawsuits there is no end; poor Sir Allan must have another trial, for which, however, his antagonist cannot be much blamed, having two Judges on his side. I am more afraid of the debts than of the House of Lords. It is scarcely to be imagined to what debts will swell, that are daily increasing by small additions, and how carelessly in a state of desperation debts are contracted. Poor Macquarry was far from thinking that when he sold his islands he should receive nothing. For what were they sold? And what was their yearly value? The admission of money into the Highlands will soon put an end to the feudal modes of life, by making those men landlords who were not chiefs. I do not know that the people will suffer by the change; but there was in the patriarchal authority something venerable and pleasing. Every eye must look with pain on a *Campbell* turning the *Macquarries* at will out of their *sedes avitæ*, their hereditary island.

Sir Alexander Dick is the only Scotsman liberal enough not to be angry that I could not find trees, where trees were not. I was much delighted by his kind letter.

I remember Rasay with too much pleasure not to

partake of the happiness of any part of that amiable family. Our ramble in the islands hangs upon my imagination, I can hardly help imagining that we shall go again. Pennant seems to have seen a great deal which we did not see: when we travel again let us look better about us.

You have done right in taking your uncle's house. Some change in the form of life, gives from time to time a new epocha of existence. In a new place there is something new to be done, and a different system of thoughts rises in the mind. I wish I could gather currants in your garden. Now fit up a little study, and have your books ready at hand; do not spare a little money, to make your habitation pleasing to yourself.

I have dined lately with poor dear Langton. I do not think he goes on well. His table is rather coarse, and he has his children too much about him. But he is a very good man.

Mrs. Williams is in the country to try if she can improve her health; she is very ill. Matters have come so about that she is in the country with very good accommodation; but age and sickness, and pride, have made her so peevish that I was forced to bribe the maid to stay with her, by a secret stipulation of half a crown a week over her wages.

Our CLUB ended its session about six weeks ago. We now only meet to dine once a fortnight. Mr. Dunning, the great lawyer, is one of our members. The Thrales are well.

I long to know how the Negro's cause will be decided. What is the opinion of Lord Auchinleck, or Lord Hailes, or Lord Monboddo?

   I am, dear Sir, your most affectionate, &c.
July 22, 1777.   SAM: JOHNSON.

529. To MRS. BOSWELL

Madam
  Though I am well enough pleased with the taste

of sweetmeats, very little of the pleasure which I
received at the arrival of your jar of marmalade arose
from eating it. I received it as a token of friendship,
as a proof of reconciliation, things much sweeter than
sweetmeats, and upon this consideration I return you,
dear Madam, my sincerest thanks. By having your
kindness I think I have a double security for the continuance of Mr. Boswell's, which it is not to be expected
that any man can long keep, when the influence of
a lady so highly and so justly valued operates against
him. Mr. Boswell will tell you that I was always
faithful to your interest, and always endeavoured to
exalt you in his estimation. You must now do the
same for me. We must all help one another, and you
must now consider me, as,

     Dear Madam, your most obliged,
      and most humble servant,
July 22, 1777.   SAM: JOHNSON.

537. To MRS. THRALE

Dear Madam   Lichfield, August 13, 1777.

Such tattle as filled your last sweet letter prevents
one great inconvenience of absence, that of returning
home a stranger and an enquirer. The variations of
life consist of little things. Important innovations
are soon heard, and easily understood. Men that
meet to talk of physicks or metaphysicks, or law or
history, may be immediately acquainted. We look
at each other in silence, only for want of petty talk
upon slight occurrences. Continue therefore to write
all that you would say.

You have Lord Westcote and every body when I am
away, and you go to Mr. Cator's, and you are so happy.

Miss Turton and Harry Jackson are dead. Mrs.
Aston is, I am afraid, in great danger. Mr. Green,
Mr. Garrick, and Mr. Newton are all well. I have been
very faint and breathless since I came hither, but
fancy myself better this day. I hope Master's walk

will be finished when I come back, and I shall perambulate it very often.

There seems to be in this country scarcely any fruit, there never indeed was much; but great things have been said of the harvest, and the only fear is of the weather. It rains here almost every day.

I dined yesterday with the corporation, and talked against a workhouse which they have in *contemplation*—there's the word now. I do not know that they minded me, for they said nothing to me.

I have had so little inclination to motion that I have always gone the shortest way to Stowhill, and hardly any where else, so that I can tell you nothing new of Green's museum, but I design to visit him, and all friends.

I hope for a letter to-morrow, for you must not forget that I am, Madam,

Your most humble servant,
SAM: JOHNSON.

P.S. Why cannot Queeney write?

542. To MRS. THRALE

Dearest Lady   [Ashbourne], Sept. 6, 1777.

It is true that I have loitered, and what is worse, loitered with very little pleasure. The time has run away, as most time runs, without account, without use, and without memorial. But to say this of a few weeks, though not pleasing, might be borne, but what ought to be the regret of him who, in a few days, will have so nearly the same to say of sixty-eight years? But complaint is vain.

If you have nothing to say from the neighbourhood of the metropolis, what can occur to me in little cities and petty towns; in places which we have both seen, and of which no description is wanted? I have left part of the company with which you dined here, to come and write this letter; in which I have nothing to tell, but that my nights are very tedious. I cannot persuade myself to forbear trying something.

As you have now little to do, I suppose you are pretty diligent at the Thraliana,[1] and a very curious collection posterity will find it. Do not remit the practice of writing down occurrences as they arise, of whatever kind, and be very punctual in annexing the dates. Chronology you know is the eye of history; and every man's life is of importance to himself. Do not omit painful casualties, or unpleasing passages, they make the variegation of existence; and there are many transactions, of which I will not promise with Æneas, *et hæc olim meminisse juvabit*.[2] Yet that remembrance which is not pleasant may be useful. There is however an intemperate attention to slight circumstances which is to be avoided, lest a great part of life be spent in writing the history of the rest. Every day perhaps has something to be noted, but in a settled and uniform course few days can have much.

Why do I write all this, which I had no thought of when I begun? The Thraliana drove it all into my head. It deserves however an hour's reflection, to consider how, with the least loss of time, the loss of what we wish to retain may be prevented.

Do not neglect to write to me, for when a post comes empty, I am really disappointed.

Boswell, I believe, will meet me here.

I am, dearest Lady,
Your, &c.,
SAM: JOHNSON.

544. To JAMES BOSWELL

Dear Sir

I write to be left at Carlisle, as you direct me; but you cannot have it. Your letter, dated Sept. 6, was not at this place till this day, Thursday, Sept. 11; and I hope you will be here before this is at Carlisle.

[1] [Mrs. Thrale's Journal.]
[2] An hour will come with pleasure to relate
Your sorrows past as benefits of Fate. Dryden.

However, what you have not going, you may have returning; and as I believe I shall not love you less after our interview, it will then be as true as it is now, that I set a very high value upon your friendship, and count your kindness as one of the chief felicities of my life. Do not fancy that an intermission of writing is a decay of kindness. No man is always in a disposition to write; nor has any man at all times something to say.

That distrust which intrudes so often on your mind is a mode of melancholy, which, if it be the business of a wise man to be happy, it is foolish to indulge; and if it be a duty to preserve our faculties entire for their proper use, it is criminal. Suspicion is very often an useless pain. From that, and all other pains, I wish you free and safe; for

I am, dear Sir, most affectionately yours,
Ashbourne, Sept. 11, 1777.   SAM: JOHNSON.

554. To MRS. THRALE

Dear Madam   Ashbourne, October 6, 1777.

You are glad that I am absent; and I am glad that you are sick. When you went away, what did you do with your aunt ? I am glad she liked my Susy ; I was always a Susy, when nobody else was a Susy. How have you managed at your new place ? Could you all get lodgings in one house, and meat at one table ? Let me hear the whole series of misery ; for, as Dr. Young says, *I love horrour.*

Methinks you are now a great way off; and if I come, I have a great way to come to you ; and then the sea is so cold, and the rooms are so dull ; yet I do love to hear the sea roar and my mistress talk—For when she talks, ye gods ! how she will talk. I wish I were with you, but we are now near half the length of England asunder. It is frightful to think how much time must pass between writing this letter and receiving an answer, if any answer were necessary.

Taylor is now going to have a ram; and then, after Aries and Taurus, we shall have Gemini. His oats are now in the wet; here is a deal of rain. Mr. Langdon bought, at Nottingham fair, fifteen tun of cheese; which, at an ounce a-piece, will suffice after dinner for four hundred and eighty thousand men. This is all the news that the place affords. I purpose soon to be at Lichfield, but know not just when, having been defeated of my first design. When I come to town, I am to be very busy about my Lives.[1]—Could not you do some of them for me?

I am glad Master unspelled you, and run you all on rocks, and drove you about, and made you stir. Never be cross about it. Quiet and calmness you have enough of—a little hurry stirs life—and,

> Brushing o'er, adds motion to the pool.

Now *pool* brings my master's excavations into my head. I wonder how I shall like them; I should like not to see them, till we all see them together. He will have no waterfall to roar like the Doctor's. I sat by it yesterday, and read Erasmus's *Militis Christiani Enchiridion*. Have you got that book?

Make my compliments to dear Queeney. I suppose she will dance at the Rooms, and your heart will go one knows not how.

> I am, dearest, and dearest Lady,
> Your most humble servant,
> SAM: JOHNSON.

559. To MRS. THRALE

Dear Madam   Lichfield, October 27, 1777.

You talk of writing and writing, as if you had all the writing to yourself. If our correspondence were printed, I am sure posterity, for posterity is always the authour's favourite, would say that I am a good writer too.—*Anch'io sono pittore*. To sit down so often with nothing to say: to say something so often, almost

[1] [*The Lives of the Poets*, published 1779–81.]

without consciousness of saying, and without any remembrance of having said, is a power of which I will not violate my modesty by boasting, but I do not believe that every body has it.

Some, when they write to their friends, are all affection; some are wise and sententious; some strain their powers for efforts of gaiety: some write news, and some write secrets; but to make a letter without affection, without wisdom, without gaiety, without news, and without a secret, is, doubtless, the great epistolick art.

In a man's letters, you know, Madam, his soul lies naked, his letters are only the mirrour of his breast; whatever passes within him is shown undisguised in its natural process; nothing is inverted, nothing distorted; you see systems in their elements; you discover actions in their motives.

Of this great truth, sounded by the knowing to the ignorant, and so echoed by the ignorant to the knowing, what evidence have you now before you! Is not my soul laid open in these veracious pages? Do not you see me reduced to my first principles? This is the pleasure of corresponding with a friend, where doubt and distrust have no place, and every thing is said as it is thought. The original idea is laid down in its simple purity, and all the supervenient conceptions are spread over it *stratum super stratum*, as they happen to be formed. These are the letters by which souls are united, and by which minds naturally in unison move each other as they are moved themselves. I know, dearest Lady, that in the perusal of this, such is the consanguinity of our intellects, you will be touched as I am touched. I have indeed concealed nothing from you, nor do I expect ever to repent of having thus opened my heart.

I am, &c.,
SAM: JOHNSON.

560. To Mrs. Thrale

Dear Madam   Lichfield, October 29, 1777.

Though after my last letter I might justly claim an interval of rest, yet I write again to tell you, that for this turn you will hear but once more from Lichfield. This day is Wednesday, on Saturday I shall write again, and on Monday I shall set out to seek adventures ; for you know,

None but the brave deserve the fair.

On Monday we hope to see Birmingham, the seat of the mechanick arts ; and know not whether our next stage will be Oxford, the mansion of the liberal arts ; or London, the residence of all the arts together. The chymists call the world *Academia Paracelsi* ; my ambition is to be his fellow-student—to see the works of nature, and hear the lectures of truth. To London therefore—London may perhaps fill me ; and I hope to fill my part of London.

In the mean time, let me continue to keep the part which I have had so long in your kindness, and my master's ; for if that should grow less, I know not where to find that which may supply the diminution. But I hope what I have been so happy as to gain I shall have the happiness of keeping.

I always omitted to tell you that Lucy's maid took the worm-powder with strict regularity, but with no great effect. Lucy has had several letters from you, but cannot prevail on herself to write ; but she is very grateful.

Mrs. Walmsley has been at Stowhill, and has invited me, when I come to Bath, to be at her house. Poor Mrs. Aston either mends not at all, or not perceptibly ; but she does not seem to grow worse.

I suppose * * * * * * * * * is by this time recovered, and perhaps grown wiser, than to shake his constitution so violently a second time.

Poor Mrs. * * * * * ! One cannot think on her but

with great compassion. But it is impossible for her husband's daughters not to triumph; and the husband will feel, as Rochefoucault says, *something that does not displease him*. You and I, who are neutral, whom her happiness could not have depressed, may be honestly sorry.

I am, dear Madam,
Your, &c.,
SAM: JOHNSON.

561. To MRS. THRALE

Dear Madam   Lichfield, November 3, 1777.

This is the last time that I shall write, in this excursion, from this place. To-morrow I shall be, I hope, at Birmingham; from which place I shall do my best to find the nearest way home. I come home, I think, worse than I went; and do not like the state of my health. But, *vive hodie*[1], make the most of life. I hope to get better, and——sweep the cobwebs. But I have sad nights. Mrs. Aston has sent me to Mr. Green to be cured.

Did you see Foote at Brighthelmstone?—Did you think he would so soon be gone?—Life, says Falstaff, is a shuttle. He was a fine fellow in his way; and the world is really impoverished by his sinking glories. Murphy ought to write his life, at least to give the world a Footeana. Now, will any of his contemporaries bewail him? Will Genius change *his sex* to weep? I would really have his life written with diligence.

It will be proper for me to work pretty diligently now for some time. I hope to get through, though so many weeks have passed. Little lives and little criticisms may serve.

Having been in the country so long, with very little to detain me, I am rather glad to look homewards.

I am, &c.,
SAM: JOHNSON.

[1] [Live for the day.]

562. To Mrs. Thrale

Dear Madam [Bolt Court], November 10, 1777.

And so, supposing that I might come to town and neglect to give you notice, or thinking some other strange thought, but certainly thinking wrong, you fall to writing about me to Tom Davies, as if he could tell you any thing that I would not have you know. As soon as I came hither, I let you know of my arrival; and the consequence is, that I am summoned to Brighthelmstone through storms, and cold, and dirt, and all the hardships of wintry journies. You know my natural dread of all those evils; yet to shew my master an example of compliance, and to let you know how much I long to see you, and to boast how little I give way to disease, my purpose is to be with you on Friday.

I am sorry for poor Nezzy, and hope she will in time be better; I hope the same for myself. The rejuvenescency of Mr. Scrase gives us both reason to hope, and therefore both of us rejoice in his recovery. I wish him well besides, as a friend to my master.

I am just come home from not seeing my Lord Mayor's shew, but I might have seen at least part of it. But I saw Miss Wesley and her brothers; she sends her compliments. Mrs. Williams is come home, I think a very little better.

Every body was an enemy to that wig.—We will burn it, and get drunk; for what is joy without drink. Wagers are laid in the city about our success, which is yet, as the French call it, problematical. Well, but seriously I think I shall be glad to see you in your own hair; but do not take too much time in combing, and twisting, and papering, and unpapering, and curling, and frizzing, and powdering, and getting out the powder, with all the other operations required in the cultivation of a head of hair; yet let it be combed at least once in three months, on the quarter-day—I could wish it might be combed once at least in six weeks; if I were to indulge my wishes, but what are wishes, without hopes, I should fancy the operation performed—one knows not when one has enough—perhaps every morning.

>I am, dearest Lady,
>Your, &c.,
>SAM: JOHNSON.

To THOMAS JOHNSON

Dear Tom

Our good friend Mr. Rann very kindly requires that I shall give you some token of reconciliation. Neither you nor I have any time to spare for quarrels or grudges. I desire you to think no more of what you may have done wrong with respect to me, and to consider me as

>Your affectionate kinsman and friend,
>
>Dec. 16, 1777. SAM: JOHNSON.

568. To JAMES BOSWELL, ESQ.

Dear Sir

To a letter so interesting as your last, it is proper to return some answer, however little I may be disposed to write.

Your alarm at your lady's illness was reasonable, and not disproportionate to the appearance of the disorder. I hope your physical friend's conjecture is now verified, and all fear of a consumption at an end: a little care and exercise will then restore her. London is a good air for ladies; and if you bring her hither, I will do for her what she did for me—I will retire from my apartments, for her accommodation. Behave kindly to her, and keep her chearful.

You always seem to call for tenderness. Know then, that in the first month of the present year I very highly esteem and very cordially love you. I hope to tell you this at the beginning of every year as long as we live; and why should we trouble ourselves to tell or hear it oftener?

Tell Veronica, Euphemia, and Alexander, that I wish them, as well as their parents, many happy years.

You have ended the negro's cause much to my mind. Lord Auchinleck and dear Lord Hailes were on the side of liberty. Lord Hailes's name reproaches me; but if he saw my languid neglect of my own affairs, he would rather pity than resent my neglect of his. I hope to mend, *ut et mihi vivam et amicis.*[1]

I am, dear Sir, your's affectionately,
January 24, 1778.   SAM: JOHNSON.
My service to my fellow-traveller, Joseph.

571. TO SAUNDERS WELCH, ESQ., AT THE ENGLISH COFFEE-HOUSE, ROME

Dear Sir

To have suffered one of my best and dearest friends to pass almost two years in foreign countries without a letter, has a very shameful appearance of inattention. But the truth is, that there was no particular time in which I had any thing particular to say; and general expressions of good will, I hope, our long friendship is grown too solid to want.

Of publick affairs you have information from the newspapers wherever you go, for the English keep no secret; and of other things, Mrs. Nollekens informs you. My intelligence could therefore be of no use; and Miss Nancy's letters made it unnecessary to write to you for information: I was likewise for some time out of humour, to find that motion, and nearer approaches to the sun, did not restore your health so fast as I expected. Of your health, the accounts have lately been more pleasing; and I have the gratification of imaging to myself a length of years which I hope you have gained, and of which the enjoyment will be improved by a vast accession of images and observations which your journeys and various residence have enabled you to make and accumulate. You have travelled with this felicity, almost peculiar to yourself, that your companion is not to part from you at your

[1] [That I may live for myself and my friends.]

journey's end; but you are to live on together, to help each other's recollection, and to supply each other's omissions. The world has few greater pleasures than that which two friends enjoy, in tracing back, at some distant time, those transactions and events through which they have passed together. One of the old man's miseries is, that he cannot easily find a companion able to partake with him of the past. You and your fellow-traveller have this comfort in store, that your conversation will be not easily exhausted; one will always be glad to say what the other will always be willing to hear.

That you may enjoy this pleasure long, your health must have your constant attention. I suppose you purpose to return this year. There is no need of haste: do not come hither before the height of summer, that you may fall gradually into the inconveniences of your native clime. July seems to be the proper month. August and September will prepare you for the winter. After having travelled so far to find health, you must take care not to lose it at home; and I hope a little care will effectually preserve it.

Miss Nancy has doubtless kept a constant and copious journal. She must not expect to be welcome when she returns, without a great mass of information. Let her review her journal often, and set down what she finds herself to have omitted, that she may trust to memory as little as possible, for memory is soon confused by a quick succession of things; and she will grow every day less confident of the truth of her own narratives, unless she can recur to some written memorials. If she has satisfied herself with hints, instead of full representations, let her supply the deficiences now while her memory is yet fresh, and while her father's memory may help her. If she observes this direction, she will not have travelled in vain; for she will bring home a book with which she may entertain herself to the end of life. If it were not now too late, I would advise her to note the impression which the first sight of any thing new and wonderful made upon her mind.

Let her now set her thoughts down as she can recollect
them; for faint as they may already be, they will
grow every day fainter.

Perhaps I do not flatter myself unreasonably when I
imagine that you may wish to know something of me.
I can gratify your benevolence with no account of
health. The hand of time, or of disease, is very heavy
upon me. I pass restless and uneasy nights, harassed
with convulsions of my breast, and flatulencies at my
stomach; and restless nights make heavy days. But
nothing will be mended by complaints, and therefore
I will make an end. When we meet, we will try to
forget our cares and our maladies, and contribute, as
we can, to the chearfulness of each other. If I had
gone with you, I believe I should have been better;
but I do not know that it was in my power.

I am, dear Sir, your most humble servant,
Feb. 3, 1778.   SAM: JOHNSON.

575. To JAMES BOSWELL

Sir

The debate between Dr. Percy and me [1] is one of
those foolish controversies, which begin upon a question
of which neither party cares how it is decided, and which
is, nevertheless, continued to acrimony, by the vanity
with which every man resists confutation. Dr. Percy's
warmth proceeded from a cause which, perhaps, does
him more honour than he could have derived from
juster criticism. His abhorrence of Pennant proceeded
from his opinion that Pennant had wantonly and
indecently censured his patron. His anger made him
resolve, that, for having been once wrong, he never
should be right. Pennant has much in his notions that
I do not like; but still I think him a very intelligent
traveller. If Percy is really offended, I am sorry; for

[1] [In the course of a dispute as to Pennant's merit as
a traveller, Johnson had said that Percy 'had the
resentment of a narrow mind against Pennant, because
he did not find everything in Northumberland'.]

he is a man whom I never knew to offend any one. He is a man very willing to learn, and very able to teach; a man, out of whose company I never go without having learned something. It is sure that he vexes me sometimes, but I am afraid it is by making me feel my own ignorance. So much extension of mind, and so much minute accuracy of enquiry, if you survey your whole circle of acquaintance, you will find so scarce, if you find it at all, that you will value Percy by comparison. Lord Hailes is somewhat like him : but Lord Hailes does not, perhaps, go beyond him in research; and I do not know that he equals him in elegance. Percy's attention to poetry has given grace and splendour to his studies of antiquity. A mere antiquarian is a rugged being.

Upon the whole, you see that what I might say in sport or petulance to him, is very consistent with full conviction of his merit.

I am, dear Sir, your most, &c.,
April 23, 1778.   SAM : JOHNSON.

578. To JAMES BOSWELL, ESQ.

Dear Sir

I have received two letters from you, of which the second complains of the neglect shewn to the first. You must not tye your friends to such punctual correspondence. You have all possible assurances of my affection and esteem; and there ought to be no need of reiterated professions. When it may happen that I can give you either counsel or comfort, I hope it will never happen to me that I should neglect you; but you must not think me criminal or cold if I say nothing when I have nothing to say.

You are now happy enough. Mrs. Boswell is recovered; and I congratulate you upon the probability of her long life. If general approbation will add anything to your enjoyment, I can tell you that I have heard you mentioned as *a man whom everybody likes*. I think life has little more to give.

Langton has gone to his regiment. He has laid down his coach, and talks of making more contractions of his expence: how he will succeed I know not. It is difficult to reform a household gradually; it may be better done by a system totally new. I am afraid he has always something to hide. When we pressed him to go to Langton, he objected the necessity of attending his navigation; yet he could talk of going to Aberdeen, a place not much nearer his navigation. I believe he cannot bear the thought of living at ——— in a state of diminution; and of appearing among the gentlemen of the neighbourhood *shorn of his beams*. This is natural, but it is cowardly. What I told him of the encreasing expence of a growing family seems to have struck him. He certainly had gone on with very confused views, and we have, I think, shewn him that he is wrong; though, with the common deficience of advisers, we have not shewn him how to do right.

I wish you would a little correct or restrain your imagination, and imagine that happiness, such as life admits, may be had at other places as well as London. Without asserting Stoicism, it may be said, that it is our business to exempt ourselves as much as we can from the power of external things. There is but one solid basis of happiness; and that is, the reasonable hope of a happy futurity. This may be had every where.

I do not blame your preference of London to other places, for it is really to be preferred, if the choice is free; but few have the choice of their place, or their manner of life; and mere pleasure ought not to be the prime motive of action.

Mrs. Thrale, poor thing, has a daughter. Mr. Thrale dislikes the times, like the rest of us. Mrs. Williams is sick; Mrs. Desmoulins is poor. I have miserable nights. Nobody is well but Mr. Levett.

I am, dear Sir, your most, &c.

London, July 3, 1778.   SAM: JOHNSON.

601. To Mrs. Garrick

Dr. Johnson sends most respectful condolence to Mrs. Garrick, and wishes that any endeavour of his could enable her to support a loss which the world cannot repair.
Feb. 2, 1779.

607. To James Boswell

Dear Sir

Why should you take such delight to make a bustle, to write to Mr. Thrale that I am negligent, and to Francis to do what is so very unnecessary. Thrale, you may be sure, cared not about it; and I shall spare Francis the trouble, by ordering a set both of the *Lives* and *Poets* to dear Mrs. Boswell,[1] in acknowledgement of her marmalade. Persuade her to accept them, and accept them kindly. If I thought she would receive them scornfully, I would send them to Miss Boswell, who, I hope, has yet none of her mamma's ill-will to me.

I would send sets of *Lives*, four volumes[2], to some other friends, to Lord Hailes first. His second volume lies by my bed-side; a book surely of great labour, and to every just thinker of great delight. Write me word to whom I shall send besides; would it please Lord Auchinleck? Mrs. Thrale waits in the coach.

I am, dear Sir, &c.,
March 13, 1779.   SAM: JOHNSON.

631. To Mrs. Thrale

Dear Madam   London, Oct. 8, 1779.

I begin to be frighted at your omission to write; do not torment me any longer, but let me know where you are, how you got thither, how you live there, and every thing else that one friend loves to know of another.

---

[1] He sent a set elegantly bound and gilt, which was received as a very handsome present. BOSWELL.

[2] [Vols. 1–4 were published in 1779.]

I will show you the way.

On Sunday the gout left my ankles, and I went very commodiously to Church. On Monday night I felt my feet uneasy. On Tuesday I was quite lame. That night I took an opiate, having first taken physick and fasted. Towards morning on Wednesday the pain remitted.—Bozzy came to me, and much talk we had. I fasted another day; and on Wednesday night could walk tolerably. On Thursday, finding myself mending, I ventured on my dinner, which I think has a little interrupted my convalescence. To-day I have again taken physick, and eaten only some stewed apples. I hope to starve it away. It is now no worse than it was at Brighthelmstone.

This, Madam, is the history of one of my toes; the history of my head would perhaps be much shorter. I thought it was the gout on Saturday. It has already lost me two dinners abroad, but then I have not been at much more charges, for I have eaten little at home.

Surely I shall have a letter to-morrow.

I am, &c.,
SAM: JOHNSON.

635. TO THE REVEREND DR. TAYLOR

Dear Sir

When I found that the Deanery had given you no uneasiness, I was satisfied, and thought no more of writing. You may indeed be very well without it, and I am glad to find that you think so yourself. You have enough, if you are satisfied.

Mr. Thrale, after whose case you will have a natural curiosity, is with his family at Brighthelmston. He rides very vigorously, and runs much into company, and is very angry if it be thought that any thing ails him. Mrs. Thrale thinks him for the present in no danger. I had no mind to go with them, for I have had what Brighthelmston can give, and I know not they much wanted me.

I have had a little catch of the gout; but as I have

had no great opinion of the benefits which it is supposed to convey, I made haste to be easy, and drove it away after two days.

Publick affairs continue to go on without much mending, and there are those still who either fright themselves or would fright others with an invasion; but my opinion is that the French neither have nor had in any part of the Summer a number of ships on the opposite coast equal to the transportation of twenty or of ten thousand Men. Such a fleet cannot be hid in a creek, it must be easily visible, and yet I believe no man has seen the man that has seen it. The ships of war were within sight of Plymouth, and only within sight.

I wish, I knew how your health stands. My friends congratulate me upon my looks, and indeed I am very free from some of the most troublesome of my old complaints, but I have gained this relief by very steady use of mercury and purgatives, with some opium, and some abstinence. I have eaten more fruit this summer than perhaps in any since I was twenty years old, but though it certainly did me no harm, I know not that I had any medicinal good from it.

Write to me soon. We are both old. How few of those whom we have known in our youth are left alive! May we yet live to some better purpose.

I am, Sir, your most humble Servant,
London, Oct. 19, 1779.   SAM: JOHNSON.
To the Rev^d Dr. Taylor in Ashbourne, Derbyshire.

636. To MRS. THRALE

Dear Madam   October 21, 1779.

Your treatment of little Perkins was undoubtedly right; when there is so strong a reason against any thing as unconquerable terrour, there ought surely to be some mighty reason for it before it is done. But for putting into the water a child already well, it is not very easy to find any reason strong or weak. That the nurses fretted, will supply me during life with an additional motive to keep every child, as far as is possible, out of a nurse's power. A nurse made of common mould will have a pride in overpowering a child's reluctance. There are few minds to which tyranny is not delightful; power is nothing but as it is felt, and the delight of superiority is proportionate to the resistance overcome.

I walked yesterday to Covent-garden, and feel to-day neither pain nor weakness. Send me, if you can, such an account of yourself and my master.

Sir Philip sent me word that he should be in town, but he has not yet called. Yesterday came Lady Lucan and Miss Bingham, and she said it was the first visit that she had paid.

Your new friend Mr. Bowen, who has sold fifty sets,[1] had but thirty to sell, and I am afraid has yet a set or two for a friend. There is a great deal of fallacy in this world. I hope you do not teach the company wholly to forsake poor Thomas.

The want of company is an inconvenience, but Mr. Cumberland is a million. Make the most of what you have. Send my master out to hunt in the morning, and to walk the rooms in the evening; and bring him as active as a stag on the mountain, back to the borough. When he is in motion he is mending.

The young ones are very good in minding their book. If I do not make something of them, *'twill reflect upon me, as I know not my trade*; for their parts are sufficiently known, and every body will have a better opinion of their industry than of mine. However, I hope when they come back, to accustom them to more lessons.

Your account of Mr. Scrase gives me no delight. He was a friend upon all occasions, whether assistance was wanted from the purse or the understanding. When he is gone, our barrier against calamity is weakened; and

[1] [Johnson believed—wrongly, as a later letter confesses—that this bookseller had only thirty sets of the first edition of the *Lives of the Poets*—that is of volumes 1-4, published in 1779.]

1779 (*aetat.* 70) 193

we must act with more caution, as we shall be in more danger. Consult him, while his advice is yet to be had.

What makes Cumberland hate Burney. Delap is indeed a rival, and can upon occasion *provoke a bugle*. But what has Burney done ? Does he not like her book ?

* * * * has passed one evening with me. He has made great discoveries in a library at Cambridge, and he finds so many precious materials, that his book must be a porter's load. He has sent me another sheet.

I am, dearest of all dear Ladies,
Your, &c.,
Sam : Johnson.

639. To James Boswell

Dear Sir

Why should you importune me so earnestly to write ? Of what importance can it be to hear of distant friends, to a man who finds himself welcome wherever he goes, and makes new friends faster than he can want them ? If to the delight of such universal kindness of reception, any thing can be added by knowing that you retain my good-will, you may indulge yourself in the full enjoyment of that small addition.

I am glad that you made the round of Lichfield with so much success : the oftener you are seen, the more you will be liked. It was pleasing to me to read that Mrs. Aston was so well, and that Lucy Porter was so glad to see you.

In the place where you now are, there is much to be observed ; and you will easily procure yourself skilful directors. But what will you do to keep away the *black dog* that worries you at home ? If you would, in compliance with your father's advice, enquire into the old tenures and old charters of Scotland, you would certainly open to yourself many striking scenes of the manners of the middle ages. The feudal system, in a country half-barbarous, is naturally productive of great anomalies in civil life. The knowledge of past times is naturally growing less in all cases not of publick record; and the past time of Scotland is so unlike the present, that it is already difficult for a Scotchman to image the œconomy of his grandfather. Do not be tardy nor negligent; but gather up eagerly what can yet be found.

We have, I think, once talked of another project, a *History of the late insurrection in Scotland*, with all its incidents. Many falsehoods are passing into uncontradicted history. Voltaire, who loved a striking story, has told what he could not find to be true.

You may make collections for either of these projects, or for both, as opportunities occur, and digest your materials at leisure. The great direction which Burton has left to men disordered like you, is this, *Be not solitary: be not idle:* which I would thus modify;— If you are idle, be not solitary; if you are solitary, be not idle.

There is a letter for you, from your humble servant,
London, October 27, 1779. SAM: JOHNSON.

647. TO MRS. THRALE

Dear Madam London, Nov. 16, 1779.

Pray how long does a letter tarry between London and Brighthelmston? Your letter of the 12th I received on the 15th.

Poor Mrs. * * * * is a feeler. It is well that she has yet power to feel. Fiction durst not have driven upon a few months such a conflux of misery. Comfort her as you can.

I have looked again into your grave letter. You mention trustees. I do not see who can be trustee for a casual and variable property, for a fortune yet to be acquired. How can any man be trusted with what he cannot possess, cannot ascertain, and cannot regulate? The trade must be carried on by somebody who must be answerable for the debts contracted. This can be none but yourself; unless you deliver up the property to some other agent, and trust the chance both of his prudence and his honesty. Do not be frighted; trade could not be managed by those who manage it, if it had much difficulty. Their great books are soon understood, and their language,

> If speech it may be call'd, that speech is none
> Distinguishable in number, mood, or tense,

is understood with no very laborious application.

The help which you can have from any man as a trustee, you may have from him as a friend; the trusteeship may give him power to perplex, but will neither increase his benevolence to assist, nor his wisdom to advise.

> Living on God, and on thyself rely.

Who should be trustee but you, for your own and your children's prosperity? I hope this is an end of this unpleasing speculation, and lighter matters may take their turn.

What Mr. Scrase says about the Borough is true, but is nothing to the purpose. A house in the square will not cost so much as building in Southwark; but buildings are more likely to go on in Southwark if your dwelling is at St. James's. Every body has some desire that deserts the great road of prosperity, to look for pleasure in a bye-path. I do not see with so much indignation Mr. Thrale's desire of being the first Brewer, as your despicable dread of living in the Borough. Ambition in little things, is better than cowardice in little things; but both these things, however little to the publick eye, are great in their consequences to yourselves. The world cares not how you brew, or where you live; but it is the business of the one to brew in a manner most advantageous to his family, and of the other to live where the general interest may best be superintended. It was by an accidental visit to the Borough that you escaped great evils last Summer. Of this folly let there be an end, at least an intermission.

I am glad that Queeney danced with Mr. Wade. She was the Sultaness of the evening; and I am glad that Mr. Thrale has found a riding companion whom he likes. Let him ride, say I, till he leaves dejection and disease behind him; and let them limp after him an hundred years without overtaking him. When he returns, let me see him frolick and airy, and social, and busy, and as kind to me as in former times.

You seem to be afraid that I should be starved before you come back. I have indeed practised abstinence with some stubbornness, and with some success; but as Dryden talks of *writing with a hat*, I am sometimes very witty with a knife and fork. I have managed myself very well; except that having no motive, I have no exercise.

At home we do not much quarrel; but perhaps the less we quarrel the more we hate. There is as much malignity amongst us as can well subsist, without any thoughts of daggers or poisons.

Mrs. —— is by the help of frequent operations still kept alive; and such is the capricious destiny of mortals, that she will die more lamented by her husband, than I will promise to usefulness, wisdom, or sanctity. There is always something operating distinct from diligence or skill. Temple therefore in his composition of a hero, to the heroick virtues adds good fortune.

I am, &c.,
SAM: JOHNSON.

650. TO DR. LAWRENCE

Dear Sir

At a time when all your friends ought to shew their kindness, and with a character which ought to make all that know you your friends, you may wonder that you have yet heard nothing from me.

I have been hindered by a vexatious and incessant cough, for which within these ten days I have been bled once, fasted four or five times, taken physick five times, and opiates, I think, six. This day it seems to remit.

The loss, dear Sir, which you have lately suffered,

I felt many years ago, and know therefore how much has been taken from you, and how little help can be had from consolation. He that outlives a wife whom he has long loved, sees himself disjoined from the only mind that has the same hopes, and fears, and interest; from the only companion with whom he has shared much good or evil; and with whom he could set his mind at liberty, to retrace the past or anticipate the future. The continuity of being is lacerated; the settled course of sentiment and action is stopped; and life stands suspended and motionless, till it is driven by external causes into a new channel. But the time of suspense is dreadful.

Our first recourse in this distressed solitude, is, perhaps for want of habitual piety, to a gloomy acquiescence in necessity. Of two mortal beings, one must lose the other; but surely there is a higher and better comfort to be drawn from the consideration of that Providence which watches over all, and a belief that the living and the dead are equally in the hands of GOD, who will reunite those whom he has separated; or who sees that it is best not to reunite.

I am, dear Sir, your most affectionate,
and most humble servant,
January 20, 1780.   SAM: JOHNSON.

655. To JAMES BOSWELL

Dear Sir

Well, I had resolved to send you the Chesterfield letter; but I will write once again without it. Never impose tasks upon mortals. To require two things is the way to have them both undone.

For the difficulties which you mention in your affairs I am sorry; but difficulty is now very general: it is not therefore less grievous, for there is less hope of help. I pretend not to give you advice, not knowing the state of your affairs; and general counsels about prudence and frugality would do you little good. You are, however, in the right not to increase your own perplexity by a journey hither; and I hope that by staying at home you will please your father.

Poor dear Beauclerk—*nec, ut soles, dabis joca.* His wit and his folly, his acuteness and maliciousness, his merriment and reasoning, are now over. Such another will not often be found among mankind. He directed himself to be buried by the side of his mother, an instance of tenderness which I hardly expected. He has left his children to the care of Lady Di, and if she dies, of Mr. Langton, and of Mr. Leicester his relation, and a man of good character. His library has been offered to sale to the Russian ambassador.

Dr. Percy, notwithstanding all the noise of the newspapers, has had no literary loss.[1] Clothes and moveables were burnt to the value of about one hundred pounds; but his papers, and I think his books, were all preserved.

Poor Mr. Thrale has been in extreme danger from an apoplectical disorder, and recovered, beyond the expectation of his physicians; he is now at Bath, that his mind may be quiet, and Mrs. Thrale and Miss are with him.

Having told you what has happened to your friends, let me say something to you of yourself. You are always complaining of melancholy, and I conclude from those complaints that you are fond of it. No man talks of that which he is desirous to conceal, and every man desires to conceal that of which he is ashamed. Do not pretend to deny it; *manifestum habemus furem*; make it an invariable and obligatory law to yourself, never to mention your own mental diseases; if you are never to speak of them, you will think on them but little, and if you think little of them, they will molest you rarely. When you talk of them, it is plain that you want either praise or pity; for praise there is no room, and pity will do you no

[1] By a fire in Northumberland-house, where he had an apartment, in which I have passed many an agreeable hour. BOSWELL.

good; therefore, from this hour speak no more, think no more, about them.

Your transaction with Mrs. Stewart gave me great satisfaction; I am much obliged to you for your attention. Do not lose sight of her; your countenance may be of great credit, and of consequence of great advantage to her. The memory of her brother is yet fresh in my mind; he was an ingenious and worthy man.

Please to make my compliments to your lady, and to the young ladies. I should like to see them, pretty loves.

I am, dear Sir, yours affectionately,
April 8, 1780.　　　　　　　　　Sam: Johnson.

657. To Mrs. Thrale

Dear Madam

On Sunday I dined with poor Lawrence, who is deafer than ever. When he was told that Dr. Moisy visited Mr. Thrale, he enquired, for what ? and said that there was nothing to be done, which Nature would not do for herself. On Sunday evening I was at Mrs. Vesey's, and there was enquiry about my master, but I told them all good. There was Dr. Barnard of Eaton, and we made a noise all the evening; and there was Pepys, and Wraxal till I drove him away. And I have no loss of my mistress, who laughs, and frisks, and frolicks it all the long day, and never thinks of poor Colin.[1]

---

[1] [The reference here and at the end of the letter is to Rowe's *Colin's Complaint*:

'Then to her new love let her go

. . . . . .

And frolick it all the long day.

. . . . . .

What though I have skill to complain

. . . . . .

Ah, Colin ! thy hopes are in vain,
Thy pipe and thy laurel resign,
Thy false one inclines to a swain
Whose musick is sweeter than thine.']

If Mr. Thrale will but continue to mend, we shall, I hope, come together again, and do as good things as ever we did; but perhaps you will be made too proud to heed me, and yet, as I have often told you, it will not be easy for you to find such another.

Queeney has been a good girl, and wrote me a letter; if Burney said she would write, she told you a fib. She writes nothing to me. She can write home fast enough. I have a good mind not to let her know, that Dr. Barnard, to whom I had recommended her novel, speaks of it with great recommendation; and that the copy which she lent me, has been read by Dr. Lawrence three times over. And yet what a gypsey it is. She no more minds me, than if I were a Brangton.[1] Pray speak to Queeney to write again.

I have had a cold and a cough, and taken opium, and think I am better. We have had very cold weather; bad riding weather for my master, but he will surmount it all. Did Mrs. Browne make any reply to your comparison of business with solitude, or did you quite down her? I am much pleased to think that Mrs. Cotton thinks me worth a frame, and a place upon her wall. Her kindness was hardly within my hope, but time does wonderful things. All my fear is, that if I should come again, my print would be taken down. I fear I shall never hold it.

Who dines with you? Do you see Dr. Woodward or Dr. Harrington? Do you go to the house where they write for the myrtle?[2] You are at all places of high resort, and bring home hearts by dozens; while I am seeking for something to say about men of whom I know nothing but their verses, and sometimes very little of them. Now I have begun, however, I do not despair of making an end. Mr. Nicholls holds that

---

[1] [The Brangtons are the vulgar Londoners of *Evelina*.]

[2] [Lady Miller's at Bath-Easton. This absurd lady 'held a Parnassus-fair every Thursday' at which 'a Roman vase, dressed with pink ribands and myrtles, received the poetry'.]

Addison is the most *taking* of all that I have done. I doubt they will not be done before you come away.

Now you think yourself the first writer in the world for a letter about nothing. Can you write such a letter as this? So miscellaneous, with such noble disdain of regularity, like Shakespeare's works; such graceful negligence of transition, like the ancient enthusiasts? The pure voice of nature and of friendship. Now of whom shall I proceed to speak? Of whom but Mrs. Montague? Having mentioned Shakespeare and Nature, does not the name of Montague force itself upon me? Such were the transitions of the ancients, which now seem abrupt, because the intermediate idea is lost to modern understandings. I wish her name had connected itself with friendship; but, ah Colin, thy hopes are in vain. One thing however is left me, I have skill to complain; but I hope I shall not complain much while you have any kindness for me. I am,

Dearest and dearest Madam,
Your, &c.,
London, April 11, 1780.   SAM: JOHNSON.
You do not date your letters.

658. To MRS. THRALE

Dearest Madam   April 15, 1780.

I did not mistake Dr. Woodward's case; nor should have wanted any explanation. But broken is a very bad word in the city.

Here has just been with me Dr. Burney, who has given—What has he given? Nothing, I believe, gratis. He has given fifty-seven lessons this week. Surely this is business.

I thought to have finished Rowe's life to-day, but I have five or six visitors who hindered me; and I have not been quite well. Next week I hope to dispatch four or five of them.

It is a great delight to hear so much good of all

of you. Fanny tells me good news of you, and you speak well of Fanny; and all of you say what one would wish of my master. And my sweet Queeney, I hope is well. Does she drink the waters? *One glass* would do her as much good as it does her father.

You and Mrs. Montague must keep Mrs. Cotton about you; and try to make a wit of her. She will be a little unskilful in her first essays; but you will see how precept and example will bring her forwards.

Surely it is very fine to have your powers. The wits court you, and the Methodists love you, and the whole world runs about you; and you write me word how well you can do without me: and so, go thy ways poor Jack.

That sovereign *glass of water* is the great medicine; and though his legs are rather too big, yet my master takes a glass of water. This is bold practice. I believe, under the protection of a glass of water drank at the pump, he may venture once a-week upon a stew'd lamprey.

I wish you all good; yet know not what to wish you which you have not. May all good continue and increase.

I am, &c.,
SAM: JOHNSON.

663. TO MRS. THRALE

Dearest Madam

Mr. Thrale never will live abstinently, till he can persuade himself to abstain by rule. I lived on potatoes on Friday, and on spinach to-day; but I have had, I am afraid, too many dinners of late. I took physick too both days, and hope to fast to-morrow. When he comes home, we will shame him, and Jebb shall scold him into regularity. I am glad, however, that he is always one of the company, and that my dear Queeney is again another. Encourage, as you can, the musical girl.

Nothing is more common than mutual dislike where

mutual approbation is particularly expected. There is often on both sides a vigilance not over benevolent; and as attention is strongly excited, so that nothing drops unheeded, any difference in taste or opinion, and some difference where there is no restraint will commonly appear, immediately generates dislike.

Never let criticisms operate upon your face or your mind; it is very rarely that an author is hurt by his criticks. The blaze of reputation cannot be blown out, but it often dies in the socket; a very few names may be considered as perpetual lamps that shine unconsumed. From the author of Fitzosborne's Letters I cannot think myself in much danger. I met him only once about thirty years ago, and in some small dispute reduced him to whistle; having not seen him since, that is the last impression. Poor Moore the fabulist was one of the company.

Mrs. Montague's long stay, against her own inclination, is very convenient. You would, by your own confession, want a companion; and she is *par pluribus*, conversing with her you may *find variety in one*.

At Mrs. Ord's I met one Mrs. Buller, a travelled lady, of great spirit, and some consciousness of her own abilities. We had a contest of gallantry an hour long, so much to the diversion of the company, that at Ramsay's last night, in a crowded room, they would have pitted us again. There were Smelt, and the Bishop of St. Asaph, who comes to every place; and Lord Monboddo, and Sir Joshua, and ladies out of tale.

The exhibition, how will you do, either to see or not to see! The exhibition is eminently splendid. There is contour, and keeping, and grace, and expression, and all the varieties of artificial excellence. The apartments were truly very noble. The pictures, for the sake of a sky light, are at the top of the house; there we dined, and I sat over against the Archbishop of York. See how I live when I am not under petticoat government.

I am, &c.,

London, May 1, 1780.   SAM: JOHNSON.

Mark that—you did not put the year to your last.

677. To Mrs. Thrale

Dear Madam   London, [Friday] June 9, 1780.

To the question, Who was impressed with consternation? it may with great truth be answered, that every body was impressed, for nobody was sure of his safety.

On Friday the good Protestants met in St. George's Fields, at the summons of Lord George Gordon, and marching to Westminster, insulted the Lords and Commons, who all bore it with great tameness. At night the outrages began by the demolition of the mass-house by Lincoln's Inn.

An exact journal of a week's defiance of government I cannot give you. On Monday, Mr. Strahan, who had been insulted, spoke to Lord Mansfield, who had I think been insulted too, of the licentiousness of the populace; and his Lordship treated it as a very slight irregularity. On Tuesday night they pulled down Fielding's house, and burnt his goods in the street. They had gutted on Monday Sir George Savile's house, but the building was saved. On Tuesday evening, leaving Fielding's ruins, they went to Newgate to demand their companions who had been seized demolishing the chapel. The keeper could not release them but by the Mayor's permission, which he went to ask; at his return he found all the prisoners released, and Newgate in a blaze. They then went to Bloomsbury and fastened upon Lord Mansfield's house, which they pulled down; and as for his goods, they totally burnt them. They have since gone to Cane-wood, but a guard was there before them. They plundered some Papists, I think, and burnt a mass-house in Moorfields the same night.

On Wednesday I walked with Dr. Scot to look at Newgate, and found it in ruins, with the fire yet glowing. As I went by, the Protestants were plundering the Sessions-house at the Old Bailey. There were not, I believe, a hundred; but they did their work at leisure, in full security, without sentinels, without trepidation, as men lawfully employed, in full day. Such is the cowardice of a commercial place. On Wednesday they broke open the Fleet, and the King's-bench, and the Marshalsea, and Woodstreet-counter, and Clerkenwell Bridewell, and released all the prisoners.

At night they set fire to the Fleet, and to the King's-bench, and I know not how many other places; and one might see the glare of conflagration fill the sky from many parts. The sight was dreadful. Some people were threatened; Mr. Strahan advised me to take care of myself. Such a time of terror you have been happy in not seeing.

The King said in council, that the magistrates had not done their duty, but that he would do his own; and a proclamation was published, directing us to keep our servants within doors, as the peace was now to be preserved by force. The soldiers were sent out to different parts, and the town is now at quiet.

What has happened at your house you will know, the harm is only a few butts of beer; and I think you may be sure that the danger is over. There is a body of soldiers at St. Margaret's Hill.

Of Mr. Tyson I know nothing, nor can guess to what he can allude; but I know that a young fellow of little more than seventy, is naturally an unresisted conqueror of hearts.

Pray tell Mr. Thrale that I live here and have no fruit, and if he does not interpose, am not likely to have much; but I think he might as well give me a little, as give all to the gardener.

Pray make my compliments to Queeney and Burney.

I am, &c.,

SAM: JOHNSON

681. To MRS. THRALE

Dear Madam   London, June 15, 1780.

Last night I told you that I was not well; and though you have much else to think on, perhaps you may be willing enough to hear, that by the help of an opiate, I think myself better to-day.

Whether I am or am not better, the town is quiet, and every body sleeps in quiet, except a few who please themselves with guarding us now the danger is over. Perkins seems to have managed with great dexterity. Every body, I believe, now sees, that if the tumult had been opposed immediately, it had been immediately suppressed; and we are therefore now better provided against an insurrection, than if none had happened.

I hope you, and Master, and Queeney, and Burney, are all well. I was contented last night to send an excuse to Vesey, and two days ago another to Mrs. Horneck; you may think I was bad, if you thought about it; and why should you not think about me who am so often thinking about you, and your appurtenances. But there is no gratitude in this world.

> But I could tell you, Doris, if I would;
> And since you treat me so, methinks I should.

So sings the sublime and pathetick Mr. Walsh. Well! and I will tell you too. Among the heroes of the Borough, who twice a-day perambulate, or perequitate High-street and the Clink, rides that renowned and redoubted knight, Sir Richard Hotham. There is magnanimity, which defies every danger that is past, and publick spirit, that stands sentinel over property that he does not own. Tell me no more of the self-devoted Decii, or of the leap of Curtius. Let fame talk henceforward with all her tongues of Hotham the Hatmaker.

I was last week at Renny's conversatione, and Renny got her room pretty well filled; and there were Mrs. Ord, and Mrs. Horneck, and Mrs. Bunbury, and other illustrious names, and much would poor Renny have given to have had Mrs. Thrale too, and Queeney, and Burney: but human happiness is never perfect; there is always *une vide affreuse*, as Maintenon complained, there is some craving void left aking in the breast. Renny is going to Ramsgate; and thus the world drops away, and I am left in the sultry town, to see the sun in the crab, and perhaps in the lion, while you are paddling with the Nereids.

I am, &c.,
SAM: JOHNSON.

686. TO MRS. THRALE

Dear Madam London, July 10, 1780.

If Mr. Thrale eats but half his usual quantity, he can hardly eat too much. It were better however to have some rule, and some security. Last week I saw flesh but twice, and I think fish once, the rest was pease.

You are afraid, you say, lest I extenuate myself too fast, and are an enemy to violence: but did you never hear nor read, dear Madam, that every man has his *genius*, and that the great rule by which all excellence is attained, and all success procured, is, to follow *genius*; and have you not observed in all our conversations that my *genius* is always in extremes; that I am very noisy, or very silent; very gloomy, or very merry; very sour, or very kind? And would you have me cross my *genius*, when it leads me sometimes to voracity and sometimes to abstinence? You know that the oracle said follow your *genius*. When we get together again, (but when alas will that be?) you can manage me, and spare me the solicitude of managing myself.

Poor Miss Owen called on me on Saturday, with that fond and tender application which is natural to misery, when it looks to every body for that help which nobody can give. I was melted; and soothed and counselled her as well as I could, and am to visit her to-morrow.

She gave a very honourable account of my dear Queeney; and says of my master, that she thinks his manner and temper more altered than his looks, but of this alteration she could give no particular account; and all that she could say ended in this, that he is now sleepy in the morning. I do not wonder at the scantiness of her narration, she is too busy within to turn her eyes abroad.

I am glad that Pepys is come, but hope that resolute temperance will make him unnecessary. I doubt he can do no good to poor Mr. Scrase.

I stay at home to work, and yet do not work diligently; nor can tell when I shall have done, nor perhaps does any body but myself wish me to have done; for what can they hope I shall do better? yet I wish the work was over, and I was at liberty. And what would I do if I was at liberty? Would I go to Mrs. Aston and Mrs. Porter, and see the old places, and sigh to find that my old friends are gone? Would I recall plans of life which I never brought into practice, and hopes of excellence which I once presumed, and never have attained? Would I compare what I now am with what I once expected to have been? Is it reasonable to wish for suggestions of shame, and opportunities of sorrow?

If you please, Madam, we will have an end of this, and contrive some other wishes. I wish I had you in an evening, and I wish I had you in a morning; and I wish I could have a little talk, and see a little frolick. For all this I must stay, but life will not stay.

I will end my letter and go to Blackmore's Life, when I have told you that

I am, &c.,
SAM: JOHNSON.

688. TO LORD WESTCOTE

Bolt Court, Fleet Street, July 27, 1780.
My Lord

The course of my undertaking will now require a short life of your brother, Lord Lyttelton. My desire is to avoid offence; and to be totally out of danger, I take the liberty of proposing to your lordship, that the historical account should be written under your direction by any friend you may be willing to employ,

and I will only take upon myself to examine the poetry.
Four pages like those of his work, or even half so much,
will be sufficient. As the press is going on, it will be
fit that I should know what you shall be pleased to
determine.
  I am,
    My Lord,
      Your lordship's most humble servant,
        SAM: JOHNSON.

689. To LORD WESTCOTE

Bolt Court, Fleet Street, July 28, 1780.
My Lord
  I wish it had been convenient to have had that
done which I proposed. I shall certainly not wantonly
nor willingly offend; but when there are such near
relations living, I had rather they would please themselves. For the life of Lord Lyttelton I shall need no
help—it was very public, and I have no need to be
minute. But I return your lordship thanks for your
readiness to help me. I have another life in hand,
that of Mr. West, about which I am quite at a loss;
any information respecting him would be of great use to,
  My Lord,
    Your lordship's most humble servant,
      SAM: JOHNSON.

704. To CHARLES LAWRENCE

Dear Sir
  Not many days ago Dr. Lawrence shewed me
a letter, in which you make mention of me: I hope,
therefore, that you will not be displeased that I
endeavour to preserve your good-will by some observations which your letter suggested to me.
  You are afraid of falling into some improprieties
in the daily service by reading to an audience that
requires no exactness. Your fear, I hope, secures you
from danger. They who contract absurd habits are

such as have no fear. It is impossible to do the same thing very often, without some peculiarity of manner: but that manner may be good or bad, and a little care will at least preserve it from being bad: to make it very good, there must, I think, be something of natural or casual felicity, which cannot be taught.

Your present method of making your sermons seems very judicious. Few frequent preachers can be supposed to have sermons more their own than yours will be. Take care to register, somewhere or other, the authours from whom your several discourses are borrowed; and do not imagine that you shall always remember, even what perhaps you now think it impossible to forget.

My advice, however, is, that you attempt, from time to time, an original sermon; and in the labour of composition, do not burthen your mind with too much at once; do not exact from yourself at one effort of excogitation, propriety of thought and elegance of expression. Invent first, and then embellish. The production of something, where nothing was before, is an act of greater energy than the expansion or decoration of the thing produced. Set down diligently your thoughts as they rise, in the first words that occur; and, when you have matter, you will easily give it form: nor, perhaps, will this method be always necessary; for by habit, your thoughts and diction will flow together.

The composition of sermons is not very difficult: the divisions not only help the memory of the hearer, but direct the judgement of the writer; they supply sources of invention, and keep every part in its proper place.

What I like least in your letter is your account of the manners of the parish; from which I gather, that it has been long neglected by the parson. The Dean of Carlisle, who was then a little rector in Northamptonshire, told me, that it might be discerned whether or no there was a clergyman resident in a parish by the civil or savage manners of the people. Such a congregation as yours stands in much need of reformation; and I would not have you think it impossible to reform them. A very savage parish was civilised by a decayed gentlewoman, who came among them to teach a petty school. My learned friend Dr. Wheeler of Oxford, when he was a young man, had the care of a neighbouring parish for fifteen pounds a year, which he was never paid; but he counted it a convenience that it compelled him to make a weekly sermon. One woman he could not bring to communion; and, when he reproved or exhorted her, she only answered, that she was no scholar. He was advised to set some good woman or man of the parish, a little wiser than herself, to talk to her in a language level to her mind. Such honest, I may call them holy artifices, must be practised by every clergyman; for all means must be tried by which souls may be saved. Talk to your people, however, as much as you can; and you will find, that the more frequently you converse with them on religious subjects, the more willingly they will attend, and the more submissively they will learn. A clergyman's diligence always makes him venerable. I think I have now only to say, that in the momentous work that you have undertaken, I pray GOD to bless you.

I am, Sir, your most humble servant,
Bolt-court, Aug. 30, 1780.   SAM: JOHNSON.

712. To WARREN HASTINGS

Sir   Jan. 9, 1781.

Amidst the importance and multiplicity of affairs in which your great office engages you, I take the liberty of recalling your attention for a moment to literature, and will not prolong the interruption by an apology which your character makes needless.

Mr. Hoole, a gentleman long known, and long esteemed in the India-House, after having translated Tasso, has undertaken Ariosto. How well he is qualified for his undertaking he has already shewn.

He is desirous, Sir, of your favour in promoting his proposals, and flatters me by supposing that my testimony may advance his interest.

It is a new thing for a clerk of the India-House to translate poets;—it is new for a Governour of Bengal to patronize learning. That he may find his ingenuity rewarded, and that learning may flourish under your protection, is the wish of,

Sir, your most humble servant,
SAM: JOHNSON.

715. To JAMES BOSWELL

Dear Sir

I hoped you had got rid of all this hypocrisy of misery. What have you to do with Liberty and Necessity ? Or what more than to hold your tongue about it ? Do not doubt but I shall be most heartily glad to see you here again, for I love every part about you but your affectation of distress.

I have at last finished my *Lives*, and have laid up for you a load of copy, all out of order, so that it will amuse you a long time to set it right. Come to me, my dear Bozzy, and let us be as happy as we can. We will go again to the Mitre, and talk old times over.

I am, dear Sir, yours affectionately,

March 14, 1781. SAM: JOHNSON.

717. To MRS. THRALE

Dearest Madam London, April 5, 1781.

Of your injunctions, to pray for you and write to you, I hope to leave neither unobserved ; and I hope to find you willing in a short time to alleviate your trouble by some other exercise of the mind. I am not without my part of the calamity. No death since that of my wife has ever oppressed me like this. But let us remember, that we are in the hands of Him who knows when to give and when to take away ; who will look upon us with mercy through all our variations of existence, and who invites us to call on him in the day of trouble. Call upon him in this great revolution of life, and call with confidence. You will then find comfort for the past, and support for the future. He that has given you happiness in marriage, to a degree of which, without personal knowledge, I should have thought the description fabulous, can give you another mode of happiness as a mother; and at last, the happiness of losing all temporal cares in the thoughts of an eternity in heaven.

I do not exhort you to reason yourself into tranquillity. We must first pray, and then labour; first implore the blessing of God, and then employ those means which he puts into our hands. Cultivated ground has few weeds; a mind occupied by lawful business, has little room for useless regret.

We read the will to-day; but I will not fill my first letter with any other account than that, with all my zeal for your advantage, I am satisfied; and that the other executors, more used to consider property than I, commended it for wisdom and equity. Yet why should I not tell you that you have five hundred pounds for your immediate expenses, and two thousand pounds a-year, with both the houses and all the goods?

Let us pray for one another, that the time, whether long or short, that shall yet be granted us, may be well spent; and that when this life, which at the longest is very short, shall come to an end, a better may begin which shall never end.

I am, dearest Madam,
Your, &c.,
SAM: JOHNSON.

722. To Mrs. Thrale

Dearest Madam London, April 12, 1781.

You will not suppose that much has happened since last night, nor indeed is this a time for talking much of loss and gain. The business of Christians is now for a few days in their own bosoms. God grant us to do it properly. I hope you gain ground on your affliction. I hope to overcome mine. You and Miss must comfort one another. May you long live happily together. I have nobody whom I expect to share my uneasiness, nor, if I could communicate it, would it be less. I give it little vent, and amuse it as I can. Let us pray for one another. And, when we meet, we may try what fidelity and tenderness will do for us.

There is no wisdom in useless and hopeless sorrow; but there is something in it so like virtue, that he who is wholly without it cannot be loved, nor will by me at least be thought worthy of esteem. My next letter will be to Queeney.

I am, Madam, your most humble servant,
SAM: JOHNSON.

746. To MRS. THRALE

Dearest Madam Lichfield, Nov. 3, 1781.

You very kindly remind me of the dear home which I have left; but I need none of your aids to recollection, for I am here gasping for breath, and yet better than those whom I came to visit. Mrs. Aston has been for three years a paralytic crawler; but, I think, with her mind unimpaired. She seems to me such as I left her; but she now eats little, and is therefore much emaciated. Her sister thinks her, and she thinks herself, passing fast away.

Lucy has had since my last visit a dreadful illness, from which her physicians declared themselves hopeless of recovering her, and which has shaken the general fabrick, and weakened the powers of life. She is unable or unwilling to move, and is never likely to have more of either strength or spirit.

I am so visibly disordered, that a medical man, who only saw me at church, sent me some pills. To those whom I love here I can give no help, and from those that love me none can I receive. Do you think that I need to be reminded of home and you?

The time of the year is not very favourable to excursions. I thought myself above assistance or obstruction from the seasons; but find the autumnal blast sharp and nipping, and the fading world an uncomfortable prospect. Yet I may say with Milton, that I do not *abate* much *of heart or hope*. To what I have done I do not despair of adding something, but *what it shall be I know not*.

I am, Madam,
Most affectionately yours,
SAM: JOHNSON.

749. TO MRS. THRALE

Dearest Madam   Ashbourne, Nov. 14, 1781.

Here is Doctor Taylor, by a resolute adherence to bread and milk, with a better appearance of health than he has had for a long time past; and here am I, living very temperately, but with very little amendment. But the balance is not perhaps very unequal: he has no pleasure like that which I receive from the kind importunity with which you invite me to return. There is no danger of very long delay. There is nothing in this part of the world that can counteract your attraction.

The hurt in my leg has grown well slowly, according to Hector's prognostick, and seems now to be almost healed: but my nights are very restless, and the days are therefore heavy, and I have not your conversation to cheer them.

I am willing however to hear that there is happiness in the world, and delight to think on the pleasure diffused among the Burneys. I question if any ship upon the ocean goes out attended with more good wishes than that which carries the fate of Burney. I love all of that breed whom I can be said to know, and one or two whom I hardly know I love upon credit, and love them because they love each other. Of this consanguineous unanimity I have had never much experience; but it appears to me one of the great lenitives of life;

but it has this deficience, that it is never found when
distress is mutual—He that has less than enough for
himself has nothing to spare, and as every man feels
only his own necessities, he is apt to think those of
others less pressing, and to accuse them of with-holding
what in truth they cannot give. He that has his foot
firm upon dry ground may pluck another out of the
water; but of those that are all afloat, none has any
care but for himself.

We do not hear that the deanery is yet given away,
and, though nothing is said, I believe much is still
thought about it. *Hope travels through*——

I am, dearest of all dear ladies,
Your, &c.,
Sam: Johnson.

766. To Edmond Malone

Dear Sir

I hope I grow better, and shall soon be able to
enjoy the kindness of my friends. I think this wild
adherence to Chatterton more unaccountable than the
obstinate defence of Ossian. In Ossian there is a
national pride, which may be forgiven, though it cannot
be applauded. In Chatterton there is nothing but the
resolution to say again what has once been said.

I am, Sir, your humble servant,
March 2, 1782. Sam: Johnson.

770. To Captain Langton,[1] in Rochester

Dear Sir

It is now long since we saw one another; and
whatever has been the reason neither you have written
to me, nor I to you. To let friendship die away by
negligence and silence, is certainly not wise. It is
voluntarily to throw away one of the greatest comforts

---

[1] Mr. Langton being at this time on duty at Rochester,
he is addressed by his military title. Boswell.

of this weary pilgrimage, of which when it is, as it must be, taken finally away, he that travels on alone, will wonder how his esteem could be so little. Do not forget me ; you see that I do not forget you. It is pleasing in the silence of solitude to think, that there is one at least, however distant, of whose benevolence there is little doubt, and whom there is yet hope of seeing again.

Of my life, from the time we parted, the history is mournful. The spring of last year deprived me of Thrale, a man whose eye for fifteen years had scarcely been turned upon me but with respect or tenderness ; for such another friend, the general course of human things will not suffer man to hope. I passed the summer at Streatham, but there was no Thrale ; and having idled away the summer with a weakly body and neglected mind, I made a journey to Staffordshire on the edge of winter. The season was dreary, I was sickly, and found the friends sickly whom I went to see. After a sorrowful sojourn, I returned to a habitation possessed for the present by two sick women, where my dear old friend, Mr. Levett, to whom as he used to tell me, I owe your acquaintance, died a few weeks ago, suddenly in his bed ; there passed not, I believe, a minute between health and death. At night, as at Mrs. Thrale's I was musing in my chamber, I thought with uncommon earnestness, that however I might alter my mode of life, or whithersoever I might remove, I would endeavour to retain Levett about me ; in the morning my servant brought me word that Levett was called to another state, a state for which, I think, he was not unprepared, for he was very useful to the poor. How much soever I valued him, I now wish that I had valued him more.

I have myself been ill more than eight weeks of a disorder, from which at the expence of about fifty ounces of blood, I hope I am now recovering.

You, dear Sir, have, I hope, a more cheerful scene ; you see George fond of his book, and the pretty misses airy and lively, with my own little Jenny equal to the best : and in whatever can contribute to your quiet or pleasure, you have Lady Rothes ready to concur. May whatever you enjoy of good be encreased, and whatever you suffer of evil be diminished.

I am, dear Sir, your humble servant,

SAM: JOHNSON.

Bolt-court, Fleet-street, March 20, 1782.

772. To EDMUND HECTOR

[Without a date, but supposed to be about this time.]

Dear Sir

That you and dear Mrs. Careless should have care or curiosity about my health, gives me that pleasure which every man feels from finding himself not forgotten. In age we feel again that love of our native place and our early friends, which in the bustle or amusements of middle life were overborne and suspended. You and I should now naturally cling to one another : we have outlived most of those who could pretend to rival us in each other's kindness. In our walk through life we have dropped our companions, and are now to pick up such as chance may offer us, or to travel on alone. You, indeed, have a sister, with whom you can divide the day : I have no natural friend left; but Providence has been pleased to preserve me from neglect; I have not wanted such alleviations of life as friendship could supply. My health has been, from my twentieth year, such as has seldom afforded me a single day of ease; but it is at least not worse : and I sometimes make myself believe that it is better. My disorders are, however, still sufficiently oppressive.

I think of seeing Staffordshire again this autumn, and intend to find my way through Birmingham, where I hope to see you and dear Mrs. Careless well.

I am, Sir, your affectionate friend,

SAM: JOHNSON.

775. To JAMES BOSWELL

Dear Sir

The pleasure which we used to receive from each other on Good-Friday and Easter-day, we must be this year content to miss. Let us, however, pray for each other, and hope to see one another yet from time to time with mutual delight. My disorder has been a cold, which impeded the organs of respiration, and kept me many weeks in a state of great uneasiness; but by repeated phlebotomy it is now relieved; and next to the recovery of Mrs. Boswell, I flatter myself, that you will rejoice at mine.

What we shall do in the summer it is yet too early to consider. You want to know what you shall do now; I do not think this time of bustle and confusion likely to produce any advantage to you. Every man has those to reward and gratify who have contributed to his advancement. To come hither with such expectations at the expence of borrowed money, which, I find, you know not where to borrow, can hardly be considered as prudent. I am sorry to find, what your solicitation seems to imply, that you have already gone the whole length of your credit. This is to set the quiet of your whole life at hazard. If you anticipate your inheritance, you can at last inherit nothing; all that you receive must pay for the past. You must get a place, or pine in penury, with the empty name of a great estate. Poverty, my dear friend, is so great an evil, and pregnant with so much temptation, and so much misery, that I cannot but earnestly enjoin you to avoid it. Live on what you have; live if you can on less; do not borrow either for vanity or pleasure; the vanity will end in shame, and the pleasure in regret: stay therefore at home, till you have saved money for your journey hither.

The Beauties of Johnson are said to have got money to the collector; if the *Deformities* have the same success, I shall be still a more extensive benefactor.

Make my compliments to Mrs. Boswell, who is,

I hope, reconciled to me; and to the young people whom I never have offended.

You never told me the success of your plea against the Solicitors.

I am, dear Sir, your most affectionate,
London, March 28, 1782.   SAM: JOHNSON.

785. To JAMES BOSWELL

Dear Sir

The earnestness and tenderness of your letter is such, that I cannot think myself shewing it more respect than it claims by sitting down to answer it the day on which I received it.

This year has afflicted me with a very irksome and severe disorder. My respiration has been much impeded, and much blood has been taken away. I am now harrassed by a catarrhous cough, from which my purpose is to seek relief by change of air; and I am, therefore, preparing to go to Oxford.

Whether I did right in dissuading you from coming to London this spring, I will not determine. You have not lost much by missing my company; I have scarcely been well for a single week. I might have received comfort from your kindness; but you would have seen me afflicted, and, perhaps, found me peevish. Whatever might have been your pleasure or mine, I know not how I could have honestly advised you to come hither with borrowed money. Do not accustom yourself to consider debt only as an inconvenience; you will find it a calamity. Poverty takes away so many means of doing good, and produces so much inability to resist evil, both natural and moral, that it is by all virtuous means to be avoided. Consider a man whose fortune is very narrow; whatever be his rank by birth, or whatever his reputation by intellectual excellence, what good can he do? or what evil can he prevent? That he cannot help the needy is evident; he has nothing to spare. But, perhaps, his advice or admonition may be useful. His poverty will destroy his influence: many more can find that he is poor, than that he is wise; and few will reverence the understanding that is of so little advantage to its owner. I say nothing of the personal wretchedness of a debtor, which, however, has passed into a proverb. Of riches, it is not necessary to write the praise. Let it, however, be remembered, that he who has money to spare, has it always in his power to benefit others; and of such power a good man must always be desirous.

I am pleased with your account of Easter. We shall meet I hope in Autumn, both well and both cheerful; and part each the better for the other's company.

Make my compliments to Mrs. Boswell, and to the young charmers.

I am, &c.,
London, June 3, 1782.   SAM: JOHNSON.

803. To JAMES BOSWELL, ESQ.

Dear Sir

I have struggled through this year with so much infirmity of body, and such strong impressions of the fragility of life, that death, whenever it appears, fills me with melancholy; and I cannot hear without emotion, of the removal of any one, whom I have known, into another state.

Your father's death had every circumstance that could enable you to bear it; it was at a mature age, and it was expected; and as his general life had been pious, his thoughts had doubtless for many years past been turned upon eternity. That you did not find him sensible must doubtless grieve you; his disposition towards you was undoubtedly that of a kind, though not of a fond father. Kindness, at least actual, is in our power, but fondness is not; and if by negligence or imprudence you had extinguished his fondness, he could not at will rekindle it. Nothing then remained between you but mutual forgiveness of each other's faults, and mutual desire of each other's happiness.

I shall long to know his final disposition of his fortune.

You, dear Sir, have now a new station, and have therefore new cares, and new employments. Life, as Cowley seems to say, ought to resemble a well-ordered poem; of which one rule generally received is, that the exordium should be simple, and should promise little. Begin your new course of life with the least show, and the least expence possible; you may at pleasure encrease both, but you cannot easily diminish them. Do not think your estate your own, while any man can call upon you for money which you cannot pay; therefore, begin with timorous parsimony. Let it be your first care not to be in any man's debt.

When the thoughts are extended to a future state, the present life seems hardly worthy of all those principles of conduct, and maxims of prudence, which one generation of men has transmitted to another; but upon a closer view, when it is perceived how much evil is produced, and how much good is impeded by embarrassment and distress, and how little room the expedients of poverty leave for the exercise of virtue, it grows manifest that the boundless importance of the next life enforces some attention to the interests of this.

Be kind to the old servants, and secure the kindness of the agents and factors; do not disgust them by asperity, or unwelcome gaiety, or apparent suspicion. From them you must learn the real state of your affairs, the characters of your tenants, and the value of your lands.

Make my compliments to Mrs. Boswell; I think her expectations from air and exercise are the best that she can form. I hope she will live long and happily.

I forget whether I told you that Rasay has been here; we dined cheerfully together. I entertained lately a young gentleman from Corrichatachin.

I received your letters only this morning.

     I am, dear Sir, yours, &c.,
London, Sept. 7, 1782.   Sam: Johnson.

804. To Mrs. Boswell

Dear Lady

I have not often received so much pleasure as from your invitation to Auchinleck. The journey thither and back is, indeed, too great for the latter part of the year; but if my health were fully recovered, I would suffer no little heat and cold, nor a wet or a rough road to keep me from you. I am, indeed, not without hope of seeing Auchinleck again; but to make it a pleasant place I must see its lady well, and brisk, and airy. For my sake, therefore, among many greater reasons, take care, dear Madam, of your health, spare no expence, and want no attendance that can procure ease, or preserve it. Be very careful to keep your mind quiet; and do not think it too much to give an account of your recovery to, Madam,

London, Sept. 7, 1782.

Yours, &c.,
SAM: JOHNSON.

813. To Sir Joshua Reynolds

Dear Sir

I heard yesterday of your late disorder, and should think ill of myself if I had heard of it without alarm. I heard likewise of your recovery, which I sincerely wish to be complete and permanent. Your country has been in danger of losing one of its brightest ornaments, and I of losing one of my oldest and kindest friends: but I hope you will still live long, for the honour of the nation: and that more enjoyment of your elegance, your intelligence, and your benevolence, is still reserved for, dear Sir,

Your most affectionate, &c.,
Brighthelmston, Nov. 14, 1782. SAM: JOHNSON.

815. To James Boswell

Dear Sir

Having passed almost this whole year in a succession of disorders, I went in October to Brighthelmston, whither I came in a state of so much weakness, that

I rested four times in walking between the inn and the lodging. By physick and abstinence I grew better, and am now reasonably easy, though at a great distance from health. I am afraid, however, that health begins, after seventy, and long before, to have a meaning different from that which it had at thirty. But it is culpable to murmur at the established order of the creation, as it is vain to oppose it. He that lives must grow old; and he that would rather grow old than die, has GOD to thank for the infirmities of old age.

At your long silence I am rather angry. You do not, since now you are the head of your house, think it worth your while to try whether you or your friend can live longer without writing, nor suspect after so many years of friendship, that when I do not write to you, I forget you. Put all such useless jealousies out of your head, and disdain to regulate your own practice by the practice of another, or by any other principle than the desire of doing right.

Your œconomy, I suppose, begins now to be settled; your expences are adjusted to your revenue, and all your people in their proper places. Resolve not to be poor: whatever you have, spend less. Poverty is a great enemy to human happiness; it certainly destroys liberty, and it makes some virtues impracticable, and others extremely difficult.

Let me know the history of your life, since your accession to your estate. How many houses, how many cows, how much land in your own hand, and what bargains you make with your tenants. . . .

Of my *Lives of the Poets*, they have printed a new edition in octavo, I hear, of three thousand. Did I give a set to Lord Hailes? If I did not, I will do it out of these. What did you make of all your copy?[1]

Mrs. Thrale and the three Misses are now for the winter in Argyll-street. Sir Joshua Reynolds has been out of order, but is well again; and

I am, dear Sir, your affectionate humble servant,
London, Dec. 7, 1782. SAM: JOHNSON.

[1] [See No. 715.]

830. To Sir Joshua Reynolds

Sir
March 4, 1783.

I have sent you back Mr. Crabbe's poem,[1] which I read with great delight. It is original, vigorous, and elegant.

The alterations which I have made I do not require him to adopt, for my lines are, perhaps, not often better than his own; but he may take mine and his own together, and perhaps between them produce something better than either. He is not to think his copy wantonly defaced; a wet sponge will wash all the red lines away, and leave the pages clean.

His Dedication will be least liked: it were better to contract it into a short sprightly address. I do not doubt of Mr. Crabbe's success.

I am, Sir,
Your most humble servant,
Sam: Johnson.

To Robert Chambers

Dear Sir
April 19, 1783.

Of the books which I now send you I sent you the first edition, but it fell by the chance of war into the hands of the French. I sent likewise to Mr. Hastings. Be pleased to have these parcels properly delivered.

Removed as We are with so much land and sea between us, We ought to compensate the difficulty of correspondence by the length of our letters, yet searching my memory, I do not find much to communicate. Of all publick transactions you have more exact accounts than I can give; you know our foreign miscarriages and our intestine discontents, and do not want to be told that we have now neither power nor peace, neither influence in other nations nor quiet amongst ourselves. The state of the Publick, and the operations of government have little influence upon the private happiness of private men, nor can I pretend that much

[1] [*The Village.*]

of the national calamities is felt by me; yet I cannot but suffer some pain when I compare the state of this kingdom, with that in which we triumphed twenty years ago. I have at least endeavoured to preserve order and support Monarchy.

Having been thus allured to the mention of myself, I shall give you a little of my story. That dreadful ilness which seized me at New inn Hall, left consequences which have I think always hung upon me. I have never since cared much to walk. My mental abilities I do not perceive that it impaired. One great abatement of all miseries was the attention of Mr. Thrale, which from our first acquaintance was never intermitted. I passed far the greater part of many years in his house where I had all the pleasure of riches without the solicitude. He took me into France one year, and into Wales another, and if he had lived would have shown me Italy and perhaps many other countries, but he died in the spring of eighty-one, and left me to write his epitaph.

But for much of this time my constitutional maladies persued me. My thoughts were disturbed, my nights were insufferably restless, and by spasms in the breast I was condemned to the torture of sleepyness without the power to sleep. These spasms after enduring them more than twenty years I eased by three powerful remedies, abstinence, opium and mercury, but after a short time they were succeeded by a strange oppression of another kind which when I lay down disturbed me with a sensation like flatulence or intumescence which I cannot describe. To this supervened a difficulty of respiration, such as sometimes makes it painful to cross a street or climb to my chamber; which I have eased by venisection till the Physician forbids me to bleed, as my legs have begun to swel. Almost all the last year past in a succession of diseases ἐκ κακῶν κακά [1] and this year till within these few days has heaped misery upon me. I have just now a lucid interval.

With these afflictions, I have the common accidents

[1] [evil upon evil.]

of life to suffer. He that lives long must outlive many, and I am now sometimes to seek for friends of easy conversation and familiar confidence. Mrs. Williams is much worn; Mr. Levet died suddenly in my house about a year ago. Doctor Lawrence is totaly disabled by a palsy, and can neither speak nor write. He is removed to Canterbury. Beauclerc died about two years ago and in his last sickness desired to be buried by the side of his Mother. Langton has eight children by Lady Rothes. He lives very little in London, and is by no means at ease. Goldsmith died partly of a fever and partly of anxiety, being immoderately and disgracefully in debt. Dier lost his fortune by dealing in the East India stock, and, I fear, languished into the grave. Boswel's father is lately dead, but has left the estate incumbered; Boswel has, I think, five children. He is now paying us his annual visit, he is all that he was, and more. Doctor Scot prospers exceedingly in the commons, but I seldom see him; He is married and has a Daughter.

Jones now Sir William, will give you the present state of the club, which is now very miscellaneous, and very heterogeneous; it is therefore without confidence, and without pleasure. I go to it only as to a kind of publick dinner. Reynolds continues to rise in reputation and in riches, but his health has been shaken. Dr. Percy is now Bishop of Dromore, but has I believe lost his only son. Such are the deductions from human happiness.

I have now reached an age which is to expect many diminutions of the good, whatever it be, that life affords; I have lost many friends, I am now either afflicted or threatened by many diseases, but perhaps not with more than are commonly incident to encrease of years, and I am afraid that I bear the weight of time with unseemly, if not with sinful impatience. I hope that God will enable me to correct this as well as my other faults, before he calls me to appear before him.

In return for this history of myself I shall expect some account of you, who by your situation have much more to tell. I hope to hear that the Ladies and the Children are all well, and that your constitution accommodates itself easily to the climate. If you have health, you may study, and if you can study, you will surely not miss the opportunity which place and power give you, beyond what any Englishman qualified by previous knowledge, ever enjoyed before, of enquiring into Asiatick Literature. Buy manuscripts, consult the scholars of the country, learn the languages, at least select one, and master it. To the Malabarick Books Europe is, I think, yet a Stranger. But my advice comes late ; what you purpose to do, you have already begun, but in all your good purposes persevere. Life is short, and you do not intend to pass all your life in India.

How long you will stay, I cannot conjecture. The effects of English Judicature are not believed here to have added anything to the happiness of the new dominions. Of you, Sir, I rejoice to say that I have heard no evil. There was a trifling charge produced in parliament, but it seems to be forgotten, nor did it appear to imply anything very blamable. This purity of character you will, I hope continue to retain. One of my last wishes for you, at a gay table was $ἀρετήν τε καὶ ὀλβόν$.[1] Let me now add in a more serious hour, and in more powerful words, *Keep innocency, and take heed to the thing that is right, for that shall bring a Man peace at the last.*

I shall think myself favoured by any help that you shall give to Mr. Joseph Fowke, or Mr. Lawrence. Fowke was always friendly to me, and Lawrence is the son of a Man, whom I have long placed in the first rank of my friends. Do not let my recommendation be without effect.

Let me now mention an occasion on which you may perhaps do great good without evil to yourself. Langton is much embarrassed by a mortgage made, I think, by his grandfather, and perhaps aggravated by his father. The Creditor calls for his money, and

[1] [virtue and wealth.]

it is in the present general distress very difficult to make a *versura*. If you could let him have six thousand pounds upon the security of the same land, you would save him from the necessity of selling part of his Estate under the great disadvantage produced by the present high price of money. This proposal needs give you no pain, for Langton knows nothing of it, and may perhaps have settled his affairs before the answer can be received. As the security is good, you should not take more than four per cent.

Nothing now, I think, remains but that I assure you, as I do, of my kindness, and good wishes, and express my hopes that you do not forget

Your old Friend and humble servant,

SAM: JOHNSON.

Bolt Court, Fleetstreet, Apr. 19, 1783.

Mr. Langton, who is just come in, sends his best respects but he knows still nothing.

837. TO MRS. THRALE

London, [Thursday] May-day, 1783.

Dear Madam

I am glad that you went to Streatham, though you could not save the dear pretty little girl. I loved her, for she was Thrale's and your's, and by her dear father's appointment in some sort mine : I love you all, and therefore cannot without regret see the phalanx broken, and reflect that you and my other dear girls are deprived of one that was born your friend. To such friends, every one that has them, has recourse at last, when it is discovered, and discovered it seldom fails to be, that the fortuitous friendships of inclination or vanity are at the mercy of a thousand accidents. But we must still our disquiet with remembering that, where there is no guilt, all is for the best. I am glad to hear that Cecily is so near recovery.

For some days after your departure I was pretty well, but I have begun to languish again, and last night was very tedious and oppressive. I excused myself to-day

from dining with General Paoli, where I love to dine,
but I was griped by the talons of necessity.

On Saturday I dined, as is usual, at the opening of
the Exhibition. Our company was splendid, whether
more numerous than at any former time I know not.
Our tables seem always full. On Monday, if I am told
truth, were received at the door one hundred and ninety
pounds, for the admission of three thousand eight
hundred spectators. Supposing the shew open ten
hours, and the spectators staying one with another
each an hour, the rooms never had fewer than three
hundred and eighty justling against each other. Poor
Lowe met some discouragement, but I interposed for
him, and prevailed.

Mr. Barry's exhibition was opened the same day,
and a book is published to recommend it, which, if you
read it, you will find decorated with some satirical
pictures of Sir Joshua Reynolds and others. I have
not escaped. You must however think with some
esteem of Barry for the comprehension of his design.

I am, Madam,
Your, &c.,
SAM: JOHNSON.

850. TO MRS. THRALE

Bolt-court, Fleet-street,
June 19, 1783.

Dear Madam

I am sitting down in no cheerful solitude to write a
narrative which would once have affected you with
tenderness and sorrow, but which you will perhaps pass
over now with the careless glance of frigid indifference.
For this diminution of regard however, I know not
whether I ought to blame you, who may have reasons
which I cannot know, and I do not blame myself, who
have for a great part of human life done you what good
I could, and have never done you evil.

I had been disordered in the usual way, and had been
relieved by the usual methods, by opium and cathar-
ticks, but had rather lessened my dose of opium.

On Monday the 16th I sat for my picture, and walked a considerable way with little inconvenience. In the afternoon and evening I felt myself light and easy, and began to plan schemes of life. Thus I went to bed, and in a short time waked and sat up, as has been long my custom, when I felt a confusion and indistinctness in my head, which lasted I suppose about half a minute ; I was alarmed, and prayed God, that however he might afflict my body, he would spare my understanding. This prayer, that I might try the integrity of my faculties, I made in Latin verse. The lines were not very good, but I knew them not to be very good : I made them easily, and concluded myself to be unimpaired in my faculties.

Soon after I perceived that I had suffered a paralytick stroke, and that my speech was taken from me. I had no pain, and so little dejection in this dreadful state, that I wondered at my own apathy, and considered that perhaps death itself when it should come would excite less horrour than seems now to attend it.

In order to rouse the vocal organs I took two drams. Wine has been celebrated for the production of eloquence. I put myself into violent motion, and I think repeated it ; but all was vain. I then went to bed, and, strange as it may seem, I think, slept. When I saw light, it was time to contrive what I should do. Though God stopped my speech he left me my hand, I enjoyed a mercy which was not granted to my dear friend Lawrence, who now perhaps overlooks me as I am writing, and rejoices that I have what he wanted. My first note was necessarily to my servant, who came in talking, and could not immediately comprehend why he should read what I put into his hands.

I then wrote a card to Mr. Allen, that I might have a discreet friend at hand to act as occasion should require. In penning this note I had some difficulty, my hand, I knew not how nor why, made wrong letters. I then wrote to Dr. Taylor to come to me, and bring Dr. Heberden, and I sent to Dr. Brocklesby, who is my neighbour. My physicians are very friendly and very disinterested, and give me great hopes, but you may imagine my situation. I have so far recovered my vocal powers, as to repeat the Lord's Prayer with no very imperfect articulation. My memory, I hope, yet remains as it was; but such an attack produces solicitude for the safety of every faculty.

How this will be received by you I know not. I hope you will sympathise with me; but perhaps

> My mistress gracious, mild, and good,
> Cries! Is he dumb? 'Tis time he shou'd.

But can this be possible? I hope it cannot. I hope that what, when I could speak, I spoke of you, and to you, will be in a sober and serious hour remembered by you; and surely it cannot be remembered but with some degree of kindness. I have loved you with virtuous affection; I have honoured you with sincere esteem. Let not all our endearments be forgotten, but let me have in this great distress your pity and your prayers. You see I yet turn to you with my complaints as a settled and unalienable friend; do not, do not drive me from you, for I have not deserved either neglect or hatred.

To the girls, who do not write often, for Susy has written only once, and Miss Thrale owes me a letter, I earnestly recommend, as their guardian and friend, that they remember their Creator in the days of their youth.

I suppose you may wish to know how my disease is treated by the physicians. They put a blister upon my back, and two from my ear to my throat, one on a side. The blister on the back has done little, and those on the throat have not risen. I bullied and bounced, (it sticks to our last sand) and compelled the apothecary to make his salve according to the Edinburgh Dispensatory, that it might adhere better. I have two on now of my own prescription. They likewise give me salt of hartshorn, which I take with no great confidence, but am satisfied that what can be done is done for me.

O God! give me comfort and confidence in Thee: forgive my sins; and if it be Thy good pleasure, relieve my diseases for Jesus Christ's sake. Amen.

I am almost ashamed of this querulous letter, but now it is written, let it go.

I am, &c.,
SAM: JOHNSON.

857. To Mrs. Thrale

Dearest Madam London, June 28, 1783.

Your letter is just such as I desire, and as from you I hope always to deserve.

The black dog I hope always to resist, and in time to drive, though I am deprived of almost all those that used to help me. The neighbourhood is impoverished. I had once Richardson and Lawrence in my reach. Mrs. Allen is dead. My house has lost Levet, a man who took interest in every thing, and therefore ready at conversation. Mrs. Williams is so weak that she can be a companion no longer. When I rise my breakfast is solitary, the black dog waits to share it, from breakfast to dinner he continues barking, except that Dr. Brocklesby for a little keeps him at a distance. Dinner with a sick woman you may venture to suppose not much better than solitary. After dinner, what remains but to count the clock, and hope for that sleep which I can scarce expect. Night comes at last, and some hours of restlessness and confusion bring me again to a day of solitude. What shall exclude the black dog from an habitation like this? If I were a little richer, I would perhaps take some cheerful female into the house.

Your Bath news shews me new calamities. I am afraid Mrs. L——s is left with a numerous family, very slenderly supplied. Mrs. Sheward is an old maid, I am afraid, yet *sur le pavé*.

——, if he were well, would be well enough liked; his daughter has powers and knowledge, but no art of making them agreeable.

I must touch my journal. Last night fresh flies were put to my head, and hindered me from sleeping. To-day I fancy myself incommoded by heat.

I have, however, watered the garden both yesterday and to-day, just as I watered the laurels in the island.

     I am, Madam,
      Your, &c.,
       SAM: JOHNSON.

863. To MRS. THRALE

Dear Madam   London, July 5, 1783.

That Dr. Pepys is offended I am very sorry, but if the same state of things should recur, I could not do better. Dr. Brocklesby is, you know, my neighbour, and could be ready at call; he had for some time very diligently solicited my friendship: I depended much upon the skill of Dr. Heberden, and him I had seen lately at Brocklesby's. Heberden I could not bear to miss, Brocklesby could not decently be missed, and to call three, had made me ridiculous by the appearance of self-importance. Mine was one of those unhappy cases in which something must be wrong. I can only be sorry.

I have now no Doctor, but am left to shift for myself as opportunity shall serve. I am going next week with Langton to Rochester, where I expect not to stay long. Eight children in a small house will probably make a chorus not very diverting. My purpose is to change the air frequently this summer.

Of the imitation of my stile, in a criticism on Gray's Churchyard, I forgot to make mention. The author is, I believe, utterly unknown, for Mr. Steevens cannot hunt him out. I know little of it, for though it was sent me I never cut the leaves open. I had a letter with it representing it to me as my own work; in such an account to the publick there may be humour, but to myself it was neither serious nor comical. I suspect the writer to be wrongheaded; as to the noise which it makes I have never heard it, and am inclined to believe that few attacks either of ridicule or invective make much noise, but by the help of those that they provoke.

I think Queeney's silence has something either of laziness or unkindness; and I wish her free from both, for both are very unamiable, and will both increase by indulgence. Susy is I believe at a loss for matter. I shall be glad to see pretty Sophy's production.

I hope I still continue mending. My organs are yet feeble.

I am, Madam,
Your, &c.,
SAM: JOHNSON.

864. To MISS SUSANNA THRALE

Dearest Miss Susy [About July 5, 1783.]

When you favoured me with your letter, you seemed to be in want of materials to fill it, having met with no great adventures either of peril or delight, nor done or suffered any thing out of the common course of life.

When you have lived longer, and considered more, you will find the common course of life very fertile of observation and reflection. Upon the common course of life must our thoughts and our conversation be generally employed. Our general course of life must denominate us wise or foolish; happy or miserable: if it is well regulated we pass on prosperously and smoothly; as it is neglected we live in embarrassment, perplexity, and uneasiness.

Your time, my love, passes, I suppose, in devotion, reading, work, and company. Of your devotions, in which I earnestly advise you to be very punctual, you may not perhaps think it proper to give me an account; and of work, unless I understood it better, it will be of no great use to say much; but books and company will always supply you with materials for your letters to me, as I shall always be pleased to know what you are reading, and with what you are pleased; and shall take great delight in knowing what impression new modes or new characters make upon you, and to observe with what attention you distinguish the tempers, dispositions, and abilities of your companions.

A letter may be always made out of the books of the morning or talk of the evening ; and any letters from you, my dearest, will be welcome to

Your, &c.,
Sam : Johnson.

870. To Miss Sophia Thrale

Dearest Miss Sophy   London, July 24, 1783.

By an absence from home, and for one reason and another, I owe a great number of letters, and I assure you that I sit down to write yours first. Why you should think yourself not a favourite, I cannot guess ; my favour will, I am afraid, never be worth much ; but be its value more or less, you are never likely to lose it, and less likely if you continue your studies with the same diligence as you have begun them.

Your proficience in arithmetick is not only to be commended, but admired. Your master does not, I suppose, come very often, nor stay very long ; yet your advance in the science of numbers is greater than is commonly made by those who, for so many weeks as you have been learning, spend six hours a day in the writing school.

Never think, my Sweet, that you have arithmetick enough ; when you have exhausted your master, buy books. Nothing amuses more harmlessly than computation, and nothing is oftener applicable to real business or speculative enquiries. A thousand stories which the ignorant tell, and believe, die away at once, when the computist takes them in his gripe. I hope you will cultivate in yourself a disposition to numerical enquiries ; they will give you entertainment in solitude by the practice, and reputation in publick by the effect.

If you can borrow *Wilkins's Real Character*, a folio, which the bookseller can perhaps let you have, you will have a very curious calculation, which you are qualified to consider, to shew that Noah's ark was capable of holding all the known animals of the world, with provision for all the time in which the earth was under water. Let me hear from you soon again.

     I am, Madam,
      Your, &c.,
       SAM: JOHNSON.

875. To MRS. THRALE

Dear Madam   London, August 13, 1783.

Your letter was brought just as I was complaining that you had forgotten me.

I am glad that the ladies find so much novelty at Weymouth. Ovid says, that the sea is undelightfully uniform. They had some expectation of shells, which both by their form and colours have a claim to human curiosity. Of all the wonders, I have had no account, except that Miss Thrale seems pleased with your little voyages.

Sophy mentioned a story which her sisters would not suffer her to tell, because they would tell it themselves but it has never yet been told me.

Mrs. Ing is, I think, a baronet's daughter, of an ancient house in Staffordshire. Of her husband's father, mention is made in the life of Ambrose Philips.

Of this world, in which you represent me as delighting to live, I can say little. Since I came home I have only been to church, once to Burney's, once to Paradise's, and once to Reynolds's. With Burney I saw Dr. Rose, his new relation, with whom I have been many years acquainted. If I discovered no reliques of disease I am glad, but Fanny's[1] trade is fiction.

I have since partaken of an epidemical disorder, but common evils produce no dejection.

Paradise's company, I fancy, disappointed him; I remember nobody. With Reynolds was the archbishop of Tuam, a man coarse of voice and inelegant of language.

I am now broken with disease, without the alleviation

[1] [Fanny Burney.]

of familiar friendship or domestick society ; I have no middle state between clamour and silence, between general conversation and self-tormenting solitude. Levet is dead, and poor Williams is making haste to die : I know not if she will ever more come out of her chamber.

I am now quite alone, but let me turn my thoughts another way.

I am, Madam,
Your, &c.,
SAM: JOHNSON.

876. To MRS. THRALE

Madam   London, August 20, 1783.

This has been a day of great emotion ; the office of the Communion of the Sick has been performed in poor Mrs. Williams's chamber. She was too weak to rise from her bed, and is therefore to be supposed unlikely to live much longer. She has, I hope, little violent pain, but is wearing out by torpid inappetence and wearisome decay ; but all the powers of her mind are in their full vigour, and when she has spirits enough for conversation, she possesses all the intellectual excellence that she ever had. Surely this is an instance of mercy much to be desired by a parting soul.

At home I see almost all my companions dead or dying. At Oxford I have just lost Wheeler, the man with whom I most delighted to converse. The sense of my own diseases, and the sight of the world sinking round me, oppress me perhaps too much. I hope that all these admonitions will not be vain, and that I shall learn to die as dear Williams is dying, who was very cheerful before and after this aweful solemnity, and seems to resign herself with calmness and hope upon eternal mercy.

I read your last kind letter with great delight ; but when I came to *love* and *honour,* what sprung in my mind ?—How loved, how honoured once, avails thee not.

I sat to Mrs. Reynolds yesterday for my picture,

perhaps the tenth time, and I sat near three hours with the patience of *mortal born to bear ;* at last she declared it quite finished, and seems to think it fine. I told her it was *Johnson's grimly ghost.* It is to be engraved, and I think *in glided,* &c.[1] will be a good inscription.

I am, Madam,
Your, &c.,
SAM: JOHNSON.

877. To MRS. THRALE

Dear Madam London, August 26, 1783.

Things stand with me much as they have done for some time. Mrs. Williams fancies now and then that she grows better, but her vital powers appear to be slowly burning out. Nobody thinks however that she will very soon be quite wasted, and as she suffers me to be of very little use to her, I have determined to pass some time with Mr. Bowles near Salisbury, and have taken a place for Thursday.

Some benefit may be perhaps received from change of air, some from change of company, and some from mere change of place. It is not easy to grow well in a chamber where one has long been sick, and where every thing seen and every person speaking revives and impresses images of pain. Though it be that no man can run away from himself, he may yet escape from many causes of useless uneasiness. That the *mind is its own place,* is the boast of a fallen angel that had learned to lie. External locality has great effects, at least upon all embodied beings. I hope this little journey will afford me at least some suspense of melancholy.

You give but an unpleasing account of your performance at Portland. Your scrambling days are then over.

[1] ' 'Twas at the silent solemn hour
   When night and morning meet;
 In glided Margaret's grimly ghost,
   And stood at William's feet.'
                              Margaret's Ghost.

I remember when no Miss and few Masters could have left you behind, or *thrown you out in the pursuit of honour* or of curiosity. But *tempus edax rerum*, and no way has been yet found to draw his teeth.

       I am, dear Madam,
         Your, &c.,
           SAM: JOHNSON.

880. TO MISS SUSANNA THRALE

Dear Miss   [Heale], September 9, 1783.

I am glad that you and your sisters have been at Portland. You now can tell what is a quarry and what is a cliff. Take all opportunities of filling your mind with genuine scenes of nature: description is always fallacious, at least till you have seen realities you cannot know it to be true. This observation might be extended to life, but life cannot be surveyed with the same safety as nature, and it is better to know vice and folly by report than by experience. A painter, says Sydney, mingled in the battle that he might know how to paint it; but his knowledge was useless, for some mischievous sword took away his head. They whose speculation upon characters leads them too far into the world, may lose that nice sense of good and evil by which characters are to be tried. Acquaint yourself therefore both with the pleasing and the terrible parts of nature, but in life wish to know only the good.

Pray shew Mamma this passage of a letter from Dr. Brocklesby: 'Mrs. Williams, from mere inanition, has at length paid the great debt to nature, about three o'clock this morning, (Sept. 6). She died without a struggle, retaining her faculties entire to the very last, and as she expressed it, having set her house in order, was prepared to leave it at the last summons of nature.'

I do not now say any thing more than that I am,
       My dearest,
         Your, &c.,
           SAM: JOHNSON.

883. To Mrs. Thrale

Dear Madam   London, Sept. 22, 1783.

Happy are you that have ease and leisure to want intelligence of air-ballons. Their existence is I believe indubitable; but I know not that they can possibly be of any use. The construction is this. The chymical philosophers have discovered a body (which I have forgotten, but will enquire), which, dissolved by an acid, emits a vapour lighter than the atmospherical air. This vapour is caught, among other means, by tying a bladder, compressed upon the bottle in which the dissolution is performed; the vapour rising swells the bladder, and fills it. The bladder is then tied and removed, and another applied, till as much of this light air is collected as is wanted. Then a large spherical case is made, and very large it must be, of the lightest matter that can be found, secured by some method, like that of oiling silk, against all passage of air. Into this are emptied all the bladders of light air, and if there is light air enough it mounts into the clouds, upon the same principle as a bottle filled with water will sink in water, but a bottle filled with æther would float. It rises till it comes to air of equal tenuity with its own, if wind or water does not spoil it on the way. Such, Madam, is an air ballon.

Meteors have been this autumn very often seen, but I have never been in their way.

Poor Williams has I hope seen the end of her afflictions. She acted with prudence and she bore with fortitude. She has left me.

> Thou thy weary task hast done,
> Home art gone, and ta'en thy wages.

Had she had good humour and prompt elocution, her universal curiosity and comprehensive knowledge would have made her the delight of all that knew her. She left her little to your charity school.

The complaint about which you enquire is a sarcocele:
I thought it a hydrocele, and heeded it but little.
Puncture has detected the mistake: it can be safely
suffered no longer. Upon inspection three days ago
it was determined *extrema ventura*. If excision should
be delayed there is danger of a gangrene. You would
not have me for fear of pain perish in putrescence. I
shall I hope, with trust in eternal mercy, lay hold of
the possibility of life which yet remains. My health
is not bad; the gout is now trying at my feet. My
appetite and digestion are good, and my sleep better
than formerly: I am not dejected, and I am not feeble.
There is however danger enough in such operations
at seventy-four.

Let me have your prayers and those of the young
dear people.

I am, dear Madam,
Your, &c.,
SAM: JOHNSON.

Write soon and often.

884. TO MRS. MONTAGU

Madam   September 22, 1783.

That respect which is always due to beneficence
makes it fit that you should be informed, otherwise
than by the papers, that, on the 6th of this month,
died your pensioner, Anna Williams, of whom it may
be truly said, that she received your bounty with
gratitude, and enjoyed it with propriety. You perhaps
have still her prayers.

You have, Madam, the satisfaction of having
alleviated the sufferings of a woman of great merit,
both intellectual and moral. Her curiosity was
universal, her knowledge was very extensive, and she
sustained forty years of misery with steady fortitude.
Thirty years and more she had been my companion,
and her death has left me very desolate.

That I have not written sooner, you may impute to

absence, to ill-health, to any thing rather than want of regard to the benefactress of my departed friend.

I am, Madam,

Your most humble servant,
SAM: JOHNSON.

892. To MRS. THRALE

London, October 9, 1783.

Two nights ago Mr. Burke sat with me a long time; he seems much pleased with his journey. We had both seen Stonehenge this summer for the first time. I told him that the view had enabled me to confute two opinions which have been advanced about it. One, that the materials are not natural stones, but an artificial composition hardened by time. This notion is as old as Camden's time; and has this strong argument to support it, that stone of that species is no where to be found. The other opinion, advanced by Dr. Charlton, is, that it was erected by the Danes.

Mr. Bowles made me observe, that the transverse stones were fixed on the perpendicular supporters by a knob formed on the top of the upright stone, which entered into a hollow cut in the crossing stone. This is a proof that the enormous edifice was raised by a people who had not yet the knowledge of mortar; which cannot be supposed of the Danes who came hither in ships, and were not ignorant certainly of the arts of life. This proves likewise the stones not to be factitious; for they that could mould such durable masses could do much more than make mortar, and could have continued the transverse from the upright part with the same paste.

You have doubtless seen Stonehenge, and if you have not, I should think it a hard task to make an adequate description.

It is, in my opinion, to be referred to the earliest habitation of the Island, as a Druidical monument of at least two thousand years; probably the most ancient work of man upon the Island. Salisbury cathedral, and its neighbour Stonehenge, are two eminent monuments of art and rudeness, and may show the first essay, and the last perfection, in architecture.

I have not yet settled my thoughts about the generation of light air, which I indeed once saw produced, but I was at the height of my great complaint. I have made enquiry, and shall soon be able to tell you how to fill a ballon.

I am, Madam,
Your, &c.,
SAM: JOHNSON.

895. TO MRS. THRALE

Madam   London, October 27, 1783.

You may be very reasonably weary of sickness; it is neither pleasant to talk nor to hear of it. I hope soon to lose the disgusting topick; for I have now neither pain nor sickness. My ancles are weak, and my feet tender. I have not tried to walk much above a hundred yards, and was glad to come back upon wheels. The Doctor and Mr. Metcalf have taken me out. I sleep uncertainly and unseasonably. This is the sum of my complaint. I have not been so well for two years past. The great malady is neither heard, seen, felt, nor—understood. But I am very solitary.

> Semperque relinqui
> Sola sibi, semper longam incomitata videtur
> Ire viam.[1]

But I have begun to look among my books, and hope that I am all, whatever that was, which I have ever been.

Mrs. Siddons in her visit to me behaved with great modesty and propriety, and left nothing behind her to be censured or despised. Neither praise nor money, the two powerful corrupters of mankind, seem to have

---

[1] 'She seems alone
To wander in her sleep through ways unknown,
Guideless and dark.' DRYDEN's Virgil.

depraved her. I shall be glad to see her again. Her brother Kemble calls on me, and pleases me very well. Mrs. Siddons and I talked of plays ; and she told me her intention of exhibiting this winter the characters of Constance, Catherine, and Isabella in Shakespeare.

I have had this day a letter from Mr. Mudge ; who, with all his earnestness for operation, thinks it better to wait the effects of time, and, as he says, to let well alone. To this the patient naturally inclines, though I am afraid of having the knife yet to endure when I can bear it less. Cruickshank was even now in doubt of the event ; but Pott, though never eager, had, or discovered, less fear.

If I was a little cross, would it not have made patient Grisel cross, to find that you had forgotten the letter that you was answering ? But what did I care, if I did not love you ? You need not fear that another should get my kindness from you ; that kindness which you could not throw away if you tried, you surely cannot lose while you desire to keep it.

I am, Madam,
Your, &c.,
SAM: JOHNSON.

I have a letter signed S. A. Thrale ; I take S. A. to be Miss Sophy : but who is bound to recollect initials ? A name should be written, if not fully, yet so that it cannot be mistaken.

900. To MRS. THRALE

Dear Madam

Since you have written to me with the attention and tenderness of ancient time, your letters give me a great part of the pleasure which a life of solitude admits. You will never bestow any share of your good will on one who deserves better. Those that have loved longest love best. A sudden blaze of kindness may by a single blast of coldness be extinguished, but that fondness which length of time has connected with many circumstances and occasions, though it may for a while be suppressed by disgust or resentment, with or without a cause, is hourly revived by accidental recollection. To those that have lived long together, every thing heard and every thing seen recals some pleasure communicated, or some benefit conferred, some petty quarrel, or some slight endearment. Esteem of great powers, or amiable qualities newly discovered, may embroider a day or a week, but a friendship of twenty years is interwoven with the texture of life. A friend may be often found and lost, but an *old friend* never can be found, and Nature has provided that he cannot easily be lost.

I have not forgotten the Davenants, though they seem to have forgotten me. I began very early to tell them what they have commonly found to be true. I am sorry to hear of their building. I have always warned those whom I loved, against that mode of ostentatious waste.

You seem to mention Lord Kilmurrey as a stranger. We were at his house in Cheshire; and he one day dined with Sir Lynch. What he tells of the epigram is not true, but perhaps he does not know it to be false. Do not you remember how he rejoiced in having *no* park? He could not disoblige his neighbours by sending them *no* venison.

The frequency of death, to those who look upon it in the leisure of Arcadia, is very dreadful. We all know what it should teach us; let us all be diligent to learn. Lucy Porter has lost her brother. But whom I have lost—let me not now remember. Let not your loss be added to the mournful catalogue. Write soon again to

    Madam,
     Your most humble servant,
London, Nov. 13, 1783. Sam: Johnson.

901. To Miss S. A. Thrale

Dear Miss

Here is a whole week, and nothing heard from your house. Baretti said what a wicked house it would be, and a wicked house it is. Of you however I have no complaint to make, for I owe you a letter. Still I live here by my own self, and have had of late very bad nights; but then I have had a pig to dinner, which Mr. Perkins gave me. Thus life is chequered.

I cannot tell you much news, because I see nobody that you know. Do you read the Tatlers? They are part of the books which every body should read, because they are the sources of conversation, therefore make them part of your library. Bickerstaff, in the Tatler, gives as a specimen of familiar letters, an account of his cat. I could tell you as good things of Lily the white kitling, who is now at full growth, and very well behaved; but I do not see why we should descend below human beings, and of one human being I can tell something that you will like to hear.

A friend, whose name I will tell when your Mamma has tried to guess it, sent to my physician to enquire whether this long train of illness had brought me into any difficulties for want of money, with an invitation to send to him for what occasion required. I shall write this night to thank him, having no need to borrow.

I have seen Mr. Seward since his return only once; he gave no florid account of my mistress's health. Tell her that I hearken every day after a letter from her, and do not be long before you write yourself to,

My dear,
Your, &c.,
Sam: Johnson.

902. To Miss Burney

Madam

You have been at home a long time, and I have never seen you nor heard from you. Have we quarreled?

I have sent a book which I have found lately, and imagine to be Dr. Burney's. Miss Charlotte will please to examine.

Pray write me a direction of Mrs. Chapone, and pray let me sometimes have the honour of telling you, how much I am,

Madam,
Your most humble servant,
Bolt-court, Nov. 19, 1783. SAM: JOHNSON.

905. TO THE RIGHT HONOURABLE WILLIAM GERARD HAMILTON

Dear Sir

Your kind enquiries after my affairs, and your generous offers, have been communicated to me by Dr. Brocklesby. I return thanks with great sincerity, having lived long enough to know what gratitude is due to such friendship; and entreat that my refusal may not be imputed to sullenness or pride. I am, indeed, in no want. Sickness is, by the generosity of my physicians, of little expence to me. But if any unexpected exigence should press me, you shall see, dear Sir, how cheerfully I can be obliged to so much liberality.

I am, Sir,
your most obedient and most humble servant,
November 19, 1783. SAM: JOHNSON.

912. TO MRS. THRALE

London, Nov. 29, 1783.

Dear Madam

The life of my dear, sweet, pretty, lovely, delicious Miss Sophy is safe; let us return thanks to the great Giver of existence, and pray that her continuance amongst us may be a blessing to herself and to those that love her. *Multos et felices*,[1] my dear girl.

[1] [many happy years.]

Now she is recovered, she must write me a little history of her sufferings, and impart her schemes of study and improvement. Life, to be worthy of a rational being, must be always in progression; we must always purpose to do more or better than in time past. The mind is enlarged and elevated by mere purposes, though they end as they begin by airy contemplation. We compare and judge, though we do not practise.

She will go back to her arithmetick again; a science which will always delight her more, as by advancing further she discerns more of its use, and a science suited to Sophy's case of mind; for you told in the last winter that she loved metaphysicks more than the Muses. Her choice is certainly as laudable as it is uncommon; but I would have her like what is good in both.

God bless you and your children; so says,
Dear Madam,
Your old Friend,
SAM: JOHNSON.

916. To SIR JOSHUA REYNOLDS

Dear Sir

It is inconvenient to me to come out, I should else have waited on you with an account of a little evening Club which we are establishing in Essex-street, in the Strand, and of which you are desired to be one. It will be held at the Essex Head, now kept by an old servant of Thrale's. The company is numerous, and, as you will see by the list, miscellaneous. The terms are lax, and the expences light. Mr. Barry was adopted by Dr. Brocklesby, who joined with me in forming the plan. We meet thrice a week, and he who misses forfeits two-pence.

If you are willing to become a member, draw a line under your name. Return the list. We meet for the first time on Monday at eight.

I am, &c.,
Dec. 4, 1783.   SAM: JOHNSON.

921. To Mrs. Thrale

Dear Madam London, Dec. 27, 1783.

The wearisome solitude of the long evenings did indeed suggest to me the convenience of a club in my neighbourhood, but I have been hindered from attending it by want of breath. If I can complete the scheme, you shall have the names and the regulations.

The time of the year, for I hope the fault is rather in the weather than in me, has been very hard upon me. The muscles of my breast are much convulsed. Dr. Heberden recommends opiates, of which I have such horrour that I do not think of them but *in extremis*. I was however driven to them last night for refuge, and having taken the usual quantity durst not go to bed, for fear of that uneasiness to which a supine posture exposes me, but rested all night in a chair with much relief, and have been to-day more warm, active, and cheerful.

You have more than once wondered at my complaint of solitude, when you hear that I am crowded with visits. *Inopem me copia fecit.*[1] Visitors are no proper companions in the chamber of sickness. They come when I could sleep or read, they stay till I am weary, they force me to attend when my mind calls for relaxation, and to speak when my powers will hardly actuate my tongue. The amusements and consolations of languor and depression are conferred by familiar and domestick companions, which can be visited or called at will, and can occasionally be quitted or dismissed, who do not obstruct accommodation by ceremony, or destroy indolence by awakening effort.

Such society I had with Levet and Williams; such I had where—I am never likely to have it more.

I wish, dear Lady, to you and my dear girls many a cheerful and pious Christmas.

I am,
Your, &c.,
Sam: Johnson.

[1] ['Abundance makes me poor.']

926. To Mrs. Thrale

London, Jan. 21, 1784.

Dear Madam

Dr. Heberden this day favoured me with a visit; and after hearing what I had to tell him of miseries and pains, and comparing my present with my past state, declared me well. That his opinion is erroneous, I know with too much certainty; and yet was glad to hear it, as it set extremities at a greater distance: he who is by his physician thought well, is at least not thought in immediate danger. They therefore whose attention to me makes them talk of my health, will, I hope, soon not drop, but lose their subject. But, alas! I had no sleep last night. and sit now panting over my paper. *Dabit Deus his quoque finem.*[1] I have really hope from spring; and am ready, like Almanzor, to bid the sun *fly swiftly*, and *leave weeks and months behind him.* The sun has looked for six thousand years upon the world to little purpose, if he does not know that a sick man is almost as impatient as a lover.

Mr. Cator gives such an account of Miss Cecy, as you and all of us must delight to hear; Cator has a rough, manly, independent understanding, and does not spoil it by complaisance; he never speaks merely to please, and seldom is mistaken in things which he has any right to know. I think well of her for pleasing him, and of him for being pleased; and at the close, am delighted to find him delighted with her excellence. Let your children, dear Madam, be *his* care, and *your* pleasure; close your thoughts upon them, and when sad fancies are excluded, health and peace will return together.

I am, dear Madam,
Your old Friend,
Sam: Johnson.

[1] 'This too the gods shall end.'

928. To the Reverend Dr. Taylor

Dear Sir

I am still confined to the house, and one of my amusements is to write letters to my friends, though they, being busy in the common scenes of life, are not equally diligent in writing to me. Dr. Heberden was with me two or three days ago, and told me that nothing ailed me, which I am glad to hear, though I knew it not to be true. My nights are restless, my breath is difficult, and my lower parts continue tumid.

The struggle, you see, still continues between the two sets of ministers: those that are *out* and *in* one can scarce call them, for who is *out* or *in* is perhaps four times a day a new question. The tumult in government is, I believe, excessive, and the efforts of each party outrageously violent, with very little thought on any national interest, at a time when we have all the world for our enemies, when the King and parliament have lost even the titular dominion of America, and the real power of Government every where else. Thus Empires are broken down when the profits of administration are so great, that ambition is satisfied with obtaining them, and he that aspires to greatness needs do nothing more than talk himself into importance. He has then all the power which danger and conquest used formerly to give; he can raise a family and reward his followers.

Mr. Burke has just sent me his Speech upon the affairs of India, a volume of above a hundred pages closely printed. I will look into it; but my thoughts seldom now travel to great distances.

I would gladly know when you think to come hither, and whether this year you will come or no. If my life be continued, I know not well how I shall bestow myself.

     I am, Sir,
      Your affectionate &c.,
London, Jan. 24, 1784.   Sam: Johnson.

938. To Mrs. Thrale

Madam   London, March 10, 1784.

You know I never thought confidence with respect to futurity any part of the character of a brave, a wise, or a good man. Bravery has no place where it can avail nothing; wisdom impresses strongly the consciousness of those faults, of which it is itself perhaps an aggravation; and goodness, always wishing to be better, and imputing every deficience to criminal negligence, and every fault to voluntary corruption, never dares to suppose the condition of forgiveness fulfilled, nor what is wanting in the crime supplied by penitence.

This is the state of the best, but what must be the condition of him whose heart will not suffer him to rank himself among the best, or among the good? Such must be his dread of the approaching trial, as will leave him little attention to the opinion of those whom he is leaving for ever; and the serenity that is not felt, it can be no virtue to feign.

The sarcocele ran off long ago, at an orifice made for mere experiment.

The water passed naturally, by God's mercy, in a manner of which Dr. Heberden has seen but few examples. The chirurgeon has been employed to heal some excoriations; and four out of five are no longer under his cure. The physician laid on a blister, and I ordered, by their consent, a salve; but neither succeeded, and neither was very easily healed.

I have been confined from the fourteenth of December, and know not when I shall get out; but I have this day dressed me, as I was dressed in health.

Your kind expressions gave me great pleasure; do not reject me from your thoughts. Shall we ever exchange confidence by the fireside again?

I hope dear Sophy is better; and intend quickly to pay my debt to Susy.

I am, Madam,
Your, &c.,
Sam: Johnson.

945. To BENNET LANGTON

March 27, 1784. Since you left me, I have continued in my own opinion, and in Dr. Brocklesby's, to grow better with respect to all my formidable and dangerous distempers; though to a body battered and shaken as mine has lately been, it is to be feared that weak attacks may be sometimes mischievous. I have, indeed, by standing carelessly at an open window, got a very troublesome cough, which it has been necessary to appease by opium, in larger quantities than I like to take, and I have not found it give way so readily as I expected; its obstinacy, however, seems at last disposed to submit to the remedy, and I know not whether I should then have a right to complain of any morbid sensation. My asthma is, I am afraid, constitutional and incurable; but it is only occasional, and unless it be excited by labour or by cold, gives me no molestation, nor does it lay very close siege to life; for Sir John Floyer, whom the physical race consider as authour of one of the best books upon it, panted on to ninety, as was supposed; and why were we content with supposing a fact so interesting, of a man so conspicuous? because he corrupted, at perhaps seventy or eighty, the register, that he might pass for younger than he was. He was not much less than eighty, when to a man of rank who modestly asked his age, he answered, 'Go look;' though he was in general a man of civility and elegance.

The ladies, I find, are at your house all well, except Miss Langton, who will probably soon recover her health by light suppers. Let her eat at dinner as she will, but not take a full stomach to bed. Pay my sincere respects to dear Miss Langton in Lincolnshire, let her know that I mean not to break our league of friendship, and that I have a set of *Lives* for her, when I have the means of sending it.

946. To James Boswell

Dear Sir

You could do nothing so proper as to haste back when you found the Parliament dissolved. With the influence which your Address must have gained you, it may reasonably be expected that your presence will be of importance, and your activity of effect.

Your solicitude for me gives me that pleasure which every man feels from the kindness of such a friend: and it is with delight I relieve it by telling, that Dr. Brocklesby's account is true, and that I am, by the blessing of GOD, wonderfully relieved.

You are entering upon a transaction which requires much prudence. You must endeavour to oppose without exasperating; to practise temporary hostility, without producing enemies for life. This is, perhaps, hard to be done; yet it has been done by many, and seems most likely to be effected by opposing merely upon general principles, without descending to personal or particular censures or objections. One thing I must enjoin you, which is seldom observed in the conduct of elections;—I must entreat you to be scrupulous in the use of strong liquors. One night's drunkenness may defeat the labours of forty days well employed. Be firm, but not clamorous; be active, but not malicious; and you may form such an interest, as may not only exalt yourself, but dignify your family.

We are, as you may suppose, all busy here. Mr. Fox resolutely stands for Westminster, and his friends say will carry the election. However that be, he will certainly have a seat. Mr. Hoole has just told me, that the city leans towards the King.

Let me hear, from time to time, how you are employed, and what progress you make.

Make dear Mrs. Boswell, and all the young Boswells, the sincere compliments of,

Sir, your affectionate humble servant,
London, March 30, 1784.   SAM: JOHNSON.

954. To Mrs. Thrale

London, April 19, 1784.

Dear Madam

I received in the morning your magnificent fish, and in the afternoon your apology for not sending it. I have invited the Hooles and Miss Burney to dine upon it to-morrow.

The club which has been lately instituted is at Sam's; and there was I when I was last out of the house. But the people whom I mentioned in my letter are the remnant of a little club that used to meet in Ivy Lane about three-and-thirty years ago, out of which we have lost Hawkesworth and Dyer, the rest are yet on this side the grave. Our meetings now are serious, and I think on all parts tender.

Miss Moore has written a poem called Le Bas Bleu; which is in my opinion a very great performance. It wanders about in manuscript, and surely will soon find its way to Bath.

I shall be glad of another letter from my dear Queeney; the former was not much to be censured. The reckoning between me and Miss Sophy is out of my head. She must write to tell me how it stands.

I am sensible of the ease that your repayment of Mr. * * * * * has given; you felt yourself *gênée* by that debt; is there an English word for it?

As you do not now use your books, be pleased to let Mr. Cator know that I may borrow what I want. I think at present to take only Calmet, and the Greek Anthology. When I lay sleepless, I used to drive the night along by turning Greek epigrams into Latin. I know not if I have not turned a hundred.

It is time to return you thanks for your present. Since I was sick, I know not if I have not had more delicacies sent me than I had ever seen till I saw your table.

It was always Dr. Heberden's enquiry, whether my appetite for food continued; it indeed never failed me. For he considered the cessation of appetite as the despair of nature yielding up her power to the force of the disease.

> I am, Madam,
> Your, &c.,
> SAM: JOHNSON.

955. To Mrs. Thrale

London, April 21, 1784.

Dear Madam

I make haste to send you intelligence, which, if I do not still flatter myself, you will not receive without some degree of pleasure. After a confinement of one hundred twenty-nine days, more than the third part of a year, and no inconsiderable part of human life, I this day returned thanks to God in St. Clement's church, for my recovery; a recovery, in my seventy-fifth year, from a distemper which few in the vigour of youth are known to surmount; a recovery, of which neither myself, my friends, nor my physicians, had any hope; for though they flattered me with some continuance of life, they never supposed that I could cease to be dropsical. The dropsy however is quite vanished, and the asthma so much mitigated, that I walked to-day with a more easy respiration than I have known, I think, for perhaps two years past. I hope the mercy that lengthens my days, will assist me to use them well.

The Hooles, Miss Burney, and Mrs. Hall (Wesley's sister), feasted yesterday with me very cheerfully on your noble salmon. Mr. Allen could not come, and I sent him a piece, and a great tail is still left.

Dr. Brocklesby forbids the club at present, not caring to venture the chillness of the evening; but I purpose to shew myself on Saturday at the Academy's feast. I cannot publish my return to the world more effectually; for, as the Frenchman says, *tout le monde s'y trouvera.*

For this occasion I ordered some cloaths; and was told by the taylor, that when he brought me a sick dress, he never expected to make me any thing of any other kind. My recovery is indeed wonderful.

     I am, dear Madam,
      Your, &c.,
        Sam: Johnson.

959. To Miss Jane Langton

My dearest Miss Jenny

 I am sorry that your pretty letter has been so long without being answered; but, when I am not pretty well, I do not always write plain enough for young ladies. I am glad, my dear, to see that you write so well, and hope that you mind your pen, your book, and your needle, for they are all necessary. Your books will give you knowledge, and make you respected; and your needle will find you useful employment when you do not care to read. When you are a little older, I hope you will be very diligent in learning arithmetick, and, above all, that through your whole life you will carefully say your prayers, and read your Bible.

 I am, my dear, your most humble servant,
May 10, 1784.   Sam: Johnson.

970. To Mrs. Thrale

Madam

 If I interpret your letter right, you are ignominiously married; if it is yet undone, let us once more talk together. If you have abandoned your children and your religion, God forgive your wickedness: if you have forfeited your fame and your country, may your folly do no further mischief. If the last act is yet to do, I who have loved you, esteemed you, reverenced you, and served you, I who long thought you the first of humankind, entreat that, before your fate is irrevocable, I may once more see you. I was, I once was,

     Madam, most truly yours,
July 2, 1784.   Sam: Johnson.

 I will come down, if you permit it.

972. To Mrs. Thrale

Dear Madam   London, July 8, 1784.

What you have done, however I may lament it, I have no pretence to resent, as it has not been injurious to me : I therefore breathe out one sigh more of tenderness, perhaps useless, but at least sincere.

I wish that God may grant you every blessing, that you may be happy in this world for its short continuance, and eternally happy in a better state ; and whatever I can contribute to your happiness I am very ready to repay, for that kindness which soothed twenty years of a life radically wretched.

Do not think slightly of the advice which I now presume to offer. Prevail upon Mr. Piozzi to settle in England : you may live here with more dignity than in Italy, and with more security : your rank will be higher, and your fortune more under your own eye. I desire not to detail all my reasons, but every argument of prudence and interest is for England, and only some phantoms of imagination seduce you to Italy.

I am afraid however that my counsel is vain, yet I have eased my heart by giving it.

When Queen Mary took the resolution of sheltering herself in England, the Archbishop of St. Andrew's, attempting to dissuade her, attended on her journey ; and when they came to the irremeable [1] stream that separated the two kingdoms, walked by her side into the water, in the middle of which he seized her bridle, and with earnestness proportioned to her danger and his own affection pressed her to return. The Queen went forward.——If the parallel reaches thus far, may it go no further.—The tears stand in my eyes.

[1] [' Occupat Æneas aditum custode sepulto,
Evaditque celer ripam irremeabilis undæ.'
' The keeper charm'd, the chief without delay
Pass'd on and took the irremeable way.'
   Dryden's Virgil.]

I am going into Derbyshire, and hope to be followed by your good wishes, for I am, with great affection,
>Your, &c.,
>>SAM: JOHNSON.

Any letters that come for me hither will be sent me.

975. TO THE REVEREND MR. BAGSHAW, AT BROMLEY

Sir

Perhaps you may remember, that in the year 1753, you committed to the ground my dear wife. I now entreat your permission to lay a stone upon her; and have sent the inscription, that, if you find it proper, you may signify your allowance.

You will do me a great favour by showing the place where she lies, that the stone may protect her remains.

Mr. Ryland will wait on you for the inscription, and procure it to be engraved. You will easily believe that I shrink from this mournful office. When it is done, if I have strength remaining, I will visit Bromley once again, and pay you part of the respect to which you have a right from, Reverend Sir,
>Your most humble servant,

July 12, 1784.   SAM: JOHNSON.

989. TO JOHN HOOLE

Aug. 13, 1784. I thank you for your affectionate letter. I hope we shall both be the better for each other's friendship, and I hope we shall not very quickly be parted. Tell Mr. Nicholls that I shall be glad of his correspondence, when his business allows him a little remission; though to wish him less business, that I may have more pleasure, would be too selfish. To pay for seats at the balloon is not very necessary, because in less than a minute, they who gaze at a mile's distance will see all that can be seen. About the wings I am of your mind; they cannot at all assist it, nor I think regulate its motion. I am now grown somewhat easier in my body, but my mind is sometimes depressed. About the Club I am in no great pain. The forfeitures go on, and the house, I hear, is improved for our future meetings. I hope we shall meet often and sit long.

995. To Sir Joshua Reynolds

August 19, 1784. Having had since our separation, little to say that could please you or myself by saying, I have not been lavish of useless letters; but I flatter myself that you will partake of the pleasure with which I can now tell you that about a week ago, I felt suddenly a sensible remission of my asthma, and consequently a greater lightness of action and motion. Of this grateful alleviation I know not the cause, nor dare depend upon its continuance, but while it lasts I endeavour to enjoy it, and am desirous of communicating, while it lasts, my pleasure to my friends. Hitherto, dear Sir, I had written before the post, which stays in this town but a little while, brought me your letter. Mr. Davies seems to have represented my little tendency to recovery in terms too splendid. I am still restless, still weak, still watery, but the asthma is less oppressive. Poor Ramsay![1] On which side soever I turn, mortality presents its formidable frown. I left three old friends at Lichfield when I was last there, and now found them all dead. I no sooner lose sight of dear Allen, than I am told that I shall see him no more. That we must all die, we always knew; I wish I had sooner remembered it. Do not think me intrusive or importunate, if I now call, dear Sir, on you to remember it.

1008. To the Lord High Chancellor [2]

My Lord
After a long and not inattentive observation of

[1] Allan Ramsay, Esq., painter to his Majesty, who died Aug. 10, 1784, in the 71st year of his age, much regretted by his friends. BOSWELL.

[2] Sir Joshua Reynolds, on account of the excellence

mankind, the generosity of your Lordship's offer raises in me not less wonder than gratitude. Bounty, so liberally bestowed, I should gladly receive, if my condition made it necessary; for, to such a mind, who would not be proud to own his obligations? But it has pleased GOD to restore me to so great a measure of health, that if I should now appropriate so much of a fortune destined to do good, I could not escape from myself the charge of advancing a false claim. My journey to the continent, though I once thought it necessary, was never much encouraged by my physicians; and I was very desirous that your Lordship should be told of it by Sir Joshua Reynolds, as an event very uncertain; for if I grew much better, I should not be willing, if much worse, not able, to migrate. Your Lordship was first solicited without my knowledge; but, when I was told that you were pleased to honour me with your patronage, I did not expect to hear of a refusal; yet, as I have had no long time to brood hope, and have not rioted in imaginary opulence, this cold reception has been scarce a disappointment; and, from your Lordship's kindness, I have received a benefit, which only men like you are able to bestow. I shall now live *mihi carior*, with a higher opinion of my own merit.

I am, my Lord, your Lordship's most obliged, most grateful, and most humble servant,

September, 1784. SAM: JOHNSON.

1020. To DR. BROCKLESBY

October 6, 1784. The fate of the balloon I do not much lament: to make new balloons, is to repeat the

both of the sentiment and expression of this letter, took a copy of it which he shewed to some of his friends; one of whom, who admired it, being allowed to peruse it leisurely at home, a copy was made, and found its way into the newspapers and magazines. It was transcribed with some inaccuracies. I print it from the original draft in Johnson's own hand-writing. BOSWELL.

jest again. We now know a method of mounting into the air, and, I think, are not likely to know more. The vehicles can serve no use till we can guide them ; and they can gratify no curiosity till we mount with them to greater heights than we can reach without ; till we rise above the tops of the highest mountains, which we have yet not done. We know the state of the air in all its regions, to the top of Teneriffe, and therefore, learn nothing from those who navigate a balloon below the clouds. The first experiment, however, was bold, and deserved applause and reward. But since it has been performed, and its event is known, I had rather now find a medicine that can ease an asthma.

1029. To Dr. Brocklesby

October 25, 1784. You write to me with a zeal that animates, and a tenderness that melts me. I am not afraid either of a journey to London, or a residence in it. I came down with little fatigue, and am now not weaker. In the smoky atmosphere I was delivered from the dropsy, which I consider as the original and radical disease. The town is my element ; there are my friends, there are my books, to which I have not yet bid farewell, and there are my amusements. Sir Joshua told me long ago that my vocation was to publick life, and I hope still to keep my station, till God shall bid me *Go in peace*.

1035. To Mrs. Aston and Mrs. Gastrell

[Lichfield, ? November, 1784.]

Mr. Johnson sends his compliments to the Ladies at Stowhill, of whom he would have taken a more formal leave, but that he was willing to spare a ceremony, which he hopes would have been no pleasure to them, and would have been painful to himself.

1036. To Dr. Burney

Mr. Johnson, who came home last night, sends his respects to dear Dr. Burney, and all the dear Burneys, little and great.

Nov. 19, 1784.

1040. To Mr. Green, Apothecary, at Lichfield

Dear Sir

I have enclosed the Epitaph for my Father, Mother, and Brother, to be all engraved on the large size, and laid in the middle aisle in St. Michael's church, which I request the clergyman and churchwardens to permit.

The first care must be to find the exact place of interment, that the stone may protect the bodies. Then let the stone be deep, massy, and hard; and do not let the difference of ten pounds, or more, defeat our purpose.

I have enclosed ten pounds, and Mrs. Porter will pay you ten more, which I gave her for the same purpose. What more is wanted shall be sent; and I beg that all possible haste may be made, for I wish to have it done while I am yet alive. Let me know, dear Sir, that you receive this.

       I am, Sir, your most humble servant,
Dec. 2, 1784.   Sam: Johnson.

1041. To Lucy Porter

Dear Madam

I am very ill, and desire your prayers. I have sent Mr. Green the Epitaph, and a power to call on you for ten pounds.

I laid this summer a stone over Tetty, in the chapel of Bromley, in Kent. The inscription is in Latin, of which this is the English. [Here a translation.]

That this is done, I thought it fit that you should know. What care will be taken of us, who can tell? May God pardon and bless us, for Jesus Christ's sake.

       I am, &c.,
Dec. 2, 1784.   Sam: Johnson.

INDEX OF CORRESPONDENTS

The references are to the numbers of the Letters.

Miss Elizabeth ('Molly') ASTON, of Stow-hill, Lichfield, 194, 221, 1035.

Mr. B—D (Bond), an American gentleman, 297.

The Rev. Mr. BAGSHAW, of Bromley, 975.

Giuseppi (Joseph) BARETTI, for some time tutor to Thrale's daughters and an inmate of his house at Streatham, 138, 142.

Frederick Augusta BARNARD, the King's Librarian, 206.

Miss Hill BOOTHBY (1708–1756; she was a year older than Johnson), 78, 81.

James BOSWELL, eldest son of Lord Auchinleck, *passim*; his wife (Margaret Montgomerie), 481, 529, 804.

Dr. BROCKLESBY, one of Johnson's physicians, 1020, 1029.

Dr. Charles BURNEY, musician, 67, 112, 113, 1036; his daughter Frances, author of *Evelina*, 902.

The Earl of BUTE, 143.

Miss Elizabeth CARTER, translator of *Epictetus*, 87.

Edward CAVE, founder of the *Gentleman's Magazine*, 4, 5, 10.

Sir Robert CHAMBERS, Principal of New Inn Hall, Oxford (where Johnson was his guest), and later a judge in India, page 225.

The Earl of CHESTERFIELD, 61.

Miss COTTERELL, Johnson's neighbour in Castle-street, 74.

Rev. Dr. William DODD, preacher and author, hanged for forgery, 523.

William DRUMMOND, of Edinburgh, 184.

James ELPHINSTON, of Edinburgh, 30.

Rev. Dr. Richard FARMER, Master of Emmanuel College, Cambridge, author of an *Essay on the Learning of Shakespeare*, 244.

INDEX OF CORRESPONDENTS

Miss FLINT, ' a *very* young lady, who had translated his Strictures at the end of Shakespeare's Plays ' (Mrs. Piozzi), 213.

David GARRICK, 269 ; his wife, 601.

Oliver GOLDSMITH, 305.

William Gerard HAMILTON, ' Single-speech Hamilton ', 905.

Warren HASTINGS, 353, 712.

Edmund HECTOR, of Birmingham, 772.

Gregory HICKMAN, 1.

John HOOLE, translator, 989.

Sarah JOHNSON (*née* Ford), Samuel Johnson's mother, 118, 120, 121, 123 ; Elizabeth (' Tetty ') his wife, formerly Mrs. Porter, 12 ; Thomas, his cousin, page 183.

Dr. William Samuel JOHNSON, of Connecticut, 299.

Bennet LANGTON, 70, 110, 116, 117, 135, 183, 358, 525, 770, 945 ; his daughter Jane, 959.

Rev. Charles LAWRENCE, 704.

Dr. Thomas LAWRENCE, one of Johnson's physicians, 650.

Robert LEVET, one of Johnson's pensioners, 437.

MACLEOD of Skye, 328.

James MACPHERSON, ' translator ' of *Ossian*, 373.

Edmond MALONE, Shakespearian scholar, 766.

Mrs. Elizabeth MONTAGU, ' Queen of the Blues ', 133, 445, 884.

Charles O'CONNOR, an Irish Antiquary, 107, 517.

Rev. Thomas PERCY, Dean of Carlisle (later Bishop of Dromore), author of *Reliques of Ancient English Poetry*, 136, 139.

Lucy PORTER, Johnson's step-daughter, 25, 122, 125–131, 1041.

Sir Joshua REYNOLDS, 813, 830, 916, 995.

Samuel RICHARDSON, 31, 49, 94.

W. SHARP, 526.

Sir George STAUNTON, 140.

William STRAHAN, printer, 35, 38, 39, 124, 364 ; his son, Rev. George Strahan, 149, 155.

Rev. Dr. John TAYLOR, of Ashbourne in Derbyshire,

where Johnson was often his guest, 106, 275, 277, 635, 928.

Hester Lynch THRALE (*née* Salisbury), wife of Henry Thrale, brewer, member of Parliament for Southwark ('The Borough'), of whose household at Streatham Johnson was for many years an inmate, *passim*. Their daughters, Susanna, 864, 880, 901; Sophia, 870.

Mrs. Thrale was born in 1741, and was thus thirty-two years Johnson's junior. Thrale died in 1781, and in 1784 she married Gabriel Piozzi.

Lord THURLOW, Lord Chancellor, 1008.

Rev. Dr. VYSE, Rector of Lambeth, 527.

Rev. Dr. Joseph WARTON, headmaster of Winchester, poet and critic, 51, 96.

Rev. Thomas WARTON, Fellow of Trinity College, Oxford, poet (laureate) and critic, 53, 56, 58, 59, 64, 114.

Saunders WELCH, 571.

John WESLEY, 451.

Lord WESTCOTE, 688, 689.

Rev. Dr. WETHERELL, Master of University College, 463.

Rev. William WHITE, Bishop of Pennsylvania, 298.

NOTE

THE Greek Epitaph on Goldsmith (see No. 358) was thus rendered by a contemporary:

> Whoe'er thou art with reverence tread
> Where Goldsmith's letter'd dust is laid.
> If nature and the historic page,
> If the sweet muse thy care engage,
> Lament him dead whose powerful mind
> Their various energies combined.

INDEX OF AUTHORS, ETC.

Addison, 6.
Aeschylus, 5.
Africa, Stories of, 13.
Ainsworth (W. Harrison), 8.
À Kempis (Thomas), 13.
Aksakoff (Serghei), 4.
American Criticism, 4, 10.
American Verse, 4.
Ancient Law, 13.
Apocrypha The (R. V.), 13.
Aristophanes, 5.
Arnold (Matthew), 11.
Aurelius (Marcus), 11, 13.
Austen (Jane), 8.
Austrian Short Stories, 13.

Bacon (Francis), 11
Bagehot (Walter) 12.
Barrow (Sir John), 10.
Beaumont and Fletcher, 6.
Blackmore (R. D.), 8.
Blake (William), 11.
Borrow (George), 3, 14.
British Colonial Policy, 13.
   Foreign Policy, 13.
Brontë Sisters, 8 11.
Browning (Robert), 6, 11.
Buckle (T. H.), 10, 12
Buddha, Sayings of the, 13.
Bunyan (John), 8.
Burke, 12.
Burns (Robert), 11.
Butler, 8.
Byron (Lord), 11.

Carlyle (Thomas), 5, 6, 10.
Cellini (Benvenuto), 4.
Cervantes, 8.
Chaucer, 11.
Chesterfield, 10.
Cobbold (Richard), 8.
Coleridge (S. T.), 10, 11.
Collins (Wilkie), 8.
Colman, 6.
Confucius, 13.
Congreve (William), 6, 11.
Cooper (J. Fenimore), 8.
Cowper (William), 10.
Crabbe, 5.
Crime and Detection, 13.
Critical Essays, 3, 7, 10.
Czech Tales, 14.

Dante, 3, 11.
Darwin (Charles), 11.
Defoe (Daniel), 8.
Dekker, 6.
De Quincey (Thomas), 4.
Dickens (Charles), 8, 14.

Disraeli (Benjamin), 8.
Dobson (Austin), 5, 7, 11.
Don Quixote, 8.
Douglas (George), 8.
Dryden, 5, 6.
Dufferin (Lord), 10, 14.

Eighteenth-Century Comedies,
Eliot (George), 8.
Elizabethan Comedies, 6.
Elizabethan Tragedies, 6.
Emerson (R. W.), 7.
English Critical Essays, 7, 10.
English Essays, 3, 4.
English Prose, 4.
English Sermons, 7.
English Short Stories, 3, 4, 14.
English Songs and Ballads, 4, 11.
English Speeches, 12.
English Verse, 4, 11.

Farquhar, 6.
Fielding (Henry), 6, 8.
Four Gospels, 13.
Francis (St.), 5, 11.
Franklin (Benjamin), 4.
French Short Stories, 14.
Froude (J. A.), 7.

Galt (John), 8.
Gaskell (Mrs.), 5, 8, 14.
Gay, 6.
German Short Stories, 14.
Ghosts and Marvels, 14.
Gibbon (Edward), 4, 10.
Gil Blas, 9.
Goethe, 6, 11, 12.
Goldsmith (Oliver), 6, 8, 11.
Gray (Thomas), 10, 11.

Harris (J. C.), 8.
Harte (Bret), 14.
Hawthorne (Nathaniel), 8, 14.
Haydon (B. R.), 5.
Hazlitt (William), 5, 7, 10.
Herrick (Robert), 11.
Holme (Constance), 8, 14.
Holmes (Oliver Wendell), 7.
Homer, 5, 12.
Hood (Thomas), 12.
Horne (R. H.), 7.
Houghton (Lord), 5.
Hunt (Leigh), 5, 7.

Ibsen (Henrik), 6, 12.
Inchbald (Mrs.), 6.
Ingoldsby Legends, 11.
International Affairs, 13.
Irving (Washington), 7, 10, 14.

INDEX OF AUTHORS, ETC.

Johnson (Samuel), 5, 10.

Keats, 12.
Keble (John), 12.
Keith (A. B.), 13.
Kingsley (Henry), 9.
Koran, The, 13.

Lamb (Charles), 7.
La Motte Fouqué, 9.
Landor (W. S.), 7.
La Rochefoucauld, 7.
Lesage, 9.
Longfellow (H. W.), 12.

Macaulay (T. B.), 5, 10, 12.
Machiavelli, 12.
Mackenzie (Compton), 9.
Maine, Sir Henry, 13.
Marcus Aurelius, 11, 13.
Marlowe (Christopher), 6, 12.
Marryat (Captain), 9.
Massinger, 6.
Maude (Aylmer), 3, 5.
Meinhold (J. W.), 9.
Melville (Herman), 9, 14.
Mill (John Stuart), 5, 13.
Milton (John), 7, 12.
Montaigne, 7.
More (Paul Elmer), 10.
Morier (J. J.), 9, 14.
Morris (W.), 12.
Morton, 6.
Motley (J. L.), 10.
Murphy, 6.

Narrative Verse, 4, 12.
New Testament, 13.

Old Testament, 13.
Otway, 6.

Palgrave (F. T.), 4.
Pamphlets and Tracts, 4, 7.
Peacock (T. L.), 9.
Peacock (W.), 4.
Persian (From the), 14.
Poe (Edgar Allan), 14.
Polish Tales, 14.
Prescott (W. H.), 10.
Pre-Shakespearean Comedies, 6.

Rabelais, 3, 9.
Reading at Random, 4.
Redman (B. R.), 4.
Restoration Tragedies, 6.
Reynolds (Frederick), 6.

Reynolds (Sir Joshua), 7.
Rossetti (Christina), 12.
Rowe, 6.
Ruskin (John), 7, 13.
Russian Short Stories, 14.
Rutherford (Mark), 7.

Sainte-Beuve, 10.
Scott (Sir W.), 5, 9, 12, 14.
Scottish Verse, 4, 12.
Sermons (English), 7, 13.
Shakespeare, 6, 12.
Shakespeare Criticism, 10.
Shakespeare's Predecessors and Contemporaries, 6.
Shelley, 12.
Sheridan (R. B.), 6.
Smith (Adam), 13.
Smith (Alexander), 7.
Smollett (T.), 7, 9, 14.
Sophocles, 5.
Southerne, 6.
Southey (Robert), 10.
Spanish Short Stories, 14.
Stanhope (Lord), 5.
Steele, 6.
Sterne (Laurence), 7, 9, 14.
Stevenson (R. L.), 7, 9.
Sturgis, 9.
Swift (Jonathan), 9.
Swinburne, 12.
Swinnerton (Frank), 9.

Taylor (Meadows), 9.
Tennyson (Lord), 12.
Thackeray (W. M.), 9.
Three Dervishes, The, 14.
Tolstoy, 3, 5, 6, 7, 9, 11, 13, 14.
Tracts and Pamphlets, 4, 7.
Trevelyan, 5.
Trollope (Anthony), 3, 5, 9, 14.

Virgil, 5, 12.

Walpole (Hugh), 9.
Walton (Izaak), 5, 8.
Watts-Dunton (Theodore), 9.
Webster, 6.
Wellington (Duke of), 5.
Wells (Charles), 12.
Wells (H. G.), 4.
Wharton (Edith), 9.
White (Gilbert), 8, 10.
Whitman (Walt), 8, 12.
Whittier (J. G.), 12.
Wordsworth (William), 12.